WHEN A KILLER CALLS

ALSO BY JOHN DOUGLAS AND MARK OLSHAKER

WHEN A KILLER CALLS

A HAUNTING STORY OF MURDER, CRIMINAL PROFILING, AND JUSTICE IN A SMALL TOWN

CASES OF THE FBI'S ORIGINAL MINDHUNTER, BOOK 2

JOHN DOUGLAS AND MARK OLSHAKER

DEY ST.

An Imprint of WILLIAM MORROW

DEY ST.

WHEN A KILLER CALLS. Copyright © 2022 by Mindhunters, Inc. All rights reserved. Printed in the United States of America. No part of this book may be used or reproduced in any manner whatsoever without written permission except in the case of brief quotations embodied in critical articles and reviews. For information, address HarperCollins Publishers, 195 Broadway, New York, NY 10007.

HarperCollins books may be purchased for educational, business, or sales promotional use. For information, please email the Special Markets Department at SPsales@harpercollins.com.

FIRST EDITION

Designed by Angela Boutin

Library of Congress Cataloging-in-Publication Data has been applied for.

ISBN 978-0-06-297979-7 (trade paperback)
ISBN 978-0-06-307447-7 (hardcover library edition)

22 23 24 25 26   LSC   10 9 8 7 6 5 4 3 2 1

For Ann Hennigan,
a vital part of our team
since the beginning

Everything can be taken from a man but one thing: the last of the human freedoms—to choose one's attitude in any given set of circumstances, to choose one's own way. . . .

And there were always choices to make.

For what then matters is to bear witness to the uniquely human potential at its best, which is to transfer a personal tragedy into a triumph, to turn one's predicament into a human achievement.

—Dr. Viktor E. Frankl

PROLOGUE

t had already been a busy day for Shari Smith. After rushing through breakfast and her parents' mandatory short devotional and prayer session for her and her fifteen-year-old brother, Robert, she'd raced to school for practice for Lexington High's Class of 1985 graduation at the University of South Carolina's Carolina Coliseum on Sunday. She and Andy Aun had been selected to sing "The Star-Spangled Banner," so they had to rehearse with Mrs. Bullock, the chorus teacher. Once she got out of school, the rest of the day would be an unending sprint from one activity to the next, much, but not all of it, in preparation for the senior class trip—a cruise to the Bahamas the following week.

Shari loved to sing, and at Lexington High she'd been the jazz band soloist, a chorus member, and a singer and dancer in the stage choir. She'd made All State Chorus Honors her sophomore and junior years and participated in the Governor's School for the Arts as a senior. That was all in addition to three years of student council. She had auditioned for a singing and dancing job for the summer at Carowinds amusement park up on the state line with North Carolina, southwest of Charlotte, where her older and look-alike sister, Dawn, was already performing. Despite the fact that they seldom took high school students, Shari had won a place, and she had looked forward to spending the summer performing with Dawn, who was living in Charlotte in an apartment with two roommates for the summer, and like Dawn, to majoring in voice and piano at Columbia College in Columbia, South Carolina. The two stunning, blue-eyed blondes had regularly sung solos and duets at Lexington Baptist Church where the Smiths belonged, and the Smith Sisters, as they came to be called, had fulfilled numerous requests to sing at other churches in the area. Shari liked to practice her dancing on the paved basketball court in front of the garage when Robert wasn't shooting hoops. Sometimes she would bring their mom and dad out to be her audience.

But Shari's dreams for the summer had been dashed. She had spent several weekends at Carowinds learning her routines for the country show. After only a few rehearsals, she became hoarse and had trouble projecting. Her mom and dad had taken her to a throat specialist, who gave them the bad news: Shari had developed nodules on her vocal cords. She would need complete voice rest for two weeks and no singing after that for another six. Shari was heartbroken that she would not be able to work at Carowinds that summer. The only consolation was that she'd be joining Dawn at Columbia College in the fall.

At about ten o'clock that morning, Shari called her mom from school and said she would call again when she was leaving so they could meet up at the bank to get traveler's checks for her trip. She called again around eleven o'clock, saying she was

not yet ready but would call back soon. Their parents generally insisted she and Robert call in frequently to let them know
where they were, but that was one of the rules she didn't object
to, because Shari liked to talk. For the yearbook's Senior Superlatives, Shari had been voted Wittiest. She'd also been voted
Most Talented, but you weren't allowed two superlatives, so
she'd relinquished that one to another girl, who was thrilled
with the honor.

There was still so much to do to get ready.

About 11:30 A.M., Shari called home again and said her
mom could meet her in half an hour at the South Carolina National Bank branch in the Lexington Town Square shopping
center. Shari asked her to bring her a bathing suit and towel for
the pool party she was going to at her friend Dana's house a few
miles away in Lake Murray after the bank. She could change
out of her baggy white shorts and black-and-white-striped pull-
over top when she got to her house.

At the bank, Shari connected with her boyfriend, Richard
Lawson, and her good friend Brenda Boozer. She was so happy
to be surrounded by three people she felt so close to. After getting the traveler's checks, Shari and Brenda headed over to the
party with Richard, leaving their cars in the shopping center
parking lot.

Shari called from Dana's at about 2:30 that afternoon and
said she was coming home, throwing a shirt and shorts on
over her two-piece bathing suit before she and Brenda left with
Richard. About fifteen minutes later the trio got back to the
shopping center, where Brenda and Shari could each retrieve
their cars. Brenda said goodbye, and Shari and Richard sat

in his car for a little while by themselves. Then Shari got into her own little blue Chevy Chevette hatchback and took off for home, with Richard following her until she turned down Highway 1, heading toward Red Bank.

The Smiths lived out in the country, in a house they built on twenty acres of land on Platt Springs Road, about ten miles outside of Lexington. The house was set back from the road on a rise, up from the 750-foot-long driveway, so there was plenty of privacy. The girls weren't thrilled about moving from their previous home on a cul-de-sac in the comfortable Irmo community in Columbia, where their friends were close by and their schools only a mile away, but their dad had been raised in the country, and he thought it would be the best way to raise his own children. At their new home, there was enough land to build a swimming pool and for Dawn and Shari to keep horses, though by the time Dawn left for college, Shari and Robert had become more interested in riding a small motorcycle around the property and the horses were sold. The two kids would ride, sometimes for hours at a time, playfully squabbling about who was getting more time on the bike. Despite her feminine, blond beauty and angelic singing voice, unlike Dawn—whom her younger sister used to tease as a "goody-goody"—Shari had a lot of tomboy in her.

Somewhere around 3:25, Shari pulled into the Smith driveway and stopped the Chevette to check for mail at the pole-mounted wooden mailbox, as she always did when she came home. Since it was only a few steps from the car, she kept the motor running and didn't bother slipping on her black plastic jelly shoes.

It was Friday, May 31, 1985.

BOB AND HILDA SMITH HAD BEEN LOUNGING AROUND THE BACKYARD POOL WHEN
Shari called to say she was leaving Dana's party. They came
in shortly after that so Bob could get ready for the golf game
he'd scheduled. Bob, an engineer who had worked for the highway department, now sold electronic scoreboards and signs for
a company called Daktronics and often worked at home. He
also volunteered to minister in prisons and boys' correctional
schools. Dawn and Shari often accompanied him to sing. Hilda
was a part-time substitute public school teacher.

As she glanced out the window, she saw Shari's blue Chevette parked at the beginning of the driveway. When the car
hadn't moved after a few minutes, Hilda concluded Shari must
have received a letter from Dawn and stopped to read it. Shari
loved hearing from Dawn, and Hilda was more than a little
afraid that Shari was living vicariously through her big sister
since her summer plans to sing and dance at Carowinds had
been wrecked by the vocal cord problem. Hilda and Bob were
devoutly religious people and had tried to bring up their three
children with the same reverence and faith. Shari was so shattered by not being able to be with Dawn that summer and
share the stage with her that Hilda sometimes questioned why
God had delivered such a big disappointment to her younger
daughter.

About five minutes later, when the front door had not
opened with a bubbly Shari rushing in, Bob looked out the window of his home office and saw her car still parked down by
the road. That was odd. Hilda told him Shari was probably still
sitting in the car reading a letter from Dawn, but Bob thought
something must be wrong. Shari had a rare medical condition
called diabetes insipidus, also known as water diabetes, that

causes persistent thirst and the frequent need for urination, so there is a near-constant danger of life-threatening dehydration. There was no cure, but Shari took medicine that replaced vasopressin, the hormone that regulates fluid balance that her body couldn't produce. When she was little, she had to have a painful shot with a large needle every other day. Later, thankfully, a nasal spray was developed to replace the injections. One container was always in Shari's purse, with another kept in the refrigerator at home. If, for some reason, Shari had not taken her medicine, she could pass out and eventually become comatose. Whatever the reason she hadn't come down the driveway yet, Bob was worried.

He quickly grabbed his keys, went to the garage, got into his own car, and headed down the long dirt driveway.

A few seconds later he was at the road. The driver's side door of Shari's car was open, and the motor was running. There were letters on the ground near the open mailbox. But he didn't see Shari. He called out to her but got no answer. He looked inside the open car door. The towel Hilda had brought Shari was on the driver's seat, Shari's handbag was on the passenger seat, and her shoes were on the floor. Bob pulled open the top of the handbag and rummaged inside. Her wallet and medicine were still there.

In the dirt, bare footprints led from the car to the mailbox, but—ominously—there were none leading back.

PART 1

IN PURSUIT OF A KILLER

CHAPTER 1

MONDAY, JUNE 3, 1985

"Hey John." Ron Walker, a member of our small team of profilers, was standing in the doorway. "We've got this kidnapping case coming in from Columbia, South Carolina. I just heard from the sheriff's office and they want Behavioral Science Unit assistance."

"What's going on?" I asked.

"I got a call from Lewis McCarty, undersheriff of Lexington County. Sharon Faye Smith, seventeen-year-old high school senior, was abducted near the mailbox in front of her house last Friday afternoon. No paperwork yet, so I only know what I heard on the phone."

"They sure she didn't run off on her own?"

"Not the type, apparently. And her car was left running,

her pocketbook with her wallet in it was on the seat, and she's some kind of severe diabetic and her medicine, which she always has with her, was in the pocketbook, too. Plus, she was scheduled to graduate yesterday, sing the national anthem at the ceremony, and then take off on a senior class cruise to the Bahamas."

Standing in front of my desk, he related the information McCarty had given him. The house was on a twenty-acre plot of land in a rural community known as Red Bank, about ten miles outside the town of Lexington, up a 750-foot driveway from Platt Springs Road. The teen, who went by Shari, had apparently stopped her car at the head of the driveway to pick up the mail. Letters to the Smiths were strewn on the ground, suggesting she was startled and overtaken. The dad, Robert Smith, known as Bob, called the sheriff's department, which sent an officer to the house. There were no obvious prints or other forensic clues.

Sheriff James Metts put on the full-court press, organizing a large search effort, which over the weekend grew to include several hundred volunteers in addition to sheriff's department officers, despite the stifling heat.

"We really don't have much to go on yet," Ron said. "Like I said, no paperwork. But the sheriff's office asked the Columbia field office to open a case file. They're submitting all of the required material that they have at this point to Columbia, and Columbia will send a package to us."

Often, I'd found that local law enforcement was not particularly thrilled to have us consulting on a case. Either they were wary of the Bureau's reputation for moving in and then claiming all the credit because they wanted to control the investigation on their own, or they were worried our analysis wouldn't conform with the theory both the police and the community had firmly in mind.

Not so with this case. Jim Metts and Lewis McCarty were both graduates of the FBI's National Academy, an eleven-week fellowship course for senior and experienced law enforcement personnel from around the nation and many overseas countries. The thirty-seven-year-old Metts had been sheriff for twelve years and was already an institution. He'd first been elected when he was twenty-five and had transformed the department from a sleepy rural office with no uniforms, cruisers, or procedures (deputies drove their own cars and wore whatever they liked) into a modern law enforcement agency. Originally an engineering student, he earned an advanced degree in criminology and taught university-level classes. Both Metts and McCarty had a high level of respect for the Bureau, the profiling program, and what they'd learned at Quantico. And once they'd become convinced that Shari Smith had been taken against her will, which didn't take long, both men agreed on bringing in the local FBI field office and us up in Behavioral Science. Metts contacted the FBI's Columbia, South Carolina, field office and spoke to the special agent in charge, or SAC, Robert Ivey, requesting Bureau involvement.

"The Columbia field office immediately ginned up their standard kidnapping protocol," Ron said. "They've got agents at the house, they put trap and trace wiretaps on the phones, and they sent out a surveillance team. Everybody was sort of sitting around waiting for the ransom note. What they got instead were these phone calls, presumably from the UNSUB. The first one came around two twenty this morning. You can imagine what that did to the family. The mom took the call and took notes. After that, Metts's office set up a recording device on all incoming calls to the house."

"Was there a ransom demand?" I asked.

"Not from this guy. There was one call over the weekend demanding a ransom, but the sheriff's office is convinced it was a hoax." This kind of thing, seeing a grief-stricken family further victimized by an opportunist without a conscience, which unfortunately is not uncommon, always enrages me. If I had my way, they'd throw the book at every single one of them they catch.

Three days and no ransom demand, I reflected; that was a bad sign right there. You try to keep an open mind at the beginning of a case, but there are only two likely scenarios in a situation like this: You have a sexually motivated kidnapping, or you have a kidnapping for ransom; and either type could also involve an element of revenge, which is just one reason we look so closely into victimology. All kidnappings are harrowing ordeals, but by the very nature of the crime, with a money-motivated abduction, there has to be interaction with the victim's family, which makes the perpetrator highly vulnerable. It doesn't always mean the victim is returned safely, but the chances are better than with most other types of predatory crime, plus we almost always catch the perp. And to my knowledge, the FBI had never actually lost a ransom package. The outcome is usually much darker when we're dealing with a sexually motivated kidnapping. In those cases, the offender's often sadistic drive for power and complete control over his victim is the reason for the crime, and he has nothing more to gain and a lot to lose by letting the victim go and possibly identify him. In a kidnap for ransom, returning the victim safely is one side of the transaction, and while the victim can still be killed, either accidentally or intentionally, she or he stands a better chance.

At this time, my title was Profiling and Consultation Program Manager, and I shared an office with my old teaching partner, Robert Ressler. Bob and I had conducted the original prison interviews with violent predators while we were out conducting "road schools" around the country with local police departments and sheriff's offices. He and I were focusing on serial killers and violent predators, with me on the operational side as manager of the Profiling and Consultation Program, and Bob on the research side as the first manager of VICAP—the Violent Criminal Apprehension Program that created a database of criminals and their specific traits throughout the United States.

My job represented the outcome of a philosophical debate that had been simmering within the Bureau ever since Bob and I first began our interviews. According to Bureau orthodoxy, the Academy was there to train FBI agents and the other law enforcement professionals who came there for courses and the FBI Academy Fellows program. Taking part in actual investigations, therefore, was not part of the Academy's core mission. But after the previous generation of instructors in Applied Criminal Psychology began doing informal case consultations with law enforcement professionals they were teaching, the idea that Applied Criminal Psychology *actually could be applied* to real-life, ongoing cases began creating its own reality.

At a point, Bob and I had conducted enough prison interviews to feel we could start correlating what was going on in
the offender's mind before, during, and after a crime with the
details of the crime scene, the victimology, and so forth. We
then began gaining the confidence not only to start offering
insights into an offender's personality and behavior, but also
to suggest proactive strategies local investigators might use
to lure the unknown subject (or UNSUB, in our parlance) out
into the open or get others who might have encountered or
dealt with him to recognize him and come forward. That, essentially, was the beginning of the formal Profiling and Consultation Program at Quantico. Bob and I were soon joined,
always on an informal basis since they were officially tied up
with teaching and research, by Roy Hazelwood, a brilliant
agent whose special area of expertise was interpersonal violence and who had gone down to Atlanta with me four years
before to work ATKID-Major Case 30: the Atlanta Child Murders, and the equally brilliant Kenneth Lanning, who focused
on crimes against children.

But the struggle for recognition of the program's useful-
ness and for the resources we needed to expand it was ongoing. Behavioral Science Unit chief Roger L. Depue was a great
champion for us and regularly went to bat on our behalf with
the Academy and Headquarters brass. Roger, a Marine Corps
veteran and former police chief in Michigan, felt strongly and
repeatedly stated that rather than being a distraction from
the Academy's mission, consultation on active cases was the
proof of concept that justified the viability of our research and
instruction—and our very existence. Of course, this put a tremendous amount of pressure on both him and us to deliver

the goods and show positive results, and thankfully we'd had some notable victories, in particular with the Atlanta Child Murders in 1981.

Not surprisingly, those early successes led to more requests for our profiling and consultative services. I had been the Bureau's first full-time profiler, and for several years I was the only one; the workload quickly became overwhelming. In January 1983, I had gone to Jim McKenzie, the assistant FBI director in charge of the Academy, told him of my exhaustion, and pleaded for more full-time help. McKenzie was sympathetic, as well as being a firm supporter of the program, like Roger Depue. He'd managed to sell Headquarters on the idea by shifting around some manpower slots at Quantico. What this meant, in essence, was "stealing" bodies from other programs to get me my first four profilers: Ron Walker, Blaine McIlwaine, Jim Horn, and Bill Hagmaier.

Ron had come to us from the Washington field office (WFO). It was his first field assignment, which was rare, because the WFO is one of the most important field offices in the FBI network, but his background supported the posting. Like me, he was an Air Force veteran. Unlike me, he was an officer with eleven years on active duty, including flying F-4 fighter planes, and he would go on to another sixteen in the reserve, where he was involved with special investigations, security, law enforcement, base defense, and antiterrorism. In 1982, we were formalizing the profiling program and establishing a profile coordinator in each field office as a liaison to the Behavioral Science Unit in Quantico. Ron was tapped by the Training Division to be the WFO's coordinator, even though he only had two years in the Bureau, because of his service record and master's degree in psychology. I first met Ron during an in-service training he attended at the Academy, so when I was able to convince Jim McKenzie to up the profiling program's manpower, Ron was a natural choice to join our team.

Now, as he stood before me, I asked, "Anyone working with you on this kidnapping?"

All the profilers had strong egos; that was a given in our occupation. To build on their confidence while protecting against its excesses, I liked having my team work together collegially and share ideas. So much of what we were doing was intuitive that I firmly believed the old adage about two heads being better than one, and Roger Depue encouraged this approach. Bob Ressler, on the other hand, preferred to work alone, with a proprietary protectiveness about his cases and projects. I can't say that was wrong or didn't produce some good results. It was just not the way I did things.

"Yeah, I looped in Jim," Ron replied.

That seemed logical. Ron shared an office with Jim Wright who, like him, came over from the WFO. He had joined the unit when we were able to score three more profiling slots, after spending more than a year investigating the assassination attempt on President Ronald Reagan outside the Washington Hilton Hotel and preparing the case for trial. Later, when we established the Investigative Support Unit as a separate operational entity within Behavioral Science and I became its chief, Jim took over from me as profiling program manager and second-in-command of the unit. Ron and Jim were both becoming fine profilers.

Within the greater FBI establishment, we were a very small organization, and it's important to understand the way, and the conditions under which, we worked. While we consulted on a wide variety of crimes—from extortion to kidnapping to sexual assault to serial murder—it quickly became a challenge to keep up with the hundreds of cases presented to us at any given time. Some could be handled with a simple phone call that suggested to local authorities the kind of person they should be looking for within a small field of suspects, and some were extremely involved and required extensive on-scene assessment and analysis, as Roy Hazelwood and I performed on the Atlanta Child Murders investigation, in cooperation with the area's police departments and the FBI field office.

So, as early as when Bob Ressler and I undertook our study of incarcerated offenders, we realized that within the spectrum of violent and predatory crime, there were certain characteristics that made it more or less likely that what we did with behavioral profiling, criminal investigative analysis, and proactive strategies would be helpful in a given case, regardless of the type of crime involved. Under longtime director J. Edgar Hoover, the Bureau had developed a reputation for wanting to be involved in every crime that came to its attention. In our case, however, there was no sense in wasting our limited resources or the local law enforcement agency's critical time if we had nothing to contribute. To put it in its simplest terms, the more common and ordinary a crime, the harder it is to solve using our methods.

Actually, it was our legendary and fictional forerunner Sherlock Holmes who stated it most plainly in an interchange between Holmes and Dr. Watson in "The Boscombe Valley Mystery," which Arthur Conan Doyle published in *Strand Magazine* in 1891.

"Have you heard anything of the case?" [Holmes]
asked.

"Not a word. I have not seen a paper for some days."

*"The London press has not had very full accounts. I
have just been looking through all the recent papers in
order to master the particulars. It seems, from what I
gather, to be one of those simple cases which are so extremely difficult."*

"That sounds a little paradoxical."

*"But it is profoundly true. Singularity is almost in-
variably a clue. The more featureless and commonplace
a crime is, the more difficult it is to bring it home."*

While motive or motivation is an important and interesting aspect of a violent crime, and something the jury almost always wants to hear about, it is often not very helpful in solving
that crime. As Ron Walker noted when he first told me about
the Shari Smith case, we knew the motive had to be money or
some kind of sexual assault, possibly with a revenge element
attached. And while it was important to figure out which it
was, that alone wouldn't tell us all that much. By the same to-
ken, the motive for a stickup in a dark alley is obvious, but not
helpful in determining the perpetrator. That is why we almost
never accepted felony murder cases—defined as a murder
that takes place in the commission of another felony, such as a
bank robbery—or other "routine" crimes. The circumstances
and behavior displayed were just not distinctive enough for us
to add much to the standard police investigation.

We looked at a number of critical components, some of
which we've mentioned previously: victimology, along with any

known verbal exchanges between the victim and perpetrator; crime scene indicators, such as any evidence of antecedent behavior or how the crime itself was carried out, how the body was disposed of and left, and evidence of postcrime behavior; how many crime scenes were involved; environment, place, and time; apparent number of offenders; degree of organization or disorganization; type of weapon(s); forensic evidence; personal items missing from the victim or purposely left at the crime scene or body disposal site; and medical examination of the living victim or postmortem examination of a deceased one. All of these factors help us profile an UNSUB and anticipate his—and it was almost always a "he" when it came to UNSUBs we would profile—next move. And the more we have to work with, the better able we are to help direct the local authorities' investigation and hunt. Elements like the phone call to the Smith family early that morning from Shari's presumed abductor gave us hope this UNSUB would give us plenty to work with in that regard.

Even with just the bare outlines of the case to work with, Ron and Jim had determined that it was doubtful the UNSUB just happened to drive by as Shari came home and stopped at the mailbox. That meant he had likely followed her or targeted her in advance. From what Lewis McCarty had said, the Smiths were prominent in the community, but not wealthy, and definitely not showy or ostentatious, so there was no particular reason to focus on her for what we classify as a criminal enterprise—a crime committed for monetary profit. But Ron had been told that she was a pretty, blue-eyed blonde, popular in school, with an outgoing personality, so some creep could have easily fixated on her as a sexual or romantic fantasy.

The fact that her dad found her car running and her purse and medicine in the front seat not only told us she did not disappear willingly, it also revealed a fair amount about the UNSUB. Clearly this was not the kind of guy who could charm or disarm a woman into trusting him with good looks and/or a gift of gab. This was someone who knew the only way he could get a woman to go with him was by force, no doubt combined with the element of surprise. If it had been a blitz style of attack in which he suddenly physically overpowered her—knocking her out with a completely unexpected blow to the head, for example—we would have expected to see evidence of that in markings left in the soft earth between the car and the mailbox, rather than the footprints going only in one direction from the car to the mailbox. More likely, he had forced her into his car at gun- or knifepoint.

"Keep me updated," I said to Ron, "and we'll have a case consultation with the whole group when we get the package from Columbia."

AFTER RON LEFT MY OFFICE, I FOUND I COULDN'T IMMEDIATELY REFOCUS ON ALL the other work piled up on my desk. As little as we knew about the Smith case at this point, my mind went back to another I had worked more than five years earlier that seemed a lot like this one.

In December 1979, Special Agent Robert Leary of the FBI resident agency (a smaller Bureau outpost than a field office) in Rome, Georgia, called with the details of a particularly troubling case. The previous week, a pretty and outgoing twelve-year-old girl named Mary Frances Stoner had disappeared after being dropped off by the school bus at the driveway to her home in Adairsville, about a half-hour from Rome. As with the Smiths', the house was set back a good distance from the road. Her body was later found in a wooded area about ten miles away. She was clothed, and a bright yellow coat covered her head.

The cause of death was blunt force trauma to the head, and in the crime scene photos, there were bloodstains on a rock near her head. Marks on her neck also indicated manual strangulation from the rear. The autopsy clearly indicated she'd been a virgin when raped by the UNSUB. When the body was discovered, one shoe was untied, and there was blood in her panties, indicating she had been hurriedly redressed after the sexual assault.

As with Shari Smith, Mary Frances had been a low-risk victim in that environment, so I had wanted to know as much as possible about the victimology. She was described as friendly, outgoing, and charming, much like Shari; a cute twelve-year-old who looked and acted her age (rather than older); sweet and innocent, a drum majorette in the school band who often wore her uniform to school. After a full briefing from Bob Leary and a study of the crime scene photos, I jotted down some basic impressions: white male, mid-to-late twenties, average to above-average IQ; no more than high school education, possibly a dropout; dishonorable or medical discharge from the military; married with problems or divorced; blue collar, possibly electrician or plumber; past criminal record for arson and/or sexual assault; drives a dark-colored vehicle, several years old, well maintained; local. From my experience, orderly, organized, compulsive people tended to favor darker-colored cars. His would be several years old, because he wouldn't be able to afford a new one, but it would be well maintained.

I thought I could visualize what happened with Mary Frances and whoever took her. Because of where the body was deposited, I figured he knew the area well. Though, like Shari's, this was a crime of opportunity, I thought that, like Shari's abductor, the UNSUB likely had seen Mary Frances either that day or before, probably observed her sunny disposition, and fantasized that he could have a relationship with her, just as I was convinced our current UNSUB had fantasized about a relationship with Shari. Like the current UNSUB, this guy probably had an idea of when she would be dropped off at her driveway. This made me consider the possibility that he did some kind of work in the area.

The one difference between the cases was that given Mary Frances's young age, I thought she might have been easier to get close to through friendly conversation. Only when the UNSUB was close enough to get her in his vehicle would he have resorted to physical force or threat with a knife or gun. Physical evidence indicated she was assaulted in his vehicle, and once that happened, he would have seen that the reality of her horror, screams, and pain was nothing like his fantasy. At that point, if not before, he would have realized he had to kill her, or his life was ruined.

Playing out the likely scenario, I imagined him after the assault trying to control Mary Frances—at that point, hysterical and terrified—by telling her to get dressed quickly and he'd let her go, then driving to the woods he knew. As soon as he let her out of the car and she turned her back on him, he'd come up behind her and strangled her until she went limp. But strangulation is not as easy as people think, and since he'd had trouble controlling her in his car, he'd take no chances. He'd drag her under a tree, pick up the nearest rock he could find, and smash it repeatedly on her head.

The coat placed over the young girl's head told me the UNSUB didn't feel good about what he'd done, and if we could catch him—and catch him fairly quickly—we could use that in the interrogation. Believing that the UNSUB was from the area, and knowing how seriously the police had taken this case, I was reasonably sure they had already interviewed him as a potential witness to anything he might have seen at the time of the abduction. I told the investigators on the phone that this guy would be organized, and feel cocky that he had gotten away with it. And while this may have been his first murder, I felt certain it was not his first sex crime.

That case, like so many in the grim ledger of our business, had ended tragically for the victim. Most of the time, the best we can do is use our skills to try to prevent more victims. As I found myself involuntarily glancing at the photos of my own two young daughters, Erika and Lauren, on my credenza, I dared to hope this case would have a better outcome.

CHAPTER 2

Back in 1985, when Lewis McCarty called us about the Smith case, Behavioral Science occupied a row of offices on the first floor of the Forensic Science Building on the FBI Academy campus, nestled in the woods on the U.S. Marine Base in Quantico, Virginia. Unlike in later years, when we were moved to a warren of offices sixty feet belowground under a gun vault and indoor firearms ranges, though we didn't have private offices, we did have windows to look out and see nature. We also shared a conference room with the Forensic Science side of the house, and they weren't always happy about it because we were taking up some of their space. We started asking them to sit in with us on some of our case consultation conferences, and many of them seemed to appreciate that.

We met on Thursday, three days after Ron's first conversion with McCarty, for a case consultation on Shari's abduction. We tried to hold these meetings at least once a week so everyone on the team could run his or her cases (Special Agents

Rosanne Russo and Patricia Kirby had come to us from the New York and Baltimore field offices, respectively, the year before as our first female profilers) by the others for assumption-challenging questions and ideas. In this instance, we had just received the Smith case package from Columbia, together with recordings of several phone calls from the UNSUB. In addition, there had been phone conversations every day with Metts or McCarty, filling us in on each new development as well as the situation at the Smith home, since sheriff's department officers were a constant presence there. The case materials and photocopied newspaper articles were spread out across the conference table.

In addition to Ron Walker, Jim Wright, and me, Blaine McIlwaine and Roy Hazelwood were there. All of them would offer their insights on the current case and go on to make substantial contributions to the profiling program in general.

Ron and Blaine also made another contribution that was to have a significant effect on the program, at least as far as I was concerned. They saved my life.

Not quite a year and a half before, in late November to early December 1983, I had taken them with me to Seattle to consult with the task force on the Green River Murders, then already shaping up to be one of the largest serial killer cases in American history. The previous summer, in mid-July, teenaged boys had spotted the body of sixteen-year-old Wendy Lee Cofield floating in the Green River in King County, Washington. When four more bodies turned up within a month—all young women, all found in or along the Green River—it became clear that someone was preying on young female runaways, prostitutes, and transients along the Seattle-Tacoma corridor.

By the time Ron, Blaine, and I went there in November 1983, at least eleven victims had been attributed to an UNSUB by then termed the "Green River Killer," a task force had been formed, and the search had become the country's largest serial murder investigation. As if the scope of the murders wasn't horrific enough, the sad reality of how many vulnerable young girls and women went missing in that one area alone—some as young as fourteen or fifteen—was heartbreaking, and it took a toll on all of us who worked the case.

It was a particularly stressful time in my own life. Even with the new associates, I was overwhelmed by the workload and having trouble sleeping. Three weeks earlier, while giving a talk on criminal personality profiling to about 350 NYPD, Transit Police, and Nassau and Suffolk County, Long Island, police officers, the stress had gotten to me—I'd had a momentary but overpowering feeling of dread, even though I'd given the speech many times before.

I recovered quickly, but I couldn't shake this sense of foreboding, so when I got back to Quantico I went to the personnel office and took out some extra life insurance and income protection insurance, in case I became disabled.

The morning after our arrival in Seattle, I made a presentation to the Green River Task Force and suggested some proactive strategies that might get the killer to come forward as a "witness," and how to interrogate him if that did happen. Ron, Blaine, and I spent the rest of the day touring body dump sites with the police to pick up more behavioral clues. November in Seattle is not the most inviting month to be outdoors, and the locals were still talking about the "Turkey Day Storm" the previous week. By the time we got back to the Hilton hotel that evening, I was wiped out, had a headache, and felt like I might be coming down with the flu.

As I was trying to unwind over drinks in the hotel bar, I told Blaine and Ron that I thought I might feel better if I spent the next day in bed while they went to the King County Courthouse to go over records and follow up with police officials on the strategies we'd discussed that morning.

The next day was a Thursday, and my fellow agents left me alone as I'd requested. I hung the DO NOT DISTURB sign on the outside doorknob. But when I didn't show up for breakfast on Friday, they were concerned. They didn't get any answer when they used the house phone to call my room and got no response when they came up and knocked on the door.

Alarmed, they went back to the front desk and demanded a key from the manager. When they went back upstairs and unlocked the door, the security chain was on, and they heard faint moaning coming from inside. They broke the door open and found me on the floor, comatose and apparently near death from what turned out to be viral encephalitis. I was in Swedish Hospital in Seattle for nearly a month and almost died several times in the first week. I didn't return to work until the following May. While away from it all, I was despondent and questioned everything about my life and commitment to this kind of work. Ron was one of the few friends I saw during that time, probably figuring that he understood and could appreciate what I was going through.

Now I was thankful to have people like Ron, Blaine, and the others on the team both to share their insights and to help absorb and defuse some of the stress.

With Ron taking lead, we reviewed the chronology together, from the time Shari disappeared up through what we knew at the moment. Much of it was based on the timeline the sheriff's office and SLED—the South Carolina Law Enforcement Division—had put together. Understanding as much as possible about the victim's personality, actions, and whereabouts before the crime, as well as the details of all her possible encounters with the UNSUB, are important in developing a useful profile. We wanted to experience the events just as the participants had, analyzing each step in terms of what the participants knew and did not know at that point.

"Since we didn't think we were dealing with a ransom kidnapping," Ron recalls, "you kind of assume it's sexually motivated. But then what? Is this a guy that just picked this particular victim for some reason? Is he a neighborhood person, for example, or somebody that knew Shari and had seen her coming and going? Or was he kind of a stalker personality that had come across her before, followed her home, and went up to her when he saw an opportunity? At this point, unfortunately, we had no specific information about the perpetrator, so we were just shot-gunning potential lines of inquiry and thinking about what would happen next and what the typical type of person for this kind of crime might be."

We had to think beyond Shari herself. Bob Smith served as a volunteer chaplain at the Lexington County Jail. He also ministered in other prisons and young men's correctional schools and institutions. So was there a possibility that the abduction was revenge for some perceived wrong by Bob against one of the inmates, or simply resentment that he represented the law that had put them behind bars?

We'd learned, too, that sometimes Dawn and Shari would

accompany their dad and sing for those in attendance. Had one of the men he'd ministered to become obsessed with one or both of his pretty daughters and decided to pursue her once he was released? Every possibility had to be checked out, and Sheriff Metts's office and SLED were devoting the necessary manpower.

The last time Hilda Smith had seen Shari the past Friday was when they met up at the South Carolina National Bank in Lexington to get the traveler's checks for the senior class trip to the Bahamas. Shari's steady boyfriend, Richard Lawson, was with her. Hilda expected Shari home after a graduation pool party at a friend's house, at which point she was going to help her daughter alter some clothing she was planning to take on the trip. Because Hilda and Bob Smith had observed Shari's blue 1978 Chevette stopped at the mailbox by the road, we pretty much knew the exact time she had disappeared.

Ron and Jim speculated that the UNSUB had probably noticed Shari downtown, and perhaps was jealous of her obvious affection for Richard, whom she was with at the shopping center both before and after the pool party, giving the UNSUB at least two opportunities to spot her that afternoon. The couple had met up first at the post office before they went to the bank, and then headed to the party in Richard's car with friend Brenda Boozer.

The UNSUB might have seen this and followed Shari in her travels, waiting in his car, near the pool party, before following the three teens back to the shopping center. It was also possible that the second trip to the shopping center was when the UNSUB first saw her, watching and waiting until she got into her own car. Either way, he could have followed her until she finally got home and was in a position where she could be quickly and efficiently neutralized and snatched away without anyone close by to respond.

After the abduction, a phone call to the Smiths told them to expect a letter from Shari around two o'clock the next afternoon, which we learned was the normal time for their mail delivery. If the UNSUB knew that, then he may have surveilled the house and might have observed that Shari generally stopped at the mailbox before heading up the driveway. Whatever the scenario, we didn't think this was simply an unlucky, chance encounter.

When Bob drove down to the mailbox but couldn't find Shari, he drove back to the house and, according to his wife's account, said, "Hilda, I don't know where Shari is, but she is gone." They then stood in the foyer and prayed for their daughter's return, prayer and devotion to God being a central tenet of the Smiths' life together.

While Bob called the Lexington County Sheriff's Office, Hilda got in her car and drove back down to the road to look for Shari herself. With her daughter's diabetes insipidus, there was a possibility Shari might have had to urinate suddenly and wouldn't have time to get back into her car and drive up to the house. But there was no sign of her, and Bob called up to Hilda and told her to come back. As soon as she got there, Bob told her to wait at the house for an officer while he took the car to go out and search the surrounding area.

When he returned without finding any trace of Shari, Hilda was pacing the driveway, praying. No one had yet arrived from the sheriff's office, and when Bob called back, a sergeant tried to reassure him. She and most of the other personnel in the department knew and admired Bob from his years of volunteer chaplaincy at the jail.

An officer finally arrived at the house about thirty minutes after Bob's first call. Soon becoming convinced that Shari was not the kind of girl who would run off, particularly without her purse and medicine, and leaving her car still running, the deputy relayed this back to his office, whereupon Sheriff Metts, who also knew and respected the Smiths, threw the weight of the entire department behind the effort to get Shari back.

"There's no doubt she was kidnapped," Captain Bob Ford of the sheriff's department told the *State* newspaper the next day. "She's not a runaway. We can't accept any theories that she ran away from home."

MEANWHILE, IN CHARLOTTE, NORTH CAROLINA, SHARI'S OLDER SISTER, DAWN, was out at a mall, shopping for a graduation gift for her. She found a hamster that she could take with her to college in the fall. When Dawn got home, her roommate met her at the door and immediately she knew something was wrong. She said, "You need to call your mom. Shari's been abducted." When she said the word "abducted," it was to Dawn as if she was speaking a foreign language. She just couldn't comprehend it. *What does that word mean?* she thought, because it was so foreign to anything she would have expected to come out of her roommate's mouth.

Dawn called her mom, who told her, "You need to pack a bag. A patrolman is coming to pick you up at your apartment."

"What? Mom," she replied, "I can't come home; my show opens tomorrow. I've got to be at the show. I'm sure Shari is fine."

"No, this is real," Hilda said. "Pack a bag. They'll be there in ten minutes."

She did, and a South Carolina Highway Patrol trooper came and drove her back to Red Bank. It felt weird getting in the patrol car with a stranger, having no idea what in the world was going on. She thought, *I was just shopping one minute and being escorted home the next minute.* Still, her first thought was that this was all going to turn out to be a mistake. *I'm going to go to all this trouble and pack my bag and go home, and Shari is going to be there when I get there. She went shopping with her friends, or she's somewhere with her boyfriend.* The reality of the situation did not sink in. It seemed more like an inconvenience that Dawn's big show was opening the next day and she was supposed to be at work to be there.

All the way home she kept vacillating between *This is ridiculous!* and *Oh my gosh, what if something's really wrong?* Back and forth her thoughts flew. The patrolman didn't tell her anything because no one knew anything. It was a very silent ride.

Bob and Hilda knew that their son, Robert, was somewhere at the country club with his friend Brad, probably playing golf. They were located on the golf course, and Brad's mother picked them up and brought them to the Smith house. Shari's boyfriend, Richard, rushed over as soon as he heard. Bob called his mother, who alerted Shari's aunts; and Hilda, in turn, alerted one of her brothers, who notified the rest of the family.

When the highway patrol car bringing Dawn home pulled up in the Smith driveway, she finally realized the seriousness of what was happening.

"It was at that moment that I realized it was not a mistake; that Shari was really missing," she said.

It was a scene that she could never imagine taking place in her front yard. There were patrol cars and law enforcement officers everywhere, family and friends and church members had come, and there was no longer any doubt that this was real. They went inside and all of the family friends and supporters gathered in the living room and Bob said, "Let's pray together." Amidst all of the tears and all of the unknowns of the moment he continued, "God, we know that while we don't know where Shari is, we know that You know where she is, and so we're going to trust You to watch over her, and we're going to look to You to bring her home and to get us through this."

Within hours, Dawn's college roommate Cindy had also come to the house, as well as various friends and members of their church, Lexington Baptist, who brought over enough food to feed everyone.

SLED sent its own investigators, led by Agent Harold S. Hill of the Missing Persons Bureau, who questioned all four of the Smiths, plus Richard, to see if they had noticed anything or could offer any leads. Lydia Glover, another SLED officer, spoke privately with Dawn about the Smith family dynamics and whether there was any reason Shari might have run away. Dawn told her that their father was strict, and sometimes she and Shari thought his discipline was overbearing. She conceded that a few times after being punished, Shari had called her at school and asked if she could go stay with her. Yet Dawn never thought she was serious, and all three children loved their parents and knew they only wanted the best for them. Dawn reiterated that under no circumstances would Shari voluntarily disappear with graduation in two days and her senior trip to the Bahamas the next week.

At Metts's request, the Emergency Preparedness Division of the governor's office sent a trailer equipped as a mobile operations and communications center to be set up in front of the Smith house. Despite the searing heat, hundreds of volunteers joined the land search and the sheriff's deputies with bloodhounds. It was about 10:30 on Friday night when one of the searchers discovered a red bandanna belonging to Shari along the side of Platt Springs Road, about a half mile from the house. We wondered if Shari had purposely dropped it as a clue. The state highway patrol also joined the search.

Neighbors reported seeing a late-model yellow Chevrolet Monte Carlo, a blue Ford pickup, and a reddish-purple General Motors car of some make—possibly an Oldsmobile Cutlass—near the Smith driveway around the time Shari disappeared. A dark-haired man with a beard was driving the Monte Carlo. The Cutlass driver appeared to be in his thirties.

The first possible break in the case came on Friday night, when the Smiths received the call demanding a ransom in exchange for Shari that Ron had alluded to. This had briefly lifted the family's spirits, but deputies were able to trace the call to a particular phone booth and staked it out for hours, waiting for the man to return with his next instructions. They were finally able to connect the call to twenty-seven-year-old Edward Robertson and determined it was a hoax. He was arrested and charged with extortion, obstruction of justice, making obscene telephone calls, and attempting to obtain money under false pretenses. "He cost this department a lot of man-hours checking the call and put this family through a lot of unnecessary pain," Metts declared.

The sheriff stayed out all night Friday, coordinating the

search. By the next morning, sheriff's department helicopters from Lexington and adjoining Richland County had fanned out in all directions hoping to pick up some trace. The FBI flew an infrared-sensing plane down from Washington.

Sunday, with the widescale search still underway, was the Lexington High School Class of 1985 graduation ceremony at Carolina Coliseum. An empty chair in the second row represented Shari, and the entire assembly joined in a silent prayer for her well-being. Many of the graduates wept. There was still some faint hope that if she had left voluntarily, she might show up at graduation. Of course, that didn't happen.

"We're touched by the absence of one of our classmates," Principal Karl Fulmer began. "Shari Smith's family knows how much every one of us cares for them in their time of need. Their request has been for our graduation ceremony to continue as planned."

Andy Aun, who was supposed to sing the national anthem with Shari, sang alone on the stage.

"I won't believe I've graduated until they find her," Rene Burton, a senior who was in the school chorus with Shari, told *State* reporter Michael Lewis. "A part of our family is missing."

Chris Caughman, another chorus member who had joined the search the day before, added, "If you don't graduate as a class, you don't graduate."

Valerie Bullock, the chorus teacher, called Shari, "probably the most talented student I ever taught. She had an innate musicality."

It wasn't just her classmates and teachers who were traumatized. If a sweet, innocent girl like Shari Smith could just disappear like that, no one in the community felt safe.

CHAPTER 3

itting around the conference room table, the profiling team began to analyze what had transpired following Sunday's graduation, looking through the case file and turning our attention to the events of the past Monday, June 3.

With their house shared by law enforcement personnel, extended family, friends, and church members since Friday afternoon, Dawn and Robert Smith had been spending the nights in their parents' bedroom. Even though sleep didn't come easily, it seemed like the only refuge for the four of them. Exhausted from the emotions of the day, they each gradually drifted off to sleep.

The telephone rang at 2:20 A.M. on Monday.

Out of his restless sleep, Bob grabbed for it, and almost before he could answer, sheriff's officers had barged into the room. A male voice asked to speak to Mrs. Smith.

"I'm Mr. Smith," he said. "Can I help you?"

The caller insisted he wanted to talk to Mrs. Smith.

Hilda got on the line and the man said he wanted to give

her some information about Shari. Hilda thought she was talking to a police officer or deputy, so she signaled Bob to reach for a pad and pen for her to make notes.

The caller said he wanted to give her some information to prove the call was not a hoax and proceeded to relate to her what Shari was wearing and that the authorities were looking in the wrong place. He told her that they would be getting a letter from Shari in the next day's mail and that Sheriff Metts should announce the next morning on WIS-TV, Channel 10, that he was calling off the search.

In her dazed confusion at a middle-of-the-night call, Hilda said it was not until she hung up that she realized it was not a law officer she had been talking to; she had been speaking directly with her daughter's kidnapper.

"That man has Shari," she told Dawn.

Dawn later told me that was the final realization that Shari had definitely been taken. But then she thought, *Well, if there is a letter coming from Shari, then that means Shari was alive to write that letter.* That gave the family hope. "When you have no answers," Dawn told us when we finally met, "you'll take anything that is any sort of answer."

The call was traced through Alltel, the telephone service provider, to a pay phone outside C. D. Taylor's Grocery store on Highway 378. It was about five miles outside of Lexington and twelve miles from the Smith home. By the time officers arrived at the scene, though, the UNSUB was gone. They processed the telephone and the immediate scene for fingerprints and any other trace evidence but came up empty. This gave us some insight about the perpetrator. He was organized and meticulous in making his call from a random location and wiping down anything he may have touched to leave no traces.

There was another behavioral clue in Hilda Smith's notes on that first call that was just as important to our developing behavioral profile. When describing the letter the UNSUB said the Smiths would be receiving from Shari, he mentioned that at the top of the page would be the heading "6/1/85," and the time would be "3:10 A.M." Then he added that the actual time had been 3:12, but he had rounded it off. This told us that he was not only meticulous in his habits, but compulsive as well. This was a guy who probably made lists and would be very methodical about his daily life. We hoped some of these traits we were amassing would help identify him.

There was no way Sheriff Metts was going to wait for the mail to be delivered in the afternoon to see what was in this supposed letter from Shari. His office called Lexington County postmaster Thomas Roof and asked him to meet officers J. E. Harris and Richard Freeman at four A.M. to open the post office and search for the letter. Together, the three men painstakingly sorted through all the mail addressed to anywhere in the county.

It was about seven A.M. when they finally found what they were looking for, in a mail sack that had arrived earlier that morning from the Columbia distribution center. It was a white, legal-size envelope addressed simply to "The Smith Family" with their rural route and box number on the second line and "Lex. S.C. 29072" on the third. There was no return address, though sometimes offenders will provide fake return addresses to throw off the investigation. The envelope was postmarked

June 1 and carried a twenty-two-cent stamp from the Folk Art series, featuring a mallard duck decoy. Roof informed the officers that the duck decoy stamps had been issued that year and were being sold currently.

I can tell you from several impressive encounters working with the United States Postal Inspection Service that anyone involved with the mail regards the sanctity and security of the postal system with utmost seriousness. Therefore, Roof had the officers bring Bob Smith to the post office so that he could take official delivery of the letter.

When Bob arrived, the letter was opened carefully with gloved hands and placed in transparent sleeves to preserve any prints, fibers, or trace evidence. Often, you don't know what unpredictable factor or element may turn out to be a crucial clue.

What the envelope contained was the most excruciating, heartrending, and at the same time, most moving, courageous, and transcendent statement I have seen in all my years in law enforcement. As we hunched over each other's shoulders reading the photocopy in our conference room, we were all left stunned and momentarily speechless. I have returned to it in my mind over and over again through the years. I certainly choked up when I read it. I can only imagine, even to this day, how Shari's family reacted when they read it. And it put the lid on any slight remaining notion or even hope that this was a kidnapping for ransom.

The letter was two blue-lined sheets from a yellow legal pad, in Shari's handwriting, with the phrase "GOD IS LOVE" written in capital letters down the left side of the first page. Below that was a heart with "ShaRichard" written above it.

6/1/85   3:10 AM   *I Love ya'll*

Last Will & Testament

> I Love you mommy, daddy,
> Robert, Dawn, & Richard and
> everyone else and all other
> friends and relatives. I'll be
> with my father now, so
> please, please don't worry!
> Just remember my witty
> personality & great special times
> we all shared together. Please
> don't ever let this ruin your
> lives just keep living one day
> at a time for Jesus. Some good
> will come out of this. My
> thoughts will always be with you &
> in you!! (casket closed) I love you
> all so *damn* much. Sorry dad,
> I had to cuss for once! Jesus
> Forgive me! Richard sweetie — I
> Really did & *always* will love
> You & treasure our special
> Moments. I ask one thing though,
> Accept Jesus as your personal
> savior. My family has been
> the greatest influence of my life.
> Sorry about the cruise money. Some
> body please go in my place.

[Page Two]

I am sorry if I ever disa-
ppointed you in any way, I only
wanted to make you proud
of me. Because I have always
been proud of my family. Mom,
dad, Robert & Dawn theres so
much I want to say that I should
have said before now. I love you!

I know y'all love me and will
Miss me very much but if
you'll stick together like we al-
ways did——y'all can do it!

Please do not become hard or
Upset. Everything works out for the
Good for those that love the
Lord.
☺

All My Love Always——
I Love Ya'll
w/All My Heart!

Sharon (Shari) Smith

P.S. Nana——I love you so much. I
kind of always felt like your

favorite. You were mine.!
I Love You A lot

As an important part of my process of working on a case, I
try to put myself in the shoes—and the head—of the victim. For
me, that is the best way to comprehend all the dynamics of the
crime, correlate what the UNSUB was thinking to the evidence
left at the crime scene and other sources such as medical examiner's report, to understand how he viewed the relationship
between himself and the victim. For example, is the victim just
an object for the offender to use, or does he invest her with a
particular significance or personality?

While striving to be empathic, those of us in law enforcement try to maintain our objectivity and a reasonable detach-
ment. But that just isn't possible when you have to try to feel
what the victim was feeling. Putting myself in Shari Smith's
head at the time she was writing this was almost unbearable.

On the one side, I felt the character, the courage, and the
faith of this extraordinary young woman who just a day before
was looking forward to her graduation, to singing before her
classmates and their parents, and to the fun and adventure of a
senior trip and cruise, now coming to terms with the sadness,
the terror of her situation, and accepting the fact that she was
going to die well before her time; that she would be deprived
of all of the joys and life events she had every right and reason
to expect. She would never see her family or boyfriend again.
She would never get to perform with her sister. She would never
get married. She would never have children or grandchildren.
And all this because of someone else's choice; someone she had

likely never seen before Friday. I didn't know if he'd sexually assaulted her. I didn't know if he was withholding the water that she needed in large amounts without her medication. But I did know that he had put her in this deadly position.

I stared at the copy of the portrait photo SLED had included in the case file, showing Shari's blond hair cascading down below her shoulders, her dimpled smile that looked like it would light up a room, and eyes so bright with hope and anticipation for the future. It had appeared at the top of the front page of the Saturday issue of the *State*. I imagined this young woman as she must have been at the moment she picked up the pen, somehow able to summon some fathomless courage and faith in writing her testament; for her to think about the effect her death would have on her loved ones was astonishing and emotionally gutting in itself. Ernest Hemingway defined courage as "grace under pressure," and I couldn't think of a more profound example. My wife, Pam, and I had two young daughters at that point, and the thought of Shari's parents reading this opened my heart to them and completely bound me to this case, as I knew it had gotten equally to Ron Walker and Jim Wright, both of whom also had young daughters.

On the other side, I perceived the man who had abducted Shari and was planning, with her full awareness, to kill her imminently. This UNSUB, whom we had already determined was incapable of luring a woman through cleverness, charm, wit, humor, or good looks, was clearly enjoying his power of life and death over this beautiful girl, sadistically luxuriating in their mutual knowledge that she would soon be dead by his hand. And once he no longer had Shari to torture emotionally, he could continue his indulgence through repeated phone calls to her family so he could torture them emotionally. As I read the letter and listened to the recordings, I hated this man I had never met, which is not particularly useful in terms of objectivity in my line of work but is sometimes unavoidable. And every one of us around the table was determined that he should be caught and made to pay for his crime.

The envelope and letter were photographed and dispatched to the SLED Questioned Documents Unit, where Lieutenant Marvin H. "Mickey" Dawson first compared the handwriting with known exemplars of Shari's and determined that she had, in fact, written it. Dawson was one of the country's top forensic document examiners. Ten years earlier, in 1975, he had established SLED's Document Laboratory.

Just as the UNSUB had wiped the telephone he'd used clean of fingerprints, there were no prints or identifying clues on the letter or envelope. Among the analyses Dawson and document examiner Gaile Heath performed was to put them through the ESDA, which stands for Electrostatic Detection Apparatus. This is a machine about the size and shape of a desktop computer printer. The questioned document is tightly covered with a specialized imaging film that, to the eye, resembles Saran Wrap. The ESDA doesn't bother with the writing on the page, but fills in subtle, even tiny indentations in the page with graphite carrier particles. It's a lengthy, painstaking process, but Dawson's thinking was that since the two pages clearly came from a thicker pad, perhaps the ESDA could reveal what had been written on previous sheets from the pad, and that might offer a clue as to the UNSUB's identity or whereabouts.

Re-creating the timeline, it was after the Last Will & Testament document was received that Undersheriff Lewis McCarty had first called Quantico and spoken to Ron Walker.

Shari's letter certainly didn't look good to us in terms of her survivability, but Monday afternoon, hopeful she could still be alive, at the suggestion of SLED captain Leon Gasque, all four of the Smiths and Sheriff Metts stood on the driveway outside the house and addressed the media. Under a broiling sun in hundred-degree temperatures, with one arm around Hilda's shoulders and the other around Dawn's, Bob Smith declared, "We just want to simply say whoever it is who has our daughter Shari, we want her back. We miss her. We love her. Please send her back home where she belongs."

Then Sheriff Metts, looking haggard from the strain of the past few days, said investigators believed Shari could still be alive and that somebody could be holding her captive. He announced a $15,000 reward for information leading authorities to Shari or to the person or persons responsible for her disappearance. "The search is not going to stop as long as there is hope," he declared.

Friends and church members were still showing up with food for everyone, and the local power company had installed extra electric lines for all the emergency equipment SLED and the sheriff's office had brought in.

It was 3:08 on Monday afternoon when the phone rang at the Smith home. As soon as Dawn picked up the receiver and answered, "Hello?" the recording device automatically clicked on.

"Mrs. Smith?"
"No, this is Dawn."

"I need to speak to your mother."

"Could I ask who's calling?"

"No."

"Okay. Okay, hold on just a second, please."

It took a few moments for Hilda to get to the phone.

"Have you received the mail today?"

"Yes, I have."

"Do you believe me now?"

"Well, I'm not really sure I believe you because I haven't had any word from Shari, and I need to know that Shari is well."

"You'll know in two or three days."

"Why two or three days?"

"Call the search off."

"Tell me if she is well, because of her disease. Are you taking care of her?"

At that point, the caller hung up.

The call was traced to a pay phone at the Eckerd pharmacy in the Lexington Town Square shopping center, about seven miles from the Smith home. It was the shopping center where Shari and her friend Brenda had parked their cars to ride with Richard to the pool party on Friday. It strengthened Ron and Jim's belief that the UNSUB might have first spotted Shari there and kept track of her whereabouts until she drove home.

The Signal Analysis Unit of the Bureau's Engineering Section had determined that the caller was using a pitch modulator, or variable speed device, to disguise his voice, which spoke to his degree of sophistication.

As we listened to the tapes and went over the elements of the file in our case consultation conference, we tried to consider all the possibilities. Victimology is always a critical consideration: How high risk for the victim was the situation in which the crime took place? Did the victim have any known enemies? Had the victim received any threats or observed any suspicious activity prior to the crime? And so on. But victimology is not always just about the individual to whom the crime occurred.

The brief call also gave us additional insight into the UNSUB. His asking if the Smiths had received the letter showed his egotism and wish to be in control of the family's emotions. We would refer to that as a signature aspect of the crime. We define *signature* as something the offender has to do to satisfy himself emotionally, not necessarily to pull off the crime successfully. For example, if he is a sadist, physical torture might be part of the signature. If he is a certain type of rapist, making the victim follow a verbal script as he assaults her might be a signature element. For David Berkowitz, the self-styled Son of Sam who terrorized New York City as the .44 Caliber Killer during the summer of 1977, masturbating at the scenes of the fires he had started, and later returning to the scenes of his murders to masturbate as he recalled the pleasure and power of his acts was part of his signature; that is, the return to the scene becomes part of the overall commission of the crime.

The other aspect, modus operandi, or M.O., is more familiar to the general public. M.O. is what the offender feels he has to do to commit the crime successfully and get away with it. For example, a burglar or robber cutting the phone lines before entering a house would be M.O. Notorious serial killer Theodore "Ted" Bundy often put a fake cast on his arm to make women feel he was not dangerous and that he needed their help carrying groceries to his car. The cast was part of his M.O. What he did to the women afterward was all signature.

The M.O. clues in our psycholinguistic analysis of the call were just as significant. The two key phrases were in the UNSUB's response when Hilda said she needed to know if Shari was well, to which he replied, "You'll know in two or three days," and then his next line, "Call the search off." While he was certainly deriving some pleasure and satisfaction from stringing the Smiths along, we were pretty sure the main reason for his not telling them anything definitive for several days, as well as his directive to call off the search, was possibly so he could spend more time alone with Shari if he had kept her alive. More likely, it was for her body to have time to degrade in the one-hundred-plus-degree heat and whatever soft, humid earth in which he had deposited it, leaving few useful forensic clues. This guy was compulsive and meticulous in his criminal methodology.

In a phone call, Sheriff Metts had told us that amidst their prayers and vain attempts to rest, Hilda, Bob, Dawn, and Robert repeatedly went over the words in Shari's letter, trying to find some glimmer of hope. Hilda felt as if she were crumbling inside, but strove to be strong for her husband and children. Dawn just couldn't get the image of the closed casket her sister had specified out of her mind and hoped it was part of some sort of code she was trying to send them. Maybe she had been drugged or was in some kind of altered mental and physical state because of her diabetic condition, but Shari's concern for her family and Richard and how they would deal with her loss seemed so direct that it was difficult to find hope or comfort in that. At the same time, Dawn was amazed at her sister's saintliness in focusing on the welfare of others rather than herself at such a time and in such a circumstance.

Then, at 8:07 P.M., the phone rang again. Dawn was out of breath by the time she raced down the stairs into the kitchen to answer it. She tried to force herself to sound calm.

"Hello?"

"Dawn?"

"Yes."

"Did you come down from Charlotte?"

"Yes, I did. Who's calling, please?"

"I need to speak to your mother."

"Okay. Get my mother. She's coming."

"Tell her to hurry."

"She's hurrying. Tell Shari I love her."

"Did y'all receive her letter today?"

"Yes, we did. Here's mother."

"This is Hilda."

"Did you read Shari Ray's letter?"

He misstated Shari's middle name, but even this was a significant indicator in our psycholinguistic analysis. Here and elsewhere, he was setting himself up with some false connection or intimacy with the family. But within the family and her circle of friends and acquaintances, Shari went only by the shortened form of her first name and never Shari Faye.

What we saw from this was that the UNSUB was creating his own relationship with her and giving her his own sense of her identity. In a way, it sounds like a perversion of the way the media almost always identifies criminals by their first and middle names as a matter of style for clarity. For example, we all know President John Kennedy's assassin as Lee Harvey Oswald, and that is his identity to history, even though he seldom used his middle name. I don't want to overstate this, but Shari's abductor appeared to feel that once he had her in his control, he could define her according to his own whim and perception.

> *"Did you receive the letter today?"*
> *"Yes, I did."*
> *"Tell me one thing it said."*
> *"Tell you one thing it said?"*
> *"Anything. Hurry!"*
> *"'ShaRichard.'"*
> *"Do what?"*
> *"There was that little heart on the side: 'ShaRichard'*
>   *written on this side, it said . . ."*
> *"How many pages?"*

We thought it significant that the caller immediately shifted away from the reference to Shari and Richard's relationship because in his own mind he had probably already constructed a relationship between himself and Shari. If he kept calling, we expected him at some point to say that Shari told him she was done with Richard.

In answer to his question, Hilda responded:

"Two pages."

"Okay, and it was a yellow legal pad?"

"Yeah."

"And on one side on the front page it said, 'Jesus is love'?"

"No. 'God is love.'"

"Well, 'God is love.'"

"Right."

"Okay, so you know now that this is not a hoax call."

"Yes, I know that."

The caller went on to complain that Sheriff Metts had not gone on television as instructed to call off the search. Then, completely disingenuously, he asserted:

*"Well, I'm trying to do everything possible to answer
    some of your prayers. So please, in the name of God,
    work with us here."*

*"Can you answer me one question, please? You . . .
    are very kind and . . . and you seem to be a
    compassionate person and . . . and I think you know
    how I feel being Shari's mother and how much I
    love her. Can you tell me, is she all right physically
    without her medication?"*

*"Shari is drinking a little over two gallons of water per
    hour and using the bathroom right afterwards."*

He tantalized Hilda by telling her that Shari was drinking plenty of water and that she should arrange to have an ambulance waiting at their house.

"Okay ... Have an ambulance ... Now, this is very
important. This has gone too far. Please forgive
me. Have an ambulance ready at any time at your
house."
"Have an ambulance ready at any ..."
"And at Shari's request ... She requests that only
immediate family come and Sheriff Metts and the
ambulance attendants. She don't want to make a
circus out of this."
"Right. Okay."

But at the same time that the UNSUB offered hope for Shari's return alive, he also brought up her request that if anything happened to her, her casket should be closed for the funeral and her hands should be placed in a position of prayer.

"And where she said 'casket closed' in parentheses, if
anything happens to me, she said, one of her requests
she did not put in there was to put her hands on her
stomach like she was praying in the casket."
"What, now?"
"Cross her hands."
"Why would anything happen to you? We don't want any
harm to you, I promise. We just want Shari well and
all right, okay?"

It was unclear to us when the UNSUB said "If anything happens to me" whether he was referring to himself or quoting Shari. Hilda clearly thought he was referring to himself and wanted to assure him that no one wanted to harm him; they just wanted Shari back alive and well. Ignoring Hilda's pleading benevolence, he referred again to the first, early-morning call that hadn't been recorded, then took on a tone of urgency.

> "I told you that morning you were looking at a wrong
>   place, right?"
> "Yes, you did."
> "I wish you would have remembered that, and I don't
>   know why."
> "I did remember that."
> "Okay, well listen to us, please. Forget Lexington County.
>   Look in Saluda County. Do you understand?"
> "Look in Saluda County."
> "Exactly. The closest to Lexington County within a
>   fifteen-mile radius, right over the line. Is that
>   understood?"
> "Yeah."
> "And please . . . And very, very soon get . . . Please, now,
>   Shari's request. Shari's request, please. No strangers
>   hardly when we give the location."

After continuing on with instructions, he then came to the most definitive statement, as far as our psycholinguistic analysis was concerned.

> "I want to tell you one other thing. Shari is now a part
>   of me—physically, mentally, emotionally, and
>   spiritually. Our souls are now one."
> "Your souls are one now with Shari?"

"Yes, and we're trying to work this out, so please do
     what we asked. You haven't been doing it. I don't
     understand, and she doesn't. We sit here and watch
     TV and we see no sheriff, we . . ."
"Why doesn't Shari talk to me? She knows me so well."
"That's why she asked me to communicate with you, not
     your husband. Aren't you aware of that?"
"Yes, I know that. I know that she would ask to talk
     with me."
"She said she does love y'all and, like she said, do not let
     this ruin your life."
"We're not going to let it ruin our . . ."
"Okay, well, it's not . . ."
"Listen, you tell Shari one thing."
"What is that?"
"There's no way my life could ever have any happiness
     in it again if Shari left this world with me bearing
     a guilt that I had failed in such a bad way, because
     I love her and I want to make her happy. I'll do
     anything to work it out. She doesn't have to come
     home. Okay? I'm serious. She does not have to come
     home. Anything."
"Well, time's up. And please now, have the ambulance
     ready at any time."

He tempted Hilda with additional pieces of information before adding:

"Shari is protected. And like I said, she is a part of me
     now, and God looks after all of us. Goodnight."

Except for the fact that we didn't know who he was, it was almost as if we were interviewing an incarcerated felon for our serial killer study. We all realized how weird and unusual this was. Because as agonizing as it must have been for Hilda to go through, the call did give us a lot to analyze as well as ample material to continue building our profile. Communication by active killers and other violent offenders is not unusual. David Berkowitz sent letters to NYPD detective captain Joseph Borelli and New York *Daily News* columnist Jimmy Breslin during his Son of Sam reign of terror over New York City in 1977. Wichita's "BTK Strangler" Dennis Rader wrote letters to the local newspaper and television stations over a period of several years. The still-unidentified Zodiac Killer posted letters to at least three San Francisco–area newspapers. All three of these serial murderers gave themselves their own nicknames.

But while we do see notoriety-seeking killers try to garner publicity through difficult-to-trace letters (and, these days, social media and other forms of digital communication), having an UNSUB repeatedly speaking to the family, indulgently giving details of his horrible deeds and at the same time trying to strike an almost conversational and intimate tone struck us as pretty unusual. The prison interviews Bob Ressler and I conducted had given us retrospective insight into what went on in the minds of serial violent offenders. Now this case was giving us an unprecedented "real-time" window into what this UNSUB was thinking.

In addition to getting a "feel" for the offender and insight into his narcissistic and sadistic teasing of the family on Shari's status, we could tell, for instance, that he was following the media reports, which is a highly useful piece of evidence because it allows us to anticipate his next move based on what he is hearing. A few years before, during the Atlanta Child Murders, a call had come into the police department in Conyers, a small town about twenty miles from Atlanta. The caller professed to be the child killer, and using a racial slur, he said he was "going to kill" more kids and named a particular spot along Sigmon Road where he claimed police would find another body.

Listening to the tape of that call, I could tell this racist jerk was an imposter; he sounded like an older white man, and we had already concluded the killer was young, Black, and not a Klan type. But the caller was taunting law enforcement and clearly felt superior, so I told the police they had to catch him because he would keep calling and distract the real investigation. I suggested they purposely look on the side of Sigmon Road opposite where he had specified, knowing he'd be watching. Maybe they could catch him at the scene; otherwise they'd be ready with a telephone trap and trace.

After the police made a very public show of "screwing up" his instructions of where to look, he did call again to gloat, and they were able to catch this aging redneck right in his own house. But even more significant, the actual killer then dumped a body along Sigmon Road, as if to show us how superior he was by dumping a body right where the police had been looking. I realized at that point that the media was a two-way street. If we could determine that an UNSUB was following news accounts, we could publicize facts that would lead him to react in a certain way. That ultimately helped us catch and prosecute Wayne B. Williams for some of the Atlanta murders. And once we knew that Shari's killer was following the media, we could tailor our proactive strategies accordingly.

We had learned over our years of research that most predators displayed three primary traits that fulfilled their emotional
aspirations in committing their crimes: manipulation, domination, and control. From the telephone dialogue we were listening to, it was clear this UNSUB was displaying all three. He
directed Hilda on what he wanted her to do, and teased her
that the sheriff's department was looking in the wrong place.
He tantalized her that Shari would be released, but also that
her physical condition might be grave and they should have an
ambulance waiting. He clearly appeared to be enjoying Hilda's
pleading.

This latest call was traced to a pay phone at the Wall Street
Store, near the intersection of Interstate 20 and state Highway 204, about eight miles from the Smith home. As before,
when officers arrived on scene the caller had vanished, leaving
no physical evidence behind.

CHAPTER 4

A mong the materials on the conference room table on Thursday were photocopies of the Tuesday editions of the local papers, both of which made the case their lead story. The *State* featured the portrait photo of Shari next to a shot of her family and Sheriff Metts at the news conference on the driveway. The headline read, SHERIFF THINKS TEEN STILL ALIVE, with the subhead MISSING GIRL'S FAMILY PLEADS FOR HER RETURN. The *Columbia Record* had the same photo of Shari and one of a SLED agent briefing volunteer searchers. Its headline read, SHERIFF EXPANDS SEARCH, with the subhead METTS STILL OPTIMISTIC TEENAGER IS ALIVE.

That Tuesday morning, the Smiths taped a television interview that they hoped Shari and her abductor would see. "Shari, we love you so much," Hilda said. "We're just not going to give up on finding you. I know you're being taken care of. We just feel such assurances from the Lord that you will be with us again."

"We're not a family without you," Dawn added.

Volunteers distributed more than 10,000 posters with

Shari's photo that had been provided by a local printer. With the addition of a $5,000 contribution from Lexington State Bank and individual contributions from private citizens, the reward quickly reached $25,000 for information about Shari or the person or persons responsible for her disappearance.

For the rest of the day the Smiths waited in anxious agony. Bob's mother's doctor prescribed sleeping pills for Bob and Hilda, since sleeping had become impossible for both of them and they'd reached the point of absolute exhaustion. Motorists and truck drivers continually slowed down and stopped at the Smith driveway on Platt Springs Road, inquiring of the deputy posted there if there was any news.

The phone rang at 9:45 that evening. Dawn ran to answer it.

"Dawn?"

"Yes."

"This is Shari Faye's request. Have your mother get on the other phone, quickly."

"To get on the other phone? Get on the other phone, Mother."

"Get a pencil and a piece of paper ready."

"Get a pencil and a piece of paper ready. Okay."

"Okay."

"She's not on the phone yet."

While he waited, he said:

"I know these calls are taped and traced, but that's irrelevant now. There's no money demanded. So

here's Shari Faye's last request: On the fifth day,
to put the family at rest, Shari Faye being freed.
Remember, we are one soul now. When located,
you locate both of us together. We are one. God has
chosen us. Respect all past and present requests,
actual events and times."

The UNSUB's words were just further confirmation of his narcissism and the sadistic glee he took in manipulation and control. "Shari Faye's last request," and "Shari Faye being freed," were contradictory statements, except in the sense of her being freed from this life or freed from her torment. "On the fifth day . . . you locate both of us together" had a biblical ring to it; we had no expectation he would be found along with Shari. We were convinced it only meant that he had determined how long he had to keep her body from authorities for any physical evidence to degrade sufficiently. There was an implication here of murder-suicide, and if the calls continued, it wouldn't be unusual for him to keep threatening/promising to kill himself. But we didn't believe for a moment that he would do it. This guy was too full of himself and his perceived power to take his own life. Since Monday, when Ron first laid out the case to me, he said it didn't seem like a one-off to him. This UNSUB liked what he was doing too much.

The recording continued:

"3:28 in the afternoon, Friday, thirty-first of May . . ."
"Wait a minute; too fast. 3:28, afternoon."
"Shari Faye was kidnapped from your mailbox with a

> *gun. She had the fear of God in her and she was at*
> *the mailbox. That's why she did not return back to*
> *her car."*

His next statements further confirmed his compulsivity, as well as the probability that he was reading from a script or notes.

> *"Okay: 4:58 A.M. No, I'm sorry; hold on a minute. 3:10 A.M.*
> *Saturday, the first of June . . . uh . . . she handwrote*
> *what you received. 4:58 A.M. Saturday, the first of*
> *June."*

The fact that he apologized for misstating the time, as opposed to, say, apologizing for kidnapping Shari, spoke to his narcissism and internal need for control. It was as if he wanted to establish the exact time so he could receive proper credit from the people whose lives he was ruining. He continued:

> *"Okay. Saturday, the first of June, 4:58 A.M. Became one*
> *soul."*
> *"Became one soul. What does that mean?"*
> *"No questions now."*

There was little doubt in our minds about the UNSUB's confusion over times and Hilda's question. 3:10 A.M., as he said, was when "she handwrote what you received." 4:58 A.M. must have been the time he killed her. Everything else was simply manipulation for his own sense of power and grandiosity. He went on:

"Prayers and release coming soon. Please learn to enjoy life. Forgive. God protects the chosen. Shari Faye's important request: Rest tonight and tomorrow. Good shall come out of this. And please tell Sheriff Metts, search no more. Blessings are near. Remember, tomorrow, Wednesday, four in the afternoon to seven in the evening. Ambulance ready. No circus."

"Okay, no circus. What does that mean?"

"You will receive last instructions for where to find us. Please forgive."

[Hilda] "Do not kill my daughter! Please! I mean, please!"

"We love and miss y'all. Get good rest tonight. Goodnight."

"Listen, wait a minute!"

[Dawn] "He's gone, Mom."

The call was traced to a pay phone attached to the brick wall outside the Fast Fare Convenience Store at Jake's Landing on Highway 6 at Lake Murray, just north of Lexington and about nine miles from the Smith home. As before, the caller had left no physical evidence. Officers set up roadblocks on both side of the Lake Murray Dam and combed the entire area, but once again the UNSUB had eluded them.

THE CRUELTY OF THE CALLER WAS OBVIOUS. WHAT WAS NOT SO OBVIOUS WAS THE motivation for the criminal narcissism that compelled him to keep calling the family. He had taken steps to disguise his voice and make calls from locations that wouldn't lead to his identification. That was all M.O. Yet the conversations with Hilda and Dawn were clearly part of his signature—what he needed to make his crime feel complete.

What was also striking was that despite the horror of what the UNSUB had done, there was neither anger nor hostility in his tone. It is, of course, manipulative and self-indulgent as hell, but the matter-of-fact quality is totally removed from, and out of keeping with, what was actually happening. He was neither glorying in his hideous crime, nor feeling bad about it. It was as if he was fulfilling a sacred destiny and it was altogether natural that the Smiths should go along with it.

His frequent invocations of God also suggested an omnipotent and invincible sense of himself, and his repeated instructions as to what Sheriff Metts should and should not do indicated a feeling of superiority over law enforcement authorities. When we see this kind of behavior from an UNSUB, directing the cops or ridiculing them for not being able to catch him, it often indicates an internal war within him over his own inadequacy, and the need to prove himself to himself. Concluding as we had that this individual did not have the self-confidence to control his victims any other way than by a surprise attack, apparently showing Shari a weapon to gain compliance, we certainly felt that this delicate emotional balancing act of entitlement derived from a sense of mental superiority coupled with deep-seated inadequacy and self-loathing was operating here.

Based on the behavioral evidence assimilated thus far, the guy was no genius, but he was criminally smart and sophisticated, meaning he had some experience. We didn't believe this was his first crime involving assaulting or otherwise harming women. It was possible he had gotten away cleanly with previous crimes, but we expected some kind of criminal record: anything from obscene phone calls or Peeping Tom encounters all the way up to actual sexual assaults. If he had any prior murders, they would be against children or young girls. Unlike a lot of serial killers, he'd be too intimidated to go after adult women—even professional sex workers, whose job makes them inherently more vulnerable.

Along with this, and based on our experience with this personality type, we expected he would collect pornography, with a particular emphasis on bondage and sadomasochism. He would always be fantasizing about his power over women. And he had either been planning his abduction of Shari Smith for a while or thinking and fantasizing about doing it to *someone*.

From the moment we first heard about the case, we figured the UNSUB was white. These types of predatory crimes were seldom interracial, and at that point, the perpetrators of these sorts of murders didn't tend to be African American or Hispanic, though that changed somewhat as previously marginalized groups became more assimilated into the general society. We also knew this particular UNSUB would be fairly homely, and probably somewhat overweight. He would have been married or had some long-term relationship with a woman, since women and what they thought of him was obviously very important to his self-esteem. But the marriage or relationship would have gone bad. If he had any children, they would live with his ex-wife and he probably wouldn't see much of them, if at all.

We were just about certain he had some kind of low- to medium-level blue collar job, maybe in electrical work based on what the Signal Analysis Unit had told us about the voice-altering device he was using. We also believed he must have a job with flexible hours so that his time was often his own, and he had mobility to travel at will.

Though the voice was disguised in the first few calls we listened to, we could detect enough of a southern twang and expressions to reinforce our belief that he was a local, familiar with the area (hence his ease locating pay phones for his calls), rather than an outsider passing through—despite the preference people have for imagining a stranger committing a horrible crime in their community instead of considering the possibility of evil in their midst. His comfortability with the environment also likely contributed to his growing confidence. As the days ticked by with law enforcement seemingly no closer to identifying him, he stopped using the voice-altering device. We saw that increasing cockiness as something we could use against him in developing proactive strategies to get him to reveal himself.

We pegged him for late twenties to early thirties, but age is one of the most difficult factors to predict accurately because a subject's chronological age does not always correspond to his emotional development age. A higher level of risk to the offender tends to skew our estimate lower, unless the crime was pulled off in a sophisticated or highly organized manner, which would tend to show some experience. As a result of our research with incarcerated offenders, we had come up with the categories *organized, disorganized,* and *mixed* to describe criminal behavior, having determined they were more useful to investigators than more abstract psychological terms such as *schizophrenic* or *borderline personality disorder,* which don't convey identifiable behavioral traits.

Disorganized UNSUBs tend to be younger or have severe mental problems or character disorders. However, we learned from anomalies to our methodology, such as when Special

Agent Gregg McCrary profiled a serial killer who was targeting prostitutes and homeless women in the Rochester, New York, area in 1988 and 1989. The profile helped police find the killer by staking out body dump sites, and it was highly accurate in every respect but one: Gregg had figured the killer to be about thirty. In fact, Arthur J. Shawcross was forty-four, and Gregg wondered why he had gotten this one part wrong. When he looked into Shawcross's background, Gregg found he had previously murdered a ten-year-old boy and raped and murdered an eight-year-old girl, for which he was (foolishly, in my opinion) allowed to plead down to manslaughter. Shawcross spent fourteen years in state prison before being released. As it turned out, those years in prison were essentially time on ice, and when he got out, he resumed life at his emotional developmental age of thirty.

Though the Shawcross case wouldn't come up for another five years, it was foreshadowed in at least one aspect of the Smith case. We kept hearing how beastly hot it was down in South Carolina, and Metts and McCarty felt badly for the hundreds of people who were braving the heat, out looking for Shari or clues. As I've said, we had already concluded that if Shari had been killed, as available indicators and most of the UNSUB's pronouncements suggested, he was probably holding the discovery off long enough for the body to decompose so that less forensic evidence would be obtainable. But in looking at the events of Tuesday, something else occurred to us as we brainstormed. We had profiled this guy as bold, megalomaniacal, and cocksure from a distance but unsophisticated and intimidated up close and personal, fantasizing about relationships with unattainable women. We realized another reason he was promising information but still withholding it was that he likely was returning to visit the body, wherever he had hidden it, and he certainly didn't want sheriff's officers or any of the searchers coming across him wherever he had deposited Shari. Whether he was actually trying to have sex with the corpse—appallingly, not all that uncommon among a certain type of serial killer—or just spending time with and "possessing" her, we thought he would continue this practice until the body degraded to the point where he no longer felt a human connection. This was a behavior we would later see with Shawcross.

Since this UNSUB had made a point of how Shari's casket was to be closed and her hands placed in a praying position, we expected he would eventually reveal where he had placed the body, either in a phone call or letter, or maybe even a direct communication with Sheriff Metts, on whom he seemed to be focused as the embodiment of law enforcement and the establishment.

He had told Dawn on the telephone that he and Shari had become "one soul." Clearly, he was not going to let go of her emotionally.

And we hoped to use that to our advantage.

CHAPTER 5

"Listen carefully. Take Highway 378 west to traffic circle, Take Prosperity exit. Go one and a half miles. Turn right at sign. Masonic Lodge Number 103. Go one quarter miles, turn left at white frame building. Go to backyard, six feet beyond. We're waiting. God chose us."

None of us in the conference room said anything after hearing the transcript of the call spoken aloud. That call had come just one day earlier, on Wednesday, and there was a sense of chilling resolution to it—the reality he'd been teasing had finally come to pass. We quickly realized that Wednesday had been the critical day: the day when the case started coming together, and lives finished falling apart.

By then, the law enforcement authorities had a plan. They would turn off most of the pay phones throughout the area and surveil the ones they left working. We thought that was a pretty good idea and hearkened back to my days as a street agent in Detroit when we tried to stop a rash of bank robberies by hardening the obvious targets, thereby forcing the robbers to hit other branches where we would be waiting for them.

Still, as she later told me, Dawn continued to lay awake, feeling helpless to do anything for her sister, knowing what five days without her medication could do to her. If Shari was still alive, even if she was drinking plenty of water, she would be in pretty bad shape. Maybe that's what the caller meant when he told them to have an ambulance standing by. Shari's boyfriend, Richard, hardly ever left the Smith house. He harbored feelings of guilt, thinking the kidnapper might have seen him and Shari kissing at the post office and become jealous. The only way he could somewhat allay his anxiety was by staying close to the Smith family.

At 11:54 A.M. Wednesday, the phone rang. Hilda answered it this time. The caller got right to the point, giving her the directions he had been withholding for days. The call was traced to a Camden Highway switch station, some forty-five miles away. It came in about fifteen minutes before most of the pay phones were scheduled to be turned off.

A helicopter dispatched from South Carolina Wildlife & Marine Resources Department spotted the body at 12:35 P.M. A crime scene team, led by Lieutenant Jim Springs and Agent Don Grindt, was immediately dispatched from SLED headquarters. Hilda wanted to go with Sheriff Metts and SLED captain Leon Gasque to the scene, but the two men strongly discouraged her, essentially not giving her a choice and ordering her, Bob, and the children to remain in the house. They said their presence would interfere with police work, but their stronger motive was not wanting the parents to see what they expected to find. The family members gathered in Dawn's room to wait, praying for a miracle, since much of the rest of the house was still occupied by law enforcement personnel, extended family, and friends.

As they waited, few words were spoken. There was simply nothing to say. They didn't know what to do, so they prayed silently, but with an overlay of dread of what the next official word would be. In spite of that, Dawn related that her mom absolutely refused to even begin to consider that Shari was not going to be found alive. She even packed a little overnight bag because she knew she'd probably have to go to the hospital. She had her nightgown and her toothbrush and all the things that she thought she would need. Even with that air of dread looming, none of them could face the possibility that the news would not be what they had just prayed and fervently hoped it would be.

The SLED officers and sheriff's team converged at the Masonic Lodge off Highway 391 in the Pleasant Grove section of Saluda County: a two-story white building with a pitched tin roof, mostly surrounded by thick woods. It was roughly sixteen miles west of where Shari was abducted. They quickly cased the area and found Shari's body just about where the caller said it would be, fifty or so feet from the back of the lodge and six or eight feet beyond the tree line. She was lying on her back, dressed in her white shorts over the yellow and black bikini bathing suit bottom and her black-and-white-striped blouse over her yellow tank top. Around her neck was the gold chain necklace that had been a gift from Richard. There was a gold stud earring in her left ear, but her right earring was missing.

She was still barefoot, as she had been when she'd stepped out of her car on Friday. And as expected, the body was badly decomposed.

The precision of the caller's description of the location confirmed for us that he had been returning to the body as long as it satisfied him to do so; and as compulsive as he seemed to be, we thought he had actually taken measurements of the various distances, whether miles on his car's odometer or feet from the back of the Masonic Lodge. It also supported our profile of him as an inveterate list maker; someone who would want everything he considered important in his life organized and under control.

As the SLED crime scene team took photos and processed the scene and surrounding area, forensic pathologist Dr. Joel Sexton of Newberry Memorial Hospital was sent for. At the same time, Captain Gasque went back to his car for the difficult drive back to the Smith house.

Dawn heard a car drive up, looked out the window, and saw it was Gasque's. She heard footsteps slowly climbing the stairs, as if in no hurry to reach the top.

"We heard the front door open and his steps coming upstairs were really slow and heavy," Dawn told us. "And I remember just having that fear of, oh my gosh, oh no!"

When they all saw the expression on the captain's face and the tears in his eyes, they knew for certain what his message was.

The scene was surreal in its horror, but Dawn thought she heard something like, "I'm so sorry. It is Shari and she's dead." And then she remembered her mom wailing, crying, and she just kept saying, "Not my baby! Oh God, not my baby!"

It seemed like an eternity to Dawn that the four of them sat in that room while Hilda continued to sob over her murdered daughter.

"We found her body behind the Masonic Lodge," Gasque said quietly, his voice choking.

"Are you sure it's Shari?" Bob asked.

They were sure, he replied, then told them how very sorry he was. Bob held Hilda as she sobbed. Robert continued sitting where he was, crying quietly. Dawn said she wanted to see her sister for herself. Gasque said he didn't want her to do that; that it would not be necessary for any family members to identify the body; that it was in too bad a condition. But they were certain it was Shari. He said again how sorry he was, and that he would leave them alone now.

Dawn, her brother, and her parents remained in her bedroom, realizing that Shari was gone forever. And the reality began sinking in that this man had been so cruel to tell them all these things that were completely untrue, that gave them the hope that he really was taking care of her as he said, having her drink sufficient volumes of water to counteract her diabetes insipidus since she didn't have her medicine. As Dawn reviewed the details of the phone calls, it made no sense to her to realize he'd killed her sister and all that time he was pushing all of those lies on the family.

When Dr. Sexton arrived on the scene behind the Masonic Lodge, he was briefed on the case and shown a copy of Shari's Last Will & Testament. From the line of bent-over saplings and bushes, it was determined that a vehicle had been driven to the back of the lodge, and the body then dragged from there into the woods where it was found. In addition to the decomposition caused by the extreme heat, Sexton noted insect infestation. Under these circumstances, he thought that the condition of the body was consistent with death early on Saturday morning, shortly after the time written on the Last Will & Testament. If that was the case, he declared, her diabetic condition would not have been the cause.

Back at the Smith home, Shari's parents and siblings hugged each other amidst their grief, silently acknowledging that their family would never again be complete. Eventually, when they had forced themselves into some degree of composure, they made their way downstairs, into the embrace of the friends and officers who had been standing vigil with them for the past five days. Dawn hugged her college roommates, Julie and Cindy. Hilda sensed that Bob had taken upon himself the additional pain of feeling he had failed to protect his family.

I have seen too many cases when the murder of a child or loved one strikes a deeply religious family. I have found that they seldom lose their faith; but nearly always, among their first thoughts is, "God, how could you let this happen?"

Dawn echoed similar thoughts, as she recounted in her 1993 book, *Grace So Amazing*:

> "God, how could You? Why would You let this happen to us? How could You let Shari suffer? Oh, God, how much she must have suffered! Did You even listen to my constant prayers all this time? Didn't You hear anything I said?"

As a law enforcement agent, my questions had to be of a more worldly nature, though the more transcendent ones Dawn posed have never been far from my mind. If there is a

God who is all good and all powerful, these are mysteries that will have to wait for a realm beyond the earthly one. I just know this: As long as individual men and women have the power and agency to exercise free will and choice, evil will continue to exist, and it must be challenged and fought.

By six o'clock in the evening, the crime scene investigation had been completed and Shari's body had been transported to Newberry Memorial Hospital, where Dr. Sexton was assisted in the autopsy by Saluda County coroner Bruce Horne. They had Shari's dental records to officially confirm her identity. Though they couldn't be certain, it did not appear that Shari had been shot, stabbed, or beaten, and it was unclear whether she had been sexually assaulted. It was possible to tell that Shari had been bound with rope ligatures and duct tape, which was removed prior to the body being deposited in the woods, as evidenced by the residue on her face.

The postmortem examination was completed at about 9:30 P.M. Though the advanced state of decomposition would not allow Sexton to make a definitive determination of the cause of death, he expressed his strong opinion that Shari had died as a result of strangulation or smothering. He concluded:

> As far as the manner of death, since the death occurred during abduction, the manner of death will still be homicide, regardless of whether it is due to depriving the decedent of water or from some type of homicidal asphyxia.

THE GRIEF EXTENDED WELL BEYOND SHARI'S IMMEDIATE FAMILY AND FRIENDS. "Shari has been in our prayers continuously since she was abducted on Friday," Lexington High principal Karl Fulmer told the *Columbia Record*. "Students, faculty, and administrators are all distraught and share the grief of the Smith family," he said. "The entire student body and the community have been deeply touched by this senseless tragedy."

The regular Wednesday evening prayer meeting at Lexington Baptist Church was transformed into a memorial service for Shari, whom all the congregants knew from her singing in the youth choir.

"We do know that Shari was murdered," Sheriff Metts told reporters at a news conference shortly before eleven P.M. We know Shari was abducted in Lexington County . . . We do not know if she was killed in Lexington or Saluda County."

As the *State* reported the next day in a story by Peter O'Boyle III and John Collins, many of those who had searched for Shari, and other interested people, continued driving by the Smith home in the afternoon to show their ongoing support.

"'Is she all right?' one passerby asked from her car Wednesday, several hours after authorities learned of Miss Smith's fate.

"'No, I'm afraid she's not,' said the deputy guarding the entrance to the Smith home."

CHAPTER 6

As we wrapped up our case consultation meeting Thursday, we told Undersheriff McCarty to keep us up to date on any new developments as they occurred to see if we could come up with any proactive strategies. Personality-wise, we felt we knew a lot about the UNSUB, but so far there wasn't much to lead us in a direction that would help Sheriff Metts's team home in on a specific individual. Columbia SAC Robert Ivey said he was preparing a telegram formally requesting the Behavioral Science Unit's ongoing assistance in the case.

The banner headline across the top of Thursday morning's edition of the *State* was POLICE HUNT "SICK" KILLER. A large aerial photo showed the Masonic Lodge and its surroundings, with a phalanx of police and rescue vehicles converged in the front. Below that was a map showing where Shari's body had been found relative to the Smith home.

Lexington County Sheriff's Office captain Bob Ford and SLED spokesman Hugh Munn publicly expressed their admiration and gratitude for the hundreds of citizens who braved the searing heat and searched for days for any sign of Shari. "They came to us as volunteers. They pleaded with us to let them do anything they could to help," Ford told the *Columbia Record*. Those who had participated in the search had equal praise for the dedication of the law enforcement officials.

The funeral was announced for Saturday so that Shari's classmates who had gone on the senior class trip would be back and able to attend.

At a noon news conference on Thursday, Sheriff Metts wanted to up the UNSUB's stress by giving him a sense of the department's resolve in the case, but also to encourage him to turn himself in if he was at all thinking in that direction.

"We are concerned that this person may take his own life if he doesn't turn himself in. We don't want him to do that," the sheriff stated. "I want to reassure him that we have no intentions of killing anyone. All we want to do is take this person into custody.

"We're trying to get this person to surrender. He needs help, and we want him to get it . . . He sounds as if he is afraid; as if he doesn't know whether to take his own life or turn himself in."

On the other hand, Metts warned, "If he's having fun jerking us around, he can continue. The investigation is going full blast and we are not stopping until we catch him, I promise!" He also announced that morning that the FBI had been called into the investigation.

A short time later, around 2:30 P.M., the UNSUB called Charlie Keyes, a prominent investigative reporter with WIS-TV in Columbia. To capture any news reports, the station routinely recorded all incoming telephone calls. We listened to the tape:

"This is concerning Shari Faye Smith. I want to use you
  as a medium. Can you handle it? Okay, now listen
  carefully. I can't live with myself, Charlie, and I need
  to turn myself in and I'm afraid, and you're a very
  intelligent person, and I want you to be there with
  Sheriff Metts and all [the] officers he wants at his
  home in the morning, and you answer the phone."
"At whose home?"
"At Sheriff Metts's home. Hurry now. Don't answer any
  questions unless I ask. You be there and answer the
  phone."

The caller went on to instruct Keyes to verify on his seven
o'clock television segment that he would be at Metts's house
and told Keyes that as soon as they hung up, Keyes was to call
Metts and describe Shari's Last Will & Testament so Metts
would know the call was not a hoax. He described the document in elaborate detail for Keyes's edification. He also said
he wanted "Shari Faye's priest there from Lexington Baptist.
Okay?" In return, he promised Keyes an exclusive interview
just after he turned himself in.

He then transitioned directly from power and manipulation to confessional mode:

"Now, Charlie . . . please . . . it just went bad. I know her
  family and her, and well, I just made a mistake. It
  went too far. All I wanted to do was to make love to
  her. I didn't know she had the rare disease, and it
  just got out of hand. I got scared and . . . I have to do

the right thing, Charlie. Now, please work with me,
'cause I feel like I can trust you and I've listened to
you many times, and that's why I picked you as the
medium."

After once more regurgitating how Sheriff Metts would know this was not a hoax, he continued with:

"Please forgive me. God forgive me and take care of me.
I need the help bad, and I want to do the right thing,
and tell them to please honor Shari Faye's request:
casket closed. Plus, take her hands and fold them
on her stomach like she's praying. You understand
that?"

We perceived this call as an escalation of his narcissism and compulsion to manipulate and control, now that the news of Shari's murder was the biggest story in the region, as well as a confirmation that he was avidly following the media. We noted the UNSUB's familiar tropes such as "listen carefully" and "this is not a hoax," and mentioning with specificity the date and time on the Last Will & Testament when he described it to the reporter. His statement "I didn't know she had the rare disease" proved we were right when we assessed the business about his being a friend of the family, which he'd also said in calls with Hilda and Dawn, as bunk. Anyone truly close to the family knew of Shari's condition. It was just another part of his fantasy, trying to draw a connection with this beautiful girl he had first seen at a distance. We also knew, despite his protestations, that he was not going to turn himself in. He was getting too much satisfaction out of this. The only true words he uttered in the entire exchange with the reporter were when he said he'd wanted "to make love to her." But whether he was able to accomplish that as a sexual assault while she lived or not, he would have known that he would have to kill her afterward.

There is a common misconception that some violent predators actually do start to feel guilty about what they've done and want to turn themselves in. And despite great literature like Fyodor Dostoyevsky's *Crime and Punishment*, in real life, this almost never happens. One of the few instances of a serial killer turning himself in was the first incarcerated subject we interviewed, Edmund Kemper, a very large and intelligent man who became infamous as the Coed Killer in Santa Cruz, California, in the early 1970s.

Having been released from custody after serving time for murdering his grandparents while still a teen, Kemper killed five college women and one high school girl after picking them up as hitchhikers. He sexually assaulted their corpses and dismembered their bodies. His crimes culminated with the bludgeoning and throat-slitting of his fifty-two-year-old mother, Clarnell Elizabeth Strandberg, as she slept in her bed. He then invited her best friend over to the house, whereupon he strangled her. After mutilating his mother's corpse, he drove more than a thousand miles straight through to Pueblo, Colorado, where he stopped at a phone booth and called the police, having a difficult time convincing them that he was an actual serial killer. When I interviewed Kemper, it became clear that all of his adult crimes were in reaction to his punitive and emotionally abusive mother, who belittled him by telling him he wasn't good enough for the beautiful coeds at the University of

California, Santa Cruz, where she worked. And once he worked up the nerve to kill her and, by association, her friend, instead of targeting the surrogate women whom she said he could never have, he was done. There was no point to his killing any longer. Turning himself in seemed the logical and prudent thing to do.

But in this regard, Ed Kemper was highly unusual. He was also unusual in the amount of insight he had into his own psyche. Shari Smith's unidentified killer was no such specimen. Did he actually feel guilty about what he'd done to Shari? Perhaps there might have been a tinge of guilt, though even that I doubted. What we firmly believed from his signature and M.O. was that if this individual was not caught, and caught soon, he would kill again.

THE NEXT CALL CAME TO THE SMITH HOUSE AT 8:57 THAT EVENING. HILDA'S sister-in-law Beverly Cartrette answered the phone. By this point everyone in the household had been alerted to look for any opportunity to get the persistent caller to identify himself, and to keep him on the line as long as possible. Earlier in my FBI career, one of my assignments had been as a hostage negotiator. This can be a very delicate balancing act with an offender you're trying to keep calm so he won't harm his hostages on one side, and a SWAT team ready to break down the door, sweep in, and neutralize the hostage holder as quickly and efficiently as possible on the other. Some of the techniques we now use in behavioral science came from that experience.

On the phone with Lewis McCarty, I had advised him to train the Smith family in basic hostage negotiation strategy; that is, to stall for time and try to "outlast" the offender, to listen carefully and then paraphrase and restate what he has told you. This should give the impression of understanding between the parties and may make the offender open up, reveal more, or even reveal what his actual wishes or intentions are. It can also help you know if you're making progress or going in the other direction. It was a technique I used when I interviewed Charles Manson. The only way I could gain any insight into his raving and lecturing was to paraphrase and restate declarations he made, and then go one level deeper and ask him to explain to me what he meant.

This Thursday night call both confirmed what we had pro-filed and gave us a more complete psychological portrait of the UNSUB.

The first voice was that of the telephone operator, then when Beverly responded, the UNSUB took over.

"I have a collect call for Dawn Smith."
"Dawn is not taking any calls. Could I have a name, please?"
"Please put Dawn on the line."
"Dawn can't come to the phone right now. This is her Aunt Beverly."
"Well, may I speak to Mrs. Smith? This is an emergency."
"Well, I'm sorry. She is being sedated and cannot come to the phone. She's asleep."
"Okay, may I speak to Bob Smith?"
"Bob has gone to the funeral home. You realize the situation with their daughter? Wait one moment . . . you asked to speak to Mrs. Smith?"

"Or Dawn. I'd rather speak to Dawn."

"To Dawn."

"Mm-hmm."

"Well, let me see if we can find her."

"Okay. Hurry up."

Beverly went to find Dawn, who was out walking the dog. She got on the phone and said:

"Hello?"

"Dawn?"

"Yes."

*"I'm calling for Shari Faye. And are you aware I'm
    turning myself in tomorrow morning?"*

"No."

"Well, have you talked to Sheriff Metts or Charlie Keyes?"

"No."

*"Well, talk to them and listen carefully. I have to tell you
    this; that Shari asked me to turn myself in after the
    fifth day, after they found her."*

He went on to explain:

*"I, uh, got to get myself straight with God and I turned
    myself completely over to him, so I have to turn myself
    over to him. And Charlie Keyes, he'll know what I'm
    talking about when you talk to him. He will not be able
    to get a personal interview from me in the morning.
    There'll be a letter that's already been mailed, an
    exact copy for you and to him and it's with pictures."*

"A copy for me?"

"Yes, and him at his home: pictures of Shari Faye from the time, even, I made her stand at her car and took two pictures, and all through the thing. And the letter will describe exactly what happened from the time I picked her up 'til the time I called and told y'all where to find her."

He gave details of how and when he was going to turn himself in, and that though he was going to be armed, he wouldn't be dangerous. Dawn asked him what that meant.

"Well, Shari Faye said if I couldn't live with myself, and she wouldn't forgive me if I didn't turn myself in or turn myself over to God, so I'm going to have to . . ."

Then he paused, and in the next thought handed us the strategy that would become the central focus of our manhunt.

"This thing got out of hand, and all I wanted to do was make love to Dawn. I've been watching her for a couple of weeks . . ."

"To who?"

"I'm sorry; to Shari. I watched her for a couple of weeks and, uh, it just got out of hand. And Dawn, Dawn, I hope you and your family forgive me for this."

We had noticed the striking similarity between the two beautiful blond Smith sisters, and apparently the UNSUB had, too. In his rape-fueled fantasies, he was conflating them.

Playing to Dawn's feigned sympathy, he talked about killing himself because:

> *"I can't live in prison and go to the electric chair. This is the only way I can get myself straight."*

She told him not to do that, that God could forgive him, which is more than I could have offered him, but the Smith family's faith was strong, and I know it was the only thing that sustained them throughout this horrific ordeal.

As I listened to the recording of the next thing he said, at the same time my stomach was turned by his self-indulgent cruelty, I was dumbfounded by what his recitation indicated about Shari's bravery and strength of character.

> *"Well, I want to say something to you that she told me."*
> *"Okay."*
> *"Oh boy . . . Shari Faye said that, uh . . . She did not cry the entire time, Dawn. She was very strong-willed, and she said that she did not want y'all to ruin your lives, and go on with your lives like the letter said. And I've never lied to y'all before, right? Everything I've told you came true, right?"*
> *"Yes."*
> *"Okay, so this is going to have to be the way it is. And she said that she wasn't scared, that she knew she was going to be an angel. And if I took the latter choice she suggested to me, that she would forgive me. But God's going to be the major judgment, and she'll probably end up seeing me in heaven, not in hell."*

He repeated his plan to surrender in the morning, then shifted into saying that Shari didn't want her boyfriend, Richard, to have the necklace she was wearing when she was abducted. We took this to mean that he had supplanted Richard in his own mind as Shari's boyfriend, and that now that he had killed her, she was all his.

Dawn then shifted him back to a previous thought.

"But Shari was not afraid, and she didn't cry or
    anything?"
"No, she didn't do anything. And, uh, can you handle it if
    I tell you how she died?"
"Yes."
"Okay, now be strong, now."
"Okay."
"She said you were strong. She told me all about the
    family and everything. We talked and . . . oh God . . .
    and I am a family friend. That's the sad part."
"You are a family friend?"
"Yeah, and that's why I can't face y'all. You'll find out in
    the morning or tomorrow. But forgive me. And Dawn,
    Shari . . . I don't know whether you should tell your
    mother this or not, but Shari Faye was not a virgin.
    She started with a guy in January. Were you aware of
    that?"
"We know that now, yes."
"Okay. And I did make love to her and we had oral sex for
    three different times. And she died. Can you handle
    this now?"
"Yes."

I'm sure that the only way Dawn could handle this outrage was that she knew that nothing he said about Shari and complicit sex was believable on any level. She steeled herself for the next part while the pain and anger rose up within her, realizing how much he was enjoying this.

> *"Okay. I tied her up to the bedpost and, uh, with electric cord, and she uh, didn't struggle or cry or anything. She let me, voluntarily, from her chin to her head, okay? Okay, I'll go ahead and tell you. And I took duct tape and wrapped it all the way around her head and suffocated her. And tell the coroner or get the information, that's how she died. And I was not aware she had this disease; I probably wouldn't have ever taken her."*

As we noted with earlier calls, his claims to be a family friend were clearly B.S., inconsistent with his assertion that he "was not aware she had this disease" (which we believed was true). On one level, this was a complex character. He was living in his own surreal fantasy world as far as his relationship with Shari and the Smiths was concerned, but he was also organized and pragmatic on a practical level. The nexus of those two traits would be where we would direct our attention in setting our trap to catch him.

The conversation went on a while longer from there. The one thing we believed out of all of it was when he told Dawn he would call again. He couldn't get enough of that power trip fantasy.

Before he hung up, Dawn told him again not to kill himself,

that God could forgive him, and even put her mother on to re-iterate the same message. And while he had their attention, he could put forth a little more of his self-indulgence and cruelty.

> [Hilda] *"You need to meet with somebody that can talk to you."*
>
> *"Well, I got a lot to think about and I'm, I'm gone, Mrs. Smith. And, uh, please, I know this might be selfish, but uh, y'all please ask a special prayer for me. Your daughter said that she was not afraid, and she was strong-willed. She knew that she was going to heaven, was going to be an angel, and like I told Dawn, she was going to be singing like crazy."*
>
> *"Did she . . ."*
>
> *"When she said that she was smiling."*
>
> *"Did you tell her you were going to kill her?"*
>
> *"Yes, I did. And I gave her the choice, like it's on the recording. I asked her if she wanted it to be drug overdose, shot, or, uh, uh, suffocated. And she picked suffocation."*
>
> *"My God, how could you?"*
>
> *"Well, forgive us, God."*
>
> *"Not us. You."*

Once again, by the time authorities traced the call to a truck stop at the intersection of Interstate 77 and State Highway 200 in Great Falls, South Carolina—about halfway between Columbia and Charlotte, North Carolina, approximately fifty miles from the Smiths' home—the UNSUB was no longer there; and again, he had left no evidence.

One more point emerged from the call. In the UNSUB's own mind he may have considered three ways to kill Shari, but we sincerely doubted he gave her a choice or that even if he had, she would have chosen the excruciatingly slow and agonizing process of suffocation. He chose this means because it prolonged his sexual thrill at the power he had over her, and the length of time he got to enjoy watching her die.

We found through our prison interviews that many, if not most, sexually oriented serial killers, though locked up, would replay the gratification of their crimes over and over in their minds. This individual was getting to do it while still a free man, and with the unwilling assistance of the very people whose lives he had shattered.

CHAPTER 7

Friday was the day we received the teletype from the Columbia field office formally requesting Behavioral Science's involvement with the Smith case. It didn't really change things, since we'd been analyzing the case and consulting with the sheriff's office all week, but now we were officially collaborating with local authorities, so there would be no questions about FBI involvement, either from officials on the scene in South Carolina or our own bosses at headquarters. It also meant the local investigators would be sharing evidence with us as soon as they obtained it, so we could aid the investigation in real time. By this point, we already had a pretty robust profile in place.

In addition to the characteristics we'd already come up with, we were now pretty sure this UNSUB would either be living alone or with his parents, or perhaps an older female relative, who would not know anything about his crimes. Building on our expectation that he'd have some sort of criminal record involving sex crimes, we figured that wherever he lived, besides the pornography we'd find a hidden collection of souvenirs from his exploits: jewelry, underwear, or other personal tokens taken from his victims—including items stolen from women he'd watched as a Peeping Tom earlier in his criminal career, breaking into their homes when they were out because he wasn't yet sophisticated enough to carry out an abduction.

Each successive phone call, with precise mentions of times and then the detailed directions to the body site, reinforced our belief that he was rigid and orderly in his personal habits, and obsessively neat. And the variable speed device he'd used to distort his voice on the early phone calls indicated he was more likely to work in the electrical field than, say, carpentry, and we felt he was too sophisticated to be an unskilled laborer.

In total, he presented a mixed personality profile including both organized and disorganized traits, a feeling of omnipotence that he didn't have to play by the same rules as everyone else and on some level believed he was smarter than the rest of the crowd, set against a conflicting and deep-seated insecurity, feelings of inadequacy, and a realization that he was not attractive or appealing to women. This, in turn, set up his ongoing fantasies of possessing and controlling them.

In response to the conversation with Dawn the previous night, I told Lewis McCarty on the phone that regardless of what the UNSUB said, he had no intention of either killing himself or surrendering. Much like his insistence that he was a "family friend," this was just one more weapon in his narcissistic psychopathology, trying to get the Smith family to understand and sympathize with him, even though he'd killed their loved one in cold blood. It was also part of his fantasy of being close to and loved by Shari. The longer this went on, I said to

McCarty, and the more reaction he gets from the family, the more comfortable and into the whole experience he would become. This would be hard on whoever had to listen to him on the phone, but each conversation was another opportunity to find out more about him and possibly get him to inadvertently slip in a clue that would help get to him.

But there was another, more ominous, aspect, I said. Once he gets over the high of this application of manipulation, domination, and control, he will likely slip back into his normal self-doubting, inadequate, and depressed personality, and then he'll be in danger of abducting and killing again. He'll look for someone very much like Shari, whom we determined was his victim of preference, but if he couldn't find someone like her, he would settle for another victim of opportunity–likely someone smaller, weaker, and easy to control.

In its continuing coverage, the previous day's *Columbia Record* had a story detailing how and where Shari's body was found. On the same front page, I noticed a story about how the federal police chief in São Paulo, Brazil, was 90 percent certain that a body found buried in a small nearby town was that of Dr. Josef Mengele, the fearsome Nazi "Angel of Death" who had conducted sadistically hideous medical experiments on inmates of the Auschwitz concentration camp in Poland and who, like many other Nazis at the end of World War II, was believed to have escaped to somewhere in South America. The article went on to report that the man in question had drowned at the Bertioga Beach on the Atlantic Ocean.

I couldn't help reflecting on the juxtaposition of stories on the discovery of these two bodies. One belonged to one of the most evil men the modern world has ever known; the other to someone completely guiltless, much like Mengele's own victims. The phrase "blood of the lamb" came into my mind, as it did from time to time when I had to work on violent crimes against children. In one biblical sense, it could refer to the slaughter of the pure and innocent. In another, it indicated the sacrifice that washed away the sins of the world. Though not on the level of the Smith family, I tried to maintain a degree of faith, yet it always plagued me to wonder if death truly was the end. On some level, that just didn't make any sense and I certainly hoped not, because that would indicate a universe without divine justice, which was a difficult thought to maintain. But every time I started thinking like that, I would remind myself that such abstractions were way above my pay grade. Whether there was heavenly justice in the universe or not, it was my responsibility to help secure the earthly justice to which each victim was entitled. And that always helped me focus.

Friday evening was the visitation service at the Caughman-Harman Funeral Home. While the Smiths received grief-stricken friends and members of the community, law enforcement officers videotaped everyone who came to the funeral home. As Shari requested in her Last Will & Testament—and as the killer had directed in his calls, and his actions had necessitated—Shari's shiny silver casket, adorned with a spray of roses in her favorite color, pink, was closed. On a table next to the casket was a frame containing her senior class photo. Outside, appropriately, violent storms lashed the area, and the National Weather Service issued a tornado warning for Lexington and the surrounding counties.

At eleven the following morning, more than a thousand

mourners filled the Lexington First Baptist Church to overflowing. Beyond the church's 825 seats, every available space along the walls of the sanctuary was filled. Law enforcement officers scanned the crowd and videotaped the funeral service. Among the pallbearers was Andy Aun, who was supposed to sing the national anthem with Shari at their high school graduation. Honorary pallbearers included retired and active members of the South Carolina Highway Patrol, SLED, and the Lexington County Sheriff's Department. The Smith family's pastor, the Reverend Lewis Abbott, presided, assisted by the Reverends Ray A. Ridgeway, Jr., and Graham Lyons, who flew in from Texas to be part of the service. Graham and his wife, Nancy, had lived next door to the Smiths in Columbia and became their best friends before moving to Texas.

Addressing the Smiths, Reverend Abbott conceded there was no answer to the question why and entreated mourners not to blame God. "God does not do what has been done here. It is because of the confusion and the sin and depravity of man that we've come to an occasion like this." Many of Shari's classmates held hands and quietly wept.

Ridgeway cited the tragedy that had befallen the Welsh coal-mining village of Aberfan in 1966 when spring rains saturated and unsettled a large slag heap and sent it sliding 700 yards down a mountain, engulfing a school in mud, sludge, and rubble, killing 116 children and 28 adults. The reverend described how one American reporter looked on the devastation and said, "I cannot believe in God after seeing this." A Welsh farmer searching for his own son said, "Friend, the God I know is here weeping with us. Don't ever forget one day He lost His child too."

"And I believe today our God is here weeping with us," Ridgeway concluded. "Our God is here. He cares. He understands."

As Hilda, Bob, Dawn, and Robert departed the church, SLED agents hovered close by, their eyes darting constantly for any signs of danger. And along the two-mile route to the cemetery, pink ribbons and bows were tied around mailboxes, front doors, and street signs at the suggestion of a local radio station.

Another graveside service was held at Lexington Memorial Cemetery, attended by several hundred mourners. As it was concluding, and just as the family was getting back into the limousine, a man in his early thirties, wearing a dark suit and standing near Sheriff Metts, shouted, "I'm sorry. I'm really sorry. Can I have your attention? Whoever is responsible for this, I believe you're here. I love you and will not hurt you. Come forward right now. There's no bitterness and hatred." He stretched out his arms in what *State* reporter Debra-Lynn Bledsoe characterized as "an evangelical pose."

The stunned crowd didn't know how to react, except for one of Shari's friends who fell to the ground screaming that she feared the man was coming to get her. Metts grabbed the man by the arm and led him away while the Smiths were hustled into their limousine.

The man was taken to the sheriff's department, where he was questioned for two hours and willingly cooperated. He had originally been on the suspect list because he was a member of the church and owned a cranberry-colored Oldsmobile similar to a car one of the witnesses had seen near the Smith driveway around the time Shari reached home. His voice was nothing like the one on the recorded phone calls, though, and ultimately investigators concluded he had nothing to do with the case. "I think he sees himself as some sort of evangelist," Metts said. "He's upset by this whole thing." But the sheriff also admitted, "This was extremely strange. This whole thing shocked me as much as anybody else."

Though Metts's office would only say that they were working day and night through a long list of suspects and clues, by this time the media had learned of the repeated calls to the Smith home and the one to Charlie Keyes. The caller's assertions that he "only wanted to make love to her" and that things "got out of hand" were all over the papers and television reports.

Captain Bob Ford declared that the strain of the case had left the sheriff's department personnel emotionally and physically strung out under great, self-applied pressure. The case hardly spared anyone in law enforcement its heavy emotional toll. Rita Y. Shuler was a forensic photographer with SLED who had been called upon to create detailed, high-quality images of Shari's Last Will & Testament for close analysis, as well as much of the other physical evidence. In her impressive book, *Murder in the Midlands,* she described her own experience processing the photographs taken at the Masonic Lodge when Shari's body was found:

> *There were times when I worked with photos and evidence and I had to fight back the tears. This was one of those times as I processed the film and printed the photographs. I lost the fight. I cried.*
>
> *I've always thought that the worst thing in the world that could happen to a mother and father is to lose a child. The Smiths had such hope, and this person had put*

them on an emotional roller coaster for five days waiting
for the phone to ring, then his words of rising hope, only
to have them fall back down to hopelessness.

Metts said his detectives were trying to reconstruct Shari's life in the weeks before she was taken. "We have a pretty good idea who her friends were, what she did, and who was with her right up to the time she vanished." One of their areas of focus was the Lexington People's Market, a flea market less than a mile from the Smith home, where Shari had a part-time job at a concession stand. Coworkers there described her as bright and cheerful and always ready to help, even with the tasks no one else wanted to do.

"We are all nervous down here because we don't know who it is who did this or whether he is here or if he's going to strike again," a female market employee who didn't want her name used told the *Columbia Record*.

"We are concentrating on the market as a good source of possible contact between Shari and whoever abducted her," Metts stated. "We've got a good list of the people who sell there and are checking them out." Among the incidents they were following up on was a report that about two weeks before the kidnapping, a man was thrown out of the market for bothering Shari and other young women. A previous story that Shari had been threatened by someone at school the morning she was kidnapped had not gone anywhere. "My personal feeling is that we are looking for someone older than high school age; maybe someone in their late twenties or early thirties," the sheriff commented.

"We want this guy real bad," Ford insisted.

Meanwhile, Raymond Johnson, a twenty-three-year-old resident of Darlington, South Carolina, was being held in the Darlington County Detention Center on charges of extortion, alleged to be the anonymous individual who had called Bob Smith five or six times on Saturday, before and after the funeral. He claimed to know who had killed Shari and said for $150, he would go to Florida and kill the man who had committed the crime. The caller was kept on the phone long enough for Metts's office to contact the Darlington County Sheriff's Department, which picked up Johnson around nine P.M. at a pay phone outside the Piggly Wiggly grocery store on Pearl Street. Sergeant Henry Middleton said Johnson was awaiting a bond hearing and mental competency evaluation.

"He called the president [Ronald Reagan] a month ago and threatened to kill him," Middleton reported. "He's crazy. As long as he takes his medicine, he's fine. But when he doesn't, he goes off the deep end."

At 2:21 on Saturday afternoon, the Smiths had returned from the cemetery and Dawn had just changed out of her dress clothes when the phone rang. She ran downstairs to pick up, wondering unbelievingly if the killer could possibly be calling again on this of all days.

The operator said she had a collect call from Shari. Dawn was incredulous at his brazenness but said she would accept the charges.

"Uh, Dawn, I'm real afraid now, and everything and . . ."
"You're what?"

"Real afraid, and I have to, uh, make a decision. I'm
going to stay in this area until God gives me the
strength to decide which way . . . And I did go to the
funeral today."
"You did?"

This we thought was possible, because he would want, at least in his own mind, to maintain the illusion that he and Shari were emotionally close and that he was a friend of the family. On the other hand, he had come up with so many lies so far that this could have just been part of his larger fantasy.

"Yes, and I, that ignorant policeman . . . the fellow even
directed me into a parking space. Blue uniform . . .
outside, and they were taking license plate numbers
down and stuff. Please tell Sheriff Metts I'm not
jerking anybody around. I'm not playing games;
this is reality and I'm not an idiot. When he finds
my background, he'll see I'm a highly intelligent
person."

It has been my experience that when someone says they're not jerking you around, they're jerking you around. When they claim they're not playing games, it means they're playing games. And highly intelligent people don't often feel the need to go around telling anyone how intelligent they are. Amidst all of these psycholinguistic indicators, though, we hoped he was telling the truth about being at the funeral, since Metts's deputies had kept track and were in the process of talking to everyone who attended.

Then he went on with his games and jerking the family around.

> *"I want to fill in some gaps here because between now and*
>   *next Saturday, the anniversary date of Shari Faye..."*
> *"Yeah?"*
> *"I'm going to do one way or the other, or if God gives me*
>   *strength before then, ever when, I'll call you."*
> *"Between now and next Saturday?"*
> *"Yes."*
> *"I think you need to make a decision before then."*

Dawn was accepting and assimilating the coaching we'd been giving her through Metts and McCarty; restating or questioning admissions he made and following up on each potentially significant statement.

> *"All right. And, uh, I could tell her casket was closed, but*
>   *did y'all honor Shari's request for folding her hands?"*
> *"Yes. Yes, we did, of course."*
> *"Okay, she ... she'll like that. That'll please her. Okay,*
>   *and uh, tell Sheriff Metts and the FBI ... Damn,*
>   *that's like the fear of God in you for sure. They treat*
>   *this like Bonnie and Clyde. They go out and gun you*
>   *down, and if I decide, if God gives me the strength*
>   *just to surrender like that, I'll call you, like I said.*
>   *When I see them drive up, I'll see Charlie Keyes and*
>   *Sheriff Metts get out of the car, they'll recognize*
>   *me. I'll approach them, and they can approach me*
>   *without shooting me and stuff, all right?"*

During this conversation, for the first time, we actually detected some real fear from the UNSUB and the possibility that he was facing up to the reality of the consequences of his actions. No remorse, certainly, but fear for himself. His professed anxiety about the FBI and how he could be treated like Bonnie and Clyde, shot to pieces in their car back in the 1930s, was a healthy sign for us and an important behavioral clue. It meant he was now likely to be showing signs of strain to those around him: drinking or drug-taking, losing weight or eating compulsively, probably talking about the case nonstop and asking others what they knew. As soon as we heard this recording, we told McCarty on the phone that this would be among the key characteristics of the profile.

The caller continued, feigning being helpful:

> *"I delivered her to Saluda County, I told you exactly how she died and so forth, and when I took the duct tape off of her, it took a lot of hair with it and so, that'll help 'em out. The examiner said they were having problems telling how she died. And uh, well, hold on a minute now and let's see . . ."*

He had lost his train of thought again and Dawn immediately bored in with:

> *"Where's the duct tape?"*
> *"Huh?"*
> *"Where's the duct tape?"*
> *"Only God knows, I don't. Okay, okay, now listen. Did you receive the thing and the pictures in the mail?"*

"They're coming?"

*"Unless the FBI intercepts them. It's written to you. I got
Shari Faye to address three or four different things,
and it's written to you in her handwriting."*

He said there would be a note "for your eyes only in her handwriting," in which he claimed she intended to break up with Richard, which we had predicted he'd say. From the victimology study, we knew this wasn't true, and just one more desperate attempt for the UNSUB to create a mythical relationship with Shari.

*"We talked from, uh . . . actually she wrote the Last Will
and Testament, 3:12 A.M. She kind of joked and said
they won't mind if I round it off to 3:10. So, from
about two o'clock in the morning from the time she
actually knew, until she died at 4:58, we talked a lot
and everything, and she picked the time. She said
she was ready to depart. God was ready to accept
her as an angel."*

Having finally expressed genuine fear, he was now attempting to mitigate the horror by suggesting that Shari joked with him, that they talked a lot about everything, and that she was ready to depart this life. But Dawn would not let him off the hook that easily.

*"So, the whole time, you told her that she was going to
die, right?"*

"Yeah."

He prattled on about messages Shari had given him for Dawn regarding Shari's birthday, and said he took part in the search. This was not unusual. We found that killers often took part in searches for their victims. They could blend in with the crowd, dispel any doubts about themselves, and get the vicarious thrill of knowing something no one else did, plus perceiving that they were smarter than everyone else because they were getting away with it.

Then Dawn pressed him further:

> "I know that you keep telling me that you're telling me the truth. But, uh, you did tell me that you would give yourself up at six o'clock this morning. Well, what happened?"
> "I didn't have the strength."
> "What?"
> "I didn't have the strength. I was scared. I'm scared as hell. I can't even hardly read my handwriting."

So he *was* reading from a script. Dawn kept pressing him, gently but insistently.

> "No matter what you've done, you know that Christ died for you so that you could be forgiven, and if you would give yourself up . . ."
> "Do you know what would happen, Dawn? Do you realize Sheriff Metts . . . Sheriff Metts would give me help for a couple of months and then find out I'm sane, and then I'd get tried and sent to the electric chair, put in

prison for the rest of my life. I'm not going to . . . uh . . .
go to the electric chair."

Here was another example of how he was starting to mentally decompensate, to lose the ability to react in a reasonable or methodical way, due to the increasing stress he was under. Logical thinking involves a progression of ideas. Saying he'd be sent to the electric chair and then put in prison for the rest of his life was illogical, regressive thinking. He was starting to come unglued from the pressure he was under. We hoped he would make a mistake that would give him away, but that kind of emotional decompensation also made him more unpredictable and dangerous. Now it was as if he was hanging onto Dawn as a lifeline. She, on the other hand, as the tone of her voice indicated, was gaining strength and resilience. She knew from what we'd told McCarty that he would be frightened by dominant women, so she challenged him:

> *"You keep telling us to forgive you. You don't realize what*
> *you've put us through. How could you think about*
> *what would happen to yourself?"*

That was one he couldn't answer, because as a psychopath, he had no concept of empathy.

> *"Okay, any other questions? I've filled in all the holes*
> *and everything. The only reason you wouldn't get*
> *that letter today, or probably Monday, is that the FBI*
> *intercepted it."*

By this point, Captain Gasque of SLED was in the room listening. He scribbled a note, "Ring?" and handed it to her. He wanted to know if the UNSUB had Shari's high school ring and was keeping souvenirs.

> *"Can you tell me where her ring is? You really don't know where it is?"*
> *"No, I don't, Dawn. I would send it to you if I did. I have no reason. I'm not asking for money, materialistic things. I don't have any reason for . . . She was not wearing a high school ring when she got in the car, so maybe she left it at the pool party she came from."*

Maybe that last statement meant we were right in speculating he had been following her all afternoon on Friday since spotting her at the shopping center. But since we were absolutely certain he was closely following the media accounts, he could have read the detail about the pool party.

> *"Uh, can you tell me where did Shari die?"*
> *"I told you: 4:58 in the morning."*
> *"No, I know the time. Where?"*
> *"Saturday morning, in, uh, Lexington County."*
> *"In Lexington County?"*
> *"Uh-huh."*
> *"Where in Lexington County?"*
> *"Anything else you want to ask me?"*
> *"That's what I'm asking you! Where?"*
> *"Uh, anything else?"*
> *"You won't answer that for me?"*

"No."

"You said anything I'd ask, you'd tell me."

"Okay, I'll tell you. Uh, number one: I don't know exactly
the location. I don't know the name of the highway;
391 or something like that, but right next to the
Saluda County line. That's all I can tell you. Okay,
anything else? I'm getting ready to go. At 4:58 in the
morning, set your alarm wherever you are, and I'll
call you. Can you hear me?"

"Yes. This morning?"

"No, next Saturday, on the anniversary date. Okay? I'll
call you and tell you the exact location, just like I did
Shari Faye's."

"I can't believe this because you've never been telling me
the truth."

"Okay, I have! You believe everything because it is the
truth! You go back and you go over everything."

"I just feel that the best thing for you to do is give . . ."

"Well, Dawn, God bless us all."

And then the line went dead.

The call was traced to a RaceTrac service station in Augusta, Georgia, about sixty miles from Lexington. Again, he left no evidence.

CHAPTER 8

The work of the sheriff's department and SLED continued. Nearly everyone who had attended the funeral was interviewed. Hilda, Bob, Dawn, and Robert each spent many hours in their den with investigators, poring over the videos of the service, identifying everyone they knew and pointing out anyone who struck them as being suspicious. Hundreds of tips came in to the sheriff's office every day, but none of them panned out. Since the caller had told Dawn several times that he might kill himself, authorities looked into all suspicious deaths in the surrounding area but didn't believe any were relevant to their case. There was no obvious connection to any of the prisoners or ex-prisoners Bob Smith had ministered to as a chaplain, nor any who seemed fixated on either Shari or Dawn. Detectives checked out hundreds of vehicles that matched witness descriptions and believed the most likely one was a late-model GMC sedan in a cranberry-reddish color. The hunt for Shari's killer was being reported as the most intensive manhunt in the state's history.

Despite what the UNSUB had said about knowing the family and being at the funeral, those working the case had reached the conclusion that the man they were looking for was a stranger who had had no contact with Shari before the day he abducted her.

"We're looking at the fact that the guy didn't even know her," Metts announced on Monday, June 8. "I think if he had known her, we would have turned up something by now."

Two days later, he was still trying to sound upbeat. "I'm optimistic," he said. "I've got to be. We are not going to give up even though time is against us. We still have a bunch of leads to check out and some very strong suspects. I won't be pessimistic until we've run down all our leads and still not come up with anything."

He admitted the ten-day investigation had been an emotional roller coaster for him and his detectives and went on to explain, "In any investigation like this, you start with a list of theories and work your way down, discounting the ones you can and getting more information on the ones you can't."

He also told reporters that his office was working directly with the Saluda County Sheriff's Department and Sheriff George C. Booth, and said that the FBI was working on a profile that had led his investigators to up their age estimate from high school to a man in his twenties to someone in his thirties or perhaps even early forties. "The experts have given us some thoughts that lead us to believe we are looking for an older man.".

He also publicly challenged the UNSUB as Dawn had done privately on the subject of suicide. "I don't think he has the guts. If he was going to do it, he'd have done it by now. He's been talk-

ing about it for five days. A person on the verge of killing themselves doesn't stall for five days."

This was a good strategy Metts was following. For one thing,
it was low risk. Despite the UNSUB's repeated promises to kill
himself or turn himself in, we expected neither. While mass
killers like school or workplace shooters often anticipate the
endgame where they either die by their own hand or by "suicide
by cop," it was not true of this kind of offender. Such a criminal
is inherently cowardly and has no intention of going out in a
blaze of glory. In addition, it would get his attention. We knew
the UNSUB was closely following the media and it was important to keep up the pressure on him. When that is the situation, having one strong presence as the spokesman and face
of law enforcement is what we want, so the UNSUB perceives
in him all the forces he is up against. The telephone recordings
had made it abundantly clear that the caller was obsessed with
Sheriff Metts, and we wanted to keep up the message that it
was only a matter of time before the sheriff caught his prey.

In addition, Special Agent Tommy Davis, the profile coordinator for the Columbia field office, detailed the creation of
our profile to the *Columbia Record*: "Basically, they [the profilers at Quantico] are trying to come up with a picture of the
individual who fits all the traits of a person who could commit
whatever crime is involved."

"We certainly have not run out of leads," added Metts. "We
wanted to have this [profile] as a tool to use as we continued to
actively run down leads."

Several times a day, Metts would meet with Saluda sheriff Booth and SLED captain Gasque to share information and
coordinate efforts. All vacation and leave were canceled until

the case was solved, and food was brought in so investigators wouldn't have to break for lunch.

Metts also contacted the local "Crime Stoppers" television program, a partnership between community media and law enforcement agencies, to film a reenactment of the abduction to encourage tips and additional information. "Somebody somewhere has seen him," Metts said. "Somebody somewhere knows him. We've got to find this person before he kills again." He warned, "Anytime you've got a killer out there who fits a profile like this, my opinion is, when a person kills once, a person will kill again."

The reward for information had now topped $30,000.

There were no more calls from the UNSUB that week, and we began to worry that the combination of Dawn's more aggressive tone and Metts's public statements had driven him underground or even farther away from the area than neighboring Georgia. At the same time, several families reported what they hoped were crank calls threatening their children. Parents became hypervigilant and gun sales rose.

"Anytime you get a case like this, it triggers other copycats to get into the act," Metts said. "One thing we've found out is there are a lot of psychotic and sociopathic people out there." He encouraged anyone who received such a call to report it to his office. "We are checking these things out. The information we need to break this case may be in one of them."

The "Crime Stoppers" reenactment was produced by a WIS-TV film crew on Friday, June 14, two weeks to the day after Shari was kidnapped, and scheduled to be aired on local television stations beginning the following Monday. It was filmed on location at the Town Square shopping center parking lot and on the Smiths' driveway. Twenty-one-year-old University of South Carolina junior Tracy Perry, a SLED agent's pretty blond daughter who resembled Shari, portrayed her. Shari's own blue Chevette was used, and her boyfriend, Richard, took part.

"We talked for a few minutes and then she drove out of the parking lot and waved," Richard said to the film crew, describing the last anyone saw of her before her encounter with her killer. When they got to the Smith house, sheriff's investigator Al Davis related to Tracy—clad in a bikini, white shorts, and a yellow top similar to Shari's and purchased at the same J. C. Penney store—what he believed happened and directed her in the scene, down to stepping out of the car barefoot. The scene ended as Tracy walked up to the mailbox.

In explaining her willingness to participate to a reporter, Tracy said, "I would be willing to do anything I can to catch this guy. It's just got everyone scared to death."

After filming the driveway scene, the crew moved on to the Saluda County Masonic Lodge location where Shari's body was found. When they got there, they found a used pair of forensic pathologist Dr. Sexton's rubber gloves lying on the grass.

THAT SAME DAY, DEBRA MAY HELMICK WAS PLAYING WITH HER BROTHER AND sister in the yard in front of the family's trailer home in the Shiloh Mobile Home Park fronting on Old Percival Road about five miles outside Columbia, in Richland County, which adjoins Lexington County to the East as Saluda County adjoins Lexington to the West. The Helmick family had lived there for about two months. Like Shari Smith, Debra May was a pretty, blue-eyed blonde. Unlike Shari, she was only nine years old. Her sister, Becky, was six and her brother, Woody, was three. Debra May was wearing white shorts and a plaid shirt. She was described as a smart and quiet child who did well in school.

It was about 3:30 in the afternoon and Debra Louise Helmick, mother of Debra May (referred to as such because they shared a first name), was about to leave for work at Ray Lever's Bar-B-Q Hut restaurant, driven there by her new neighbor Vicky Orr, who lived in one of the other twelve white siding-clad trailers in the park with her husband, Clay, and their two children. The two women planned to take the Helmick children with them for the ride, then they would stay with Vicky until Debra's thirty-two-year-old husband, Sherwood, got home from his job as a construction worker. But just as they were leaving, Sherwood arrived, so Debra May and Woody stayed there and continued playing in the yard. Becky went along with her mother and Vicky.

About a half hour later, a silver-gray car with red racing stripes drove into the park's only entrance and down the short driveway, which ended at a grove of trees. The car paused, then turned around and slowly cruised back toward the street. The driver stopped near the Helmicks' trailer, and with the motor still running, opened the door.

Ricky Morgan, who worked as a roofer and lived across the driveway and four trailers down from the Helmicks, was in his kitchen. Though it was another unusually hot day, still in the upper nineties, the nineteen-year-old Morgan was not running his air conditioner and instead had the windows open. He heard something indistinct, looked out, and saw a white male get out of the car, approach Debra May, grab her around the waist, pull her into the car with him, and speed off as Debra May screamed.

"Oh my God!" Morgan exclaimed to his wife as the car sped away. He ran out of his trailer and over to the Helmicks'.

Sherwood Helmick did have the air conditioning on in his trailer and was in the bedroom changing his clothes, so what he heard was a muffled yell. He thought it was just the two children playing some game. But his friend Johnny Flake, who worked with him and had given him a ride home, called out to him from the trailer's front room, "One of your kids is yelling and hollering out there."

Sherwood rushed to the front door just as Ricky Morgan ran up. Three-year-old Woody had crawled under a large bush at the side of the trailer, trembling in fear and yelling something unintelligible.

"Did you see that man take your daughter?" Morgan shouted breathlessly.

Sherwood ran around the trailer and then out to the road, not finding Debra May or any trace of the car. He rushed back to where Johnny was standing and together they got in the car and raced down Old Percival Road in pursuit. When they got to the intersection with Alpine Road, Sherwood got out and stopped passing cars, asking if anyone had seen the silver-gray car. He saw a Richland County Sheriff's Department cruiser and flagged it down. He leaned in the window and hollered to the deputy, "Someone has taken my daughter!"

The officer called for assistance, and soon a ground search was underway.

Debra Helmick was in the back storeroom of the Bar-B-Q Hut when she heard the phone ring. As she walked to the kitchen with the can of pork and beans she had gone to get, the manager ran up to her and said, "Get your pocketbook. Your mother-in-law is coming to pick you up."

When Sherwood's mother arrived minutes later, she filled Debra in on what had happened. The Helmicks had lived with her after moving down from Canton, Ohio, until they moved into the Shiloh Mobile Home Park.

As soon as Richland County sheriff Frank Powell got word, he wondered if it was related to the abduction of Shari Smith. It was exactly two weeks, almost to the hour, since Shari had been taken in front of her house. Both girls were pretty, blond, and blue-eyed. The Helmicks lived about twenty-four miles from the Smiths. Powell got in touch with the sheriffs of the other two counties and called in every officer he had to assist in the search. A plane and helicopter soon went up for an air search.

Ricky Morgan was the only one who had seen the incident, and he described to detectives and a sketch artist a white male, approximately thirty to thirty-five years of age, around five-foot-nine, somewhat over two hundred pounds and with a beer belly, a short brown beard and mustache, and a receding hairline. He thought the car might have been either a Chevrolet Monte Carlo or Pontiac Grand Prix, silver-gray in color and of a fairly recent model year. He recognized the South Carolina license plate but was only able to catch a "D" as the first letter in the sequence. The suspect was wearing shorts and a light-colored sleeveless top. As he approached the children, he appeared to be talking to them, but then suddenly grabbed Debra May. Morgan said the slight nine-year-old put up a fearsome fight, kicking and screaming and bracing her legs against the roof of the car until the offender managed to pull her inside.

When officers questioned young Woody, who was still terrified, he told them, "The bad man said he was coming back to get me!"

"At this point, we don't know what the situation is there," Sheriff Powell told the press. "It's ironic that it's the two-week anniversary, so to speak, within an hour of the time that Shari Smith disappeared. However, at this point I want to emphasize that we have nothing to indicate any connection other than the fact that this girl is missing, and we feel like there has been a crime committed."

The family waited for some word, even a ransom call or letter. They didn't have a phone in their trailer, but Debra May knew the phone number in the manager's office. It was monitored all night and into the next day, but neither the child nor anyone connected to her disappearance ever called.

PART 2

ON THE SCENE

CHAPTER 9

By Monday, June 17, Debra May Helmick's photo was all over the media, just as Shari Smith's continued to be. The Associated Press ran a story headlined OFFICERS SEEKING SUSPECTS IN RASH OF ABDUCTIONS that placed photos of the two girls side by side. Composite drawings of the bearded man appeared in all the local and regional papers, and were shown on television.

Police officials are quick to point out that composites, generally created with the Smith & Wesson Identi-Kit, are not presumed to look exactly like an unknown subject but are useful, rather, in helping witnesses eliminate as many suspects as possible. Months later, the Identi-Kit would become famous for its effectiveness in identifying Night Stalker killer Richard Ramirez at a liquor store in Los Angeles. Interestingly, some Identi-Kit artists say that women and children are better at recalling and describing faces than men, and young children are sometimes invited to play with the kit themselves to come up with the beginnings of a composite.

Now, with two possibly related abductions, Undersheriff Lewis McCarty flew up to Quantico to meet with us. As Richland sheriff Powell had suggested, we couldn't be sure the two abductions were related, but there was enough similarity that the authorities were taking no chances. We had been concerned that Shari's killer would strike again, and those of us in Behavioral Science are, among other things, in the pattern recognition business. The two-week interval between the crimes was just too coincidental to ignore.

Right after lunch, Ron Walker and I met McCarty in the Academy entrance lobby, in front of the wide reception desk. He was a well-built guy of medium height, with light-colored hair and wearing gold-rimmed aviator-style glasses. He was friendly and seemed glad to be back at Quantico, but I could tell almost right away from his voice and body language that he had been under a lot of strain. We hoped that just by being there, he would feel that he had colleagues willing to share that strain with him and his associates. We told him we had arranged one of our private VIP rooms with a bath for him in the dormitory building so he wouldn't have to share with any other resident.

We walked him back down the long corridor to the Forensic Science Building where our offices were located and took him to Roger Depue's office so we could introduce him to the Behavioral Science unit chief. Roger had always been a big supporter of ours and whenever we had a local law enforcement official in for a consultation, he always made that person feel welcome and assured of Bureau support. We then took McCarty down the hall and introduced him to all the other BSU agents. Having dispensed with formalities, we went right to the Forensic Science conference room where Jim Wright and about four other profilers were already assembled. We also had two Forensic Science Section agents sit in with us, which had become something of a regular practice for major case consultations because they could answer questions for us relative to any forensic findings or scientific tests that had been done or which they could recommend.

I had to admit that it was difficult to remain objective about this unfolding case. My older daughter, Erika, was nine, the same age as Debra May, and also a blue-eyed blonde. Her sister, Lauren, was just five, and they often played together outside in the yard, just as Debra May and Woody had been doing. There is no way to avoid the sense of "This could have been my child!" gnawing constantly at the edge of your consciousness.

If it was the same offender, we firmly believed that as the pressure built up in him following the gratification of kidnapping and killing Shari, and then the inevitable emotional letdown, the urge to do the same kind of thing would grow stronger and stronger. He didn't want to kill himself or turn himself in; he wanted another Shari to possess. If he couldn't find one, he would take the closest victim of opportunity he could find—in this case a nine-year-old girl who could not put up much resistance and would be completely in his power. He was probably surprised by how hard Debra May fought.

McCarty filled us in on the victimology. Everyone detectives had spoken to described Debra May as a sweet girl, obedient and well-behaved, and somewhat shy compared to other children. She was not a risk-taker, and this was a low-risk crime for her and a high-risk crime for the perpetrator, since her father was only about fifteen feet away from her at the time and there was only one vehicular entrance to the trailer park.

Though the Helmicks had only lived there for two months, they were well liked and had become friendly with several of the neighbors. By the time Debra May's mother had returned from the restaurant, a group of concerned neighbors had collected outside their trailer, offering support and waiting for news.

If Shari Smith's murder had sent chills through the community, McCarty noted, Debra May Helmick's abduction just about put everyone over the edge. Things like this were not supposed to happen in small-town places like this. And Shari and Debra May's cases came on top of the still-unsolved murder of seventeen-year-old Marilee Whitten, whose nude and partially decomposed body was discovered in lower Richland County four days after she went missing just weeks before Shari Smith's abduction. Marilee had been beaten with what turned out to be a metal lamp base and died from blunt force trauma. Police had already questioned a young man who worked with her part time at a local animal clinic, but didn't have enough to arrest him, so there was some consideration of her killer being the same UNSUB as Shari and Debra May's. (Whitten's coworker James Fossick was ultimately tried and convicted of the murder.) The community was also still reeling from the disappearances of former Columbia police chief Arthur Hess, whose bloodstained car was found in a shopping center June 6, and Mary McEachern, an associate in the real estate firm where Hess worked, who went missing a few weeks later.

Things would get even scarier with reports that a female nineteen-year-old University of South Carolina student was abducted at gunpoint when a man jumped into her car as she was stopped at a traffic light while driving to her job at a fast-food restaurant in Columbia. The man pulled out a revolver and demanded to be driven to Charleston. He got out of the car and left her unharmed six hours later, after they reached Charleston, delayed for a while by severe thunderstorms. The victim described the offender as being in his mid to late twenties, about five-foot-eleven and 180 pounds, with short blond hair and a Marine Corps tattoo on his left arm.

Authorities didn't believe any of those cases were related to Shari's or Debra May's, but the entire situation was increasingly unnerving, forcing people to question the basic assumptions they held about the safety and security of the area in which they lived.

And they were angry. Robert Gillespie, a store clerk in Lexington County, told the *Charlotte Observer*, "Just about everybody says if they caught [Shari's killer] before the police, it would be their pleasure to save the state the electricity expense [of the electric chair]."

Richland County sheriff Powell said that as of Monday, his department had already checked into 186 tips as to the identity of Debra May's kidnapper, but none of them had panned out. He also worried publicly that the number of abductions and missing persons would prompt copycat crimes, releasing a statement that read, "Due to the tremendous amount of publicity in recent kidnappings in the Midlands area, it may give individuals the idea to do the same thing. Unfortunately, we have some depraved individuals who may act out their bizarre fantasies in a copycat manner." He further noted that the public level of fear was hampering the efficiency of law enforcement because people were calling the sheriff's department if their spouses or children were fifteen or thirty minutes late getting home. It even got to the point that church officials were calling for advice on how to reassure their parishioners.

McCarty told us they did have a promising witness. A woman driving past the Smith home moments before Shari was abducted described seeing a man appearing to talk to Shari as she approached her mailbox. He fit the description of the man who had later taken Debra May. It also partially matched the description provided by two other witnesses nearby on Platt Springs Road at the time. A minute or two later, the woman noticed a reddish, late-model General Motors car speeding up from behind and swerving in front of her into her lane of traffic, and then slowing down dramatically. The driver didn't seem to be paying attention to the road, instead leaning over and focused on speaking to the girl in the passenger seat, who appeared to be the same one the witness had seen at the mailbox. The woman honked her horn and the reddish car swerved back into the other lane. She went on her way and didn't think much about it until the story of the kidnapping and murder played heavily in the media and she started connecting it to what she had observed.

Metts was still skeptical that the two abductions were related, because with Debra May, the UNSUB physically grabbed her rather than threatening her at gunpoint, and he hadn't made any phone calls to the victim's family. There had also been two different car descriptions. We told McCarty this wasn't necessarily significant. An individual of the type we had profiled wouldn't feel confident that he could physically wrestle a mature teen into his car and would figure he could control her more efficiently with a gun. A four-foot-tall, nine-year-old girl, on the other hand, wouldn't necessarily respond to a gun, might even think it was a toy, but would be much easier to physically control. And the difference in ages between the two victims was no surprise. If he was going to kidnap another young woman, as we had said, he would be looking for someone like Shari. But if he couldn't easily find his victim of preference, he would take what he could get, as long as she was easy to control. We suspected the fact that Debra May was also pretty and blond factored heavily in his choice of victims.

We didn't put our profile in written form, which was often our practice in ongoing cases when we didn't want any documents to be leaked. Instead, McCarty took copious notes as we sat around the conference table with him.

Particularly after the Helmick abduction, assuming it was the same guy and he was still holding Debra May, he would be under extreme mental pressure. A change of appearance would be noticeable to people around him. If he had a beard and mustache, as the composite sketch indicated, he was likely to shave them off, and he could be gaining or losing weight. The UNSUB would be following the media reports closely, likely cutting out and saving newspaper articles. If he was as meticulous and compulsive in his habits as we thought, he was probably arranging them in chronological order. He would also be unable to refrain from discussing the case in detail with anyone who would listen. His friends and family members would be surprised by his obsession with the murder of Shari Smith and the disappearance of Debra May Helmick, not understanding why he seemed so fixated on them.

Ron Walker and Jim Wright reviewed all the decision-making that had led to the profile we were presenting to Mc-Carty and said that the most recent events had given them no reason to alter it. We then expanded the scope of our discussion to give McCarty examples of how profile elements could be useful with other aspects of the investigation. For example, given our expectation that the UNSUB would have a collection of pornography focused on bondage and sadomasochism, we advised that if they identified a suspect, this was something they could include in a search warrant application.

Though the timing is different for each offender, we explained that our research into the mindset of the serial killer showed that the crime begins as a fantasy in his mind, and generally can be interpreted as some form of personal and sexual empowerment. The fantasy will build and build until he is ready to act on it. But the reality is never as good as he imagined it, and he will become let down and have something of a cooling-off period before the cycle begins again. With this UNSUB, who had already killed at least once, just as he was conflicted between a sense of personal grandiosity and deep-seated inadequacy, he also would be conflicted between feeling the growing pressure he was under and glorying in his anonymous celebrity and power over the entire community, together with his specific power to manipulate the grieving Smith family. The longer and more times he gets away with a violent crime, the more he will refine his M.O., and the more confident he will feel about the next time. This makes him even more dangerous.

Beyond the Helmick family not having a phone, there could be another reason he hadn't apparently made any attempt to contact them, we advised. While Shari would seem a grown-up and appropriate partner for him, someone he had to kill only because he otherwise would have forfeited his freedom, Debra May was only nine, a four-foot slip of a girl who would not be an appropriate romantic or sexual partner for him under any circumstances. He wouldn't feel particularly good about her abduction, and he couldn't pull off the illusion that he was a friend of the family and had any kind of reasonable relationship with her. If he had any image of self-worth at all, this is a crime he would be ashamed of.

Our goal, we told McCarty, was somehow to draw him out while Debra May could still be alive—and before he could kill again.

After about five hours in the conference room, we adjourned upstairs to the Boardroom for a few drinks and to unwind from the intensity of the discussion. The Boardroom was the official name of the Academy's bar and social lounge, and it was a very popular place after the workday. We continued discussing the case with McCarty while we imbibed and then through dinner in the dining hall.

Throughout the day, I felt as if I had developed a strong bond with McCarty. Part of it was probably because he was a National Academy program graduate, but I also sensed a powerful empathy for all victims and their families in him, together with a strong dedication to his profession. As a sheriff or undersheriff, you pretty much have to divide yourself between the administrative and political side of the job, and the investigative part. I knew that like Sheriff Metts, McCarty was a strong administrator. But after many hours with him, he was the one who was running the investigative end of the case on a day-by-day basis, and Ron and I really wanted to do right by him if we could.

McCarty left the next day, after saying goodbye to all of the agents he had met and thanking Roger Depue for the hospitality. He went home with what he said was a twenty-two-point list of conclusions and characteristics relating to the UNSUB. "I know the man," he announced upon his return. "Now all we have to find out is his name." And since this now appeared to be an active potential serial killer case that was drawing a tremendous amount of publicity and fear in the Midlands region of South Carolina, both Columbia SAC Robert Ivey and Sheriff Metts requested that we offer on-site consultation to the law enforcement effort.

It would mean putting all of my other cases on hold, but I thought I should go down there myself, and I asked Ron to accompany me.

"There was a flurry of calls back and forth," Ron Walker remembers, "and it was like, 'Hey, we've got to go down there now.' And so we decided to saddle up and go. I remember it was a real short notice to go down there on the day we did."

Ron and I both knew that this was a case—a set of cases now—that was affecting the entire community; and maybe if we were on site, we could offer more help. We hastily packed our bags and flew down to Lexington.

CHAPTER 10

cCarty picked us up at Columbia Metropolitan Airport and wasted no time in familiarizing us with the area. He drove us to each of the crime scenes—the Smiths' driveway and mailbox, the Saluda Masonic Lodge, and the Shiloh Mobile Home Park. He hadn't been exaggerating about the heat. It was pretty damn hot and humid, even by our miserable Virginia summer standards. It was the main reason we decided to dress casually, rather than in the standard FBI agent uniform of dark, sharply pressed suit, white shirt, and conservative tie.

On the drive between the locations, McCarty related some of the problems in dealing with different jurisdictions. Since the Helmick abduction, there had been a degree of conflict between the Saluda and Richland sheriffs. It sounded like each was trying to grab some of the headlines and use political influence to manage the case.

The area was a notable contrast from where Ron and I both lived in Virginia, where everything had been so built up that everywhere you looked, another housing development or shopping center was under construction. Lexington was a moderate-size southern town, actually kind of a suburb of Columbia. But the area around it was pretty rural, with farms, woods, and a lot of open space, much of it covered in kudzu. Maybe it was just because we came from the high-pressure world of the FBI, but it did seem the pace was slower and more relaxed. On the other hand—and maybe this was either me projecting or what Lew McCarty was telling us—it did seem like there was tension in the air from the string of unsolved cases.

Earlier in the week, someone had discovered bones in the woods of Richland County and rumors started flying that they were the remains of Debra May or some other unknown victim. Sheriff Powell's office investigated, and they turned out to be from a deer. Neighborhoods started forming their own watch initiatives. Diane Beardslee, the news director of a Columbia area radio station and mother of three teens, who was behind the pink ribbon campaign in honor of Shari, was now organizing a Pink Ribbon Crusade that would provide speakers and self-protection seminars. "These recent horrible crimes really affect all of us," Beardslee said. "Because Columbia is such a tight-knit community, we're starting to know the people that these terrible things are happening to. Just when you're thinking, 'It will never happen to me,' it happens to your next-door neighbor."

She spoke for the entire community when she said, "Every time one of my children walks out the door, I pray to God that they'll come back safely."

Strangers were receiving suspicious stares, unfamiliar cars had their license plates noted and written down, and a parent who lived in the large North Gate trailer park across the street from Shiloh Mobile Home Park told a reporter, "There are not many people who let their children play out by themselves anymore. It's a direct result of the kidnapping. It scared a lot of people, and if you excuse my language, it scared the hell out of me."

Waiting for some word, the Helmicks were in a bad way, just as the Smiths had been. In a story by Aad van Kampen in the *Columbia Record*, Sherwood Helmick said he was recovering from the "breakdown" he had suffered after Debra May was kidnapped from the front yard the previous Friday and was clinging to hopes and prayers that she would be found alive. He added, though, that he was prepared for the worst and that his wife was severely depressed, had not been able to return to work, and was under a doctor's care. "I don't even know right now whether she's fully aware of what's going on." All completely understandable.

"We've been hearing so much lately," he told the reporter. "Yesterday, there was a report they had found my little girl in the woods somewhere. And this week, I received three phone calls from people who said they knew where she was. Those people are real sickos."

He said he had not been going to work this week, either, and he wouldn't let his other two children out of his sight. "You've got a whacko out there, and you never know what he might do."

But as with the Smiths, the outpouring of love and care from the community had meant a lot to him, and this kind of thing always moved and impressed me every time I saw it. There are a lot of clichés about small-town life, but I have seen over and over again how people come out to support each other in times of trouble or crisis.

"I'm really grateful to the community," Sherwood Helmick said. "Every day, up to eighty people come out here offering food and money. It's fantastic and I just want to thank them for their support." As had happened with the Smiths, friends and neighbors arranged to bring them food and the Reverend Max Pettyjohn, associate minister of the Woodfield Park Baptist Church in Dentsville, opened a trust account to benefit the Helmicks, even though the Helmicks were not congregants there, and welcomed parishioners and the public to contribute. Other friends organized a fundraising dinner.

Pettyjohn said he had been visiting the family regularly, trying to provide some "relief of the enormous tension through my being there."

Sherwood expressed appreciation for what Sheriff Powell's department was doing, along with optimism that "he will crack this case in a couple of days."

TRAIPSING AROUND IN THE WOODS BEHIND THE MASONIC LODGE, I BECAME MORE convinced than ever that the UNSUB had to be a local who knew the area intimately. You wouldn't just stumble upon a place like this. And the fact that the three sites were in three different counties made us wonder if he was criminally sophisticated enough to realize that even neighboring law enforcement agencies often have trouble communicating and coordinating with each other, so it was to his advantage to spread his work around. I remembered a case up in Idaho in which two adjoining counties had very similar murders around the same time and neither police department realized it. It wasn't an instance of linkage blindness—that is, when investigators are unable to see that two or more cases are connected. Each department literally hadn't heard what had happened in the other county.

McCarty dropped us off at the motel he'd booked for us. It was a one-story affair, as I recall, not terribly luxurious, but it met our basic needs, which were to shower and sleep.

The next morning, he picked us up and drove us to a nearby diner, where he insisted that we enjoy a real "southern breakfast." We had chicken-fried steak, eggs, grits, buttered toast, and probably a bunch of other items as well. It was the first time either Ron or I had had steak for breakfast. There was another deputy having a similar meal at another table, and I think it was Ron who asked Lew if they ate like this every morning.

We went from the diner directly to the Lexington County Sheriff's Department to meet with all the key people on the case. Jim Metts seemed glad to see us. He was one of those larger-than-life characters, with a commanding bearing and that ability which the most successful politicians have to make you feel that you're the most important person in the room, no matter how many other people he's just talked to. Quickly sizing up the dynamics of the department, it seemed clear that while McCarty was a top investigative professional and that they had a good rapport, Metts was the human embodiment of law and order in these parts. It reminded me of the Old West stories about Judge Roy Bean in Texas, who was referred to as "the Law West of the Pecos."

Metts's office was equally impressive, maybe thirty feet long, with a ten- or twelve-foot-high ceiling. The walls were completely covered with plaques, certificates, photographs, testimonials for solving murder cases, and other memorabilia.

He seemed to have photos of himself with every Brownie or Girl Scout he had ever bought a box of cookies from. Where I come from, we call that an "ego wall." Ron said when he was in the military, it was referred to as a "love-me wall." Either way, it was obvious why the sheriff was such a vital fixture in the area, and why it had been a wise move for him to be the public face of law enforcement in this case.

It was also obvious that aside from his feelings about the young woman who had been murdered and the girl who was missing in Richland County, he had a deep respect for Bob Smith for all his work with prisoners and troubled young men and considered him a personal friend. Clearly, he wanted to do right by him to the extent the law could.

Metts took his place behind an appropriately massive desk. McCarty, Bob Ivey, Ron, and I sat in a semicircle facing him.

Ron and I repeated to the others that they should forget about the UNSUB killing himself. He was enjoying the attention and his power to manipulate everyone too much. Whatever affected depression or despondency he had indicated in his calls with Dawn would have been alleviated by the thrill and satisfaction of taking Debra May. Even though we didn't think he felt particularly good about that one, he now would have confidence that he could snatch away another young woman any time he wanted and get away with it. He was also probably starting to have his animosity and contempt for law enforcement strengthened and confirmed by its perceived inability to catch him. And while it was possible Debra May was still alive and he was attempting to assault and abuse her, he wouldn't see how he could return her without her giving a full description of him.

We thought the best hope would be to figure out where he was holding her and mount a quick-strike SWAT operation to rescue her. But despite what Metts would have to say to the media, we didn't want to get the hopes up of anyone in the meeting.

The phone calls the UNSUB made to the Smith family were extremely painful for them, and they were clearly part of the cat-and-mouse game he was playing with the authorities and the media, but they remained one of our best shots for learning as much as we could about him and forcing an error on his part, so it was worrisome to the investigators that he appeared to have stopped communicating.

"He's stopped calling the Smiths," Metts lamented.

"I'll get him to call again," I said. I figured that was part of why I was there.

CHAPTER 11

The Smith home was a good-size brick house with a pitched roof and two dormer windows in the main section, and from the entrance to the driveway where the mailbox was on Platt Springs Road, it looked fairly far away up the long drive. I could see why the offender wasn't particularly concerned about anyone inside the house seeing what he was doing.

McCarty drove us out and introduced us to each of the remaining four family members. They were clearly distraught, with what I would characterize as a helpless, hopeless feeling in their eyes. But they weren't crying and seemed to be maintaining a sense of emotional control. The deputies and SLED agents still occupying the house contributed to the atmosphere of uneasiness and anxiety. I didn't talk much with Robert, who seemed to want to let his parents do the communicating with Ron and me. Even in her grief, Dawn was very beautiful and looked remarkably like pictures of her sister. She seemed young-looking but at the same time mature, and I speculated about how much of that maturity had been thrust on her in the last two weeks.

The house was traditionally furnished and well maintained. I profiled the owners as being careful and detail-oriented, but not going overboard about it. All the indications were of a normal middle-class family, conservative in their behavior and habits, but not rigidly so.

I asked if we could see Shari's room, and Dawn led us up the stairs. They had left it completely intact and unchanged from the last time Shari had been there. As you might expect, this is not uncommon among families that have lost a child suddenly and tragically. There were matching flowered curtains and bedspread in shades of blue and beige that Dawn said had been given to Shari by their Smith grandparents. She said she had the same ones in her room, set against walls that she had painted pink herself. I told Dawn I thought I could get a good feel for Shari from her room.

Aside from the neatness, it looked like a typical teenage girl's bedroom, albeit one with a religious dimension. There was a cross mounted on one wall and a couple of biblically themed pictures, as well as the usual dolls and school-related memorabilia. But what was most notable was a large collection of stuffed koala bears of all sorts and sizes. Dawn said she had started collecting them because the koala was the Columbia College mascot and her sister had taken it over. Shari treasured the collection, Dawn said, and all her friends knew it, many contributing to it.

The plan was coming together in my mind. We had two positive factors to work with: Dawn looked so much like Shari, and from the way he kept playing up to her on the phone and the fact that he had confused the two of them on one call, the UNSUB was clearly obsessed with her.

I looked carefully at all the koalas, imagining Shari holding them, petting them, arranging them on her shelves. And then I imagined the UNSUB having one as a souvenir of Shari. I bet he'd like that, another way of possessing her. I wondered if I could somehow dangle one in front of him the way you'd dangle a baited fishing line in the water. Finally, I picked up a very small one. When you squeezed its shoulders, its arms opened as if it was about to hug you. This was the one I wanted. What if this could be the bait and Dawn the fisherman?

Let's be honest, Douglas, I thought to myself, *you're the fisherman and Dawn's the bait.*

In the upstairs hallway, I took Ron aside. "What kind of strategy could we come up with that might lure the UNSUB out in the open?" I asked.

"Maybe putting the koala bear on her grave?" Ron said.

"That's kind of what I was thinking," I replied.

"But we've got to let him know it's there."

"Right. And we know he reacts to the media." I thought of asking Charlie Keyes to work with us to come up with some kind of publicity since the UNSUB had reached out to him. But for that very reason, he might perceive it as the trap it would be. This guy had already proven himself to be pretty savvy about eluding capture. It would have to be something more subtle that wasn't obviously directed at the killer.

Despite her grief, there was a steely bearing in Dawn that suggested she would do whatever it took to help bring her sister's killer to justice. If Dawn was courageous enough, and every indication we'd had so far from listening to her on tape was that she was, and if Hilda, Bob, and Jim Metts would go along with it, we would try to come up with a way to use Dawn to lure her sister's killer out into the open.

We went back downstairs and sat in the den with Mr. and Mrs. Smith, Dawn, and McCarty. I told them I thought the profile we'd developed would provide a valuable aid in the police investigation and could be useful or decisive at any time. But as things now stood, particularly with Debra May Helmick still missing, it wasn't enough. We had to go proactive and try to force the UNSUB out in the open. The Smiths listened quietly and with interest, apparently willing to go along with anything that would further the case and help the Helmicks, for whom they said they were fervently praying.

For the last several minutes I had been going over the plan in my mind. With all that this family had been through already, did I dare take the chance of making Dawn a central part of the plan? What if something went wrong? Would she be in any real danger? I didn't think so because we and Sheriff Metts's deputies would be nearby. But I also knew that when you're dealing with this many variables and unknowns, you can't predict everything. God knew I'd been surprised many times in the past by the actions of violent offenders, and not in a good way. Did I have the right to potentially put someone else in jeopardy? If anything happened to Dawn, the family would never recover.

And though you try not to think in those terms, I couldn't help considering what it would mean to me and the still fairly new profiling program if any harm were to come to Dawn, even psychological harm. On the other hand—and in this business there is almost always an other hand—if Dawn could help us catch this guy before he killed again, wasn't the risk worth it?

Only if it worked.

That was when I nervously and somewhat hesitatingly said, "My idea involves Dawn."

An obvious look of concern spread over both parents' faces.

I explained that the idea had first started forming back in Quantico, when we were listening to the tape of the specific phone call in which the UNSUB confuses Dawn for Shari. And then when I got to meet Dawn in person, it was clear that this guy who was so attracted to Shari would be equally attracted to Dawn. I said I wanted to stage a public event, a memorial service of some kind for Shari that would be highly publicized by the media, with Dawn as the focal point. I turned to Dawn and asked her how she felt about that.

"I'll do anything to help catch my sister's killer," she replied, without hesitating.

Bob didn't seem as convinced, and I couldn't blame him. I had severe uncertainties and doubts about it myself. I was essentially proposing that in our attempt to catch the UNSUB, we use Dawn as the trap.

I held up the tiny koala I had taken from Shari's room and said I was recommending that in a few days, just enough time to get full newspaper and television coverage, we should hold a memorial service at Shari's grave at Lexington Memorial Cemetery. With the public invited to gather round, Dawn would attach the stuffed animal to a stick holding a bouquet of pink flowers. I thought we would have a good chance of drawing Shari's killer to the event, and an even better chance of having him go to the scene sometime after the ceremony to take the koala as a tangible souvenir of his "relationship" with Shari. At the very least, I thought the publicity could get him to start calling again.

With support from McCarty, I tried to reassure Bob Smith—and myself—that the UNSUB was a coward and would not come after Dawn amidst such intense publicity, scrutiny, and police presence. But she could provide the lure to get him to make another move. And I told him Ron and I were convinced that Dawn was smart and courageous enough to play her part effectively.

"It was beyond unnerving," Dawn later told us. "I felt I was bait at that point—bait to the man who had murdered my sister. But I remember almost not feeling like I was allowed to actually feel what a normal person would have felt in those circumstances, because I felt like it was my job, my responsibility, my assignment, to place the koala, do this, do that, be this way. Do what you have to do in order to get this to come to an end, to catch this man, for this nightmare to end."

With understandable hesitation, Bob and Hilda agreed to the plan. When they mentioned that Tuesday, June 25, would have been Shari's eighteenth birthday, we all agreed that would be the day.

ON FRIDAY, JUNE 21, SAC ROBERT IVEY AND SHERIFF JAMES METTS HELD A NEWS conference at the FBI field office in Columbia. Attempting to up what we in my unit referred to as the "ass-pucker factor" for the UNSUB, we basically wanted to make him start to sweat a bit more in the hope the added stress would push him to make a mistake that would reveal himself or make his unusual or erratic behavior more obvious to those around him. Also, if he felt law enforcement was on the verge of apprehending him, there was always the possibility he'd hesitate before trying to attempt another abduction and murder.

Ivey announced, "A rather complete psychological profile has been developed" on the man who kidnapped Shari Smith. "We are very optimistic this will allow us to bring other resources to bear on the case." He was referring specifically to the FBI laboratories, which Metts clarified, were checking out "additional evidence." He tantalized the attendees by stating that the profile of the prime suspect provided a few surprises, and even contradicted early theories investigators had about the individual.

Neither man would go into the details of the profile, which the sheriff said was helping investigators fit together "large pieces of the puzzle," noting that only officers directly involved with the case would be able to see the profile. Rumors about it were already leaking out, with one saying we believed the killer to be "an intelligent schizophrenic." While I did believe the UNSUB was criminally sophisticated, "intelligent" sounded a little strong. And while he clearly had some severe character defects, we had never characterized him as a schizophrenic, which is a psychotic disorder that often leads to delusions. This guy had a "sick" mind, but he knew exactly what he was doing, and he wanted to continue.

When a reporter asked why the two lawmen had called the press conference if they were not going to release any details of the profile, Metts responded, "The profile has been a tremendous boost to this investigation, but it wouldn't be advantageous to us to release it to the public."

Ivey said, "Seventy to eighty percent of the cases where

a suspect is eventually caught do meet the profile that was prepared. There are some profiles that have been directly responsible for solving cases." He also elaborated that the profile evolved from taped conversations with the offender, a study of the crime scene, and other previously undisclosed physical evidence. He added, "I'm very much aware of the media interest in this case. We feel the completion of this profile is significant enough to let the media know." He did not have to state that one of the reasons for the publicity was to reassure the public that law enforcement was still doing everything it could to solve the two cases, and he wasn't about to spell out that an additional reason was to increase the UNSUB's ass-pucker factor to the point that he would get sloppy and make a mistake.

It didn't take long for Ivey and Metts's public statements to have an effect, but the news it brought was not what we wanted to hear.

Ron and I were spending a lot of our time at the Smith home, and Friday night Dawn couldn't sleep. It had been three weeks since her sister had been abducted, two since the UNSUB had called, one week since Debra May was taken, and the memorial on Shari's birthday was coming up. All of this weighed heavily on her. It would have been impossible for her to feel like life was returning to normal under any circumstances since she had been suddenly uprooted from her apartment and roommates in Charlotte, and her family home had just about been taken over by law enforcement personnel like us. SLED agent Rick McCloud had been watching over her and Robert constantly and, on many days, he provided their only real companionship. With other agents helping to provide security, he would occasionally sneak them out of the house so they wouldn't go stir crazy, and he frequently brought in pizza and other treats. They came to think of him as a true friend and loved him.

"Because we'd gotten so close to the authorities living in our house, they had become like family overnight because they were so compassionate and so wonderful to us," Dawn observed. "That's something I think I'll never ever be able to express: the gratitude that my family feels for law enforcement. And it's so much more than a job because they felt the pain along with the family."

It was clear that the UNSUB wanted to speak to the Smith women and not the men. This didn't surprise us, since his mode was always to go for someone he felt was less imposing or intimidating. Hilda had held up extremely well for the first few phone calls but had grown increasingly distraught when she realized her daughter's life was in jeopardy, and then when she knew Shari was gone. Since it had become clear that the killer was infatuated with Dawn, I asked her if she would be okay continuing to answer the calls even though I knew it was painful for her. Like everything else we asked of her, she gamely complied. So we focused most of our attention on Dawn in terms of coaching on strategies to keep him on the line as long as possible and learn as much as we could. To do that, I said to try to appear very kind, compassionate, and calm. Let him be in charge and appear compassionate and understanding, even if he makes you want to retch.

"And so that's what we did," Dawn recalled. "He was so cruel, but I just kept it together because I knew that our only link to him at that point were these phone calls."

Just after Friday night turned into Saturday morning, the telephone at the Smith's home rang. It was 12:17 A.M. and Ron and I were still there. Still awake, Dawn answered. The operator asked if she would accept a collect call from Shari Faye Smith. Dawn knew what that meant. After all our coaching, she wanted the UNSUB to call. She tried to fortify herself for what she knew would be a distressing conversation. It quickly turned out to be worse than that.

> *"You know this isn't a hoax, correct?"*
> *"Right."*
> *"Did you find Shari Faye's ring?"*
> *"No, I didn't."*
> *"Okay, I don't know where it is, okay?"*

Then came the statement that I will admit struck terror into all of our hearts.

> *"Okay, you know, God wants you to join Shari Faye.*
>   *This month, next month, this year, next year. You*
>   *can't be protected all the time. You know about the*
>   *Helmick girl."*

Any thoughts he might possibly have entertained about dying by suicide or turning himself in he had clearly gotten past. He confirmed this in his next breath when he asked:

> *"Have you heard about Debra May Hamrick?"*
> *"Uh, no."*

In the typically meticulous way we had come to recognize, he corrected himself.

"The ten-year-old: H-E-L-M-I-C-K."

"Richland County?"

"Yeah."

"Uh-huh."

"Okay, now listen carefully. Go One North . . . well, One West, turn left at Peach Festival Road, or Bill's Grill. Go three and a half miles through Gilbert, turn right. Last dirt road before you come to a stop sign at Two Notch Road, go through chain and no trespassing sign. Go fifty yards and to the left. Go ten yards. Debra May is waiting. God forgive us all."

I was quickly scribbling notes and handing them to Dawn, reminding her to try to keep him on the phone and ask personal questions. Watching her for the first time handling one of these phone calls, I was both moved and impressed by her self-control, not letting her inner turmoil or the knowledge of what this face-less man would have liked to do to her distract her from her mission. She was speaking *to* the UNSUB, but she was speaking *for* her sister, for Debra May, and for the entire community that was still under threat from this man's violent desires. It very much brought to my mind the amazing grace and composure of Shari's Last Will & Testament. Whatever family tensions there might have been in the Smith household, I resolved to commend Hilda and Bob for the way they had raised both their daughters.

Dawn said to the caller:

"Hey, listen!"

"What?"

"Uh . . . just out of curiosity, how old are you?"

But he didn't take the bait.

"Dawn E., your time is near. God forgive us and protect us all. Good night for now, Dawn E. Smith."

"Wait a second here! What happened to the pictures that you said you were going to send me? What happened to those pictures that you were going to send?"

"Apparently, the FBI must have them."

"No sir! Because when they have something, we get it, too, you know. Are you going to send them?"

"Oh, yes."

"I think you're jacking me around, because you said they were coming and they're not here."

"Dawn E. Smith, I must go."

"Listen, you said you were going to wait for God's direction."

"Goodnight, Dawn, for now."

"You did not give me those pictures!"

"I'll call you later."

He hung up. This time the call was traced to a pay phone outside the Kentucky Fried Chicken restaurant at the Palmetto Plaza Shopping Center in Sumter, South Carolina, about fifty miles away. Though there were no obvious clues at the scene, SLED agents removed the phone from the wall and brought it to their lab in Columbia for analysis.

The UNSUB was still having everything his own way, the fear and anxiety he had expressed during the previous call having now vanished with the confidence he had regained through kidnapping Debra May. He was growing bolder and cockier, no longer using the voice-altering device. He apparently felt he didn't need it for protection any longer.

As soon as Dawn got off the phone, she had time to reflect rather than simply react. "I felt terrified," she acknowledged. "I felt terrified all along. That's why we had around-the-clock police protection, because the fear was that he would come after me as well. And so to hear those words come out of his mouth, I remember thinking, *Well, what are these people going to do to protect me for the rest of my life if this man is never caught?* And he was so good at not getting caught. He would stay on the phone until just before the call would be traced. And every time he'd be gone by the time someone would arrive at the destination. We couldn't even grieve Shari's death properly because this man was still taunting our family and then threatening me. It was just a horrifying, terrible feeling. Words could never describe the fear that I felt."

Dawn had tried to take down the directions as the caller gave them, and as soon as he hung up, we replayed the recording to check. Then Sheriff Metts, Captain Gasque, and other officers got in their cars to follow the directions. She said she hoped to God that they would lead to a live little girl, but we replied that it wasn't likely. She asked why we thought the perpetrator had called there instead of to the Helmicks. We explained that they didn't have a phone in their trailer, but beyond that practical consideration, since the UNSUB felt he had a relationship with her, this was a way of sharing his latest act with her and, by extension, with Shari. That was why he had promised that God, meaning himself, wanted her to "join Shari Faye." One of the officers—I think it might have been Rick McCloud—assured Dawn that she would be protected at all times, even when she was out in public at the ceremony we had planned for Shari's eighteenth birthday. I was still second-guessing my own plan, though, weighing the risks against the possible payoff. I knew how quickly things can happen when you don't have a completely controlled environment. But we were all committed now and determined to see where this strategy would get us.

LEXINGTON SHERIFF'S COLONELS LESTER "BUTCH" REYNOLDS AND MELVIN SEBOE as well as SLED lieutenant Horace "Hoss" Horton also rushed to the scene and met up with the officers who had been at the house. The area the caller had described was just outside the Gilbert city limits, about seventy-five yards off Main Street. They found a female child's body at the bottom of a hill, lying in a wooded area behind the chain and NO TRESPASSING sign the UNSUB had mentioned. Like Shari's, the body was badly decomposed from the heat and the environment, lying in a pile of leaves and underbrush. Attached to one clump of blond hair was a pink barrette. The site was about ten miles from where Shari Smith's body was found.

Though the state of the body left immediate identification ambiguous, if anyone had any doubt about the two abductions being related, the caller's similarly detailed instructions to Dawn on where to find both sites made it clear to us that we were dealing with a repeat killer. SLED lieutenant Kenneth Habben, an expert in forensic pathology, supervised the transportation of the body to Lexington County Hospital, where pathologist Dr. Erwin Shaw began the autopsy around ten o'clock in the morning. Habben took the clothing back to SLED headquarters for analysis.

Dawn and Shari Smith, holding baby Robert. (Courtesy of Dawn Smith Jordan)

Bob and Hilda Smith and Dawn, Shari, and Robert, in front of their home in Columbia, South Carolina, before they moved to the property on Platt Springs Road. (Courtesy of Dawn Smith Jordan)

Shari and Dawn Smith, who became known as the singing Smith Sisters. (Courtesy of Dawn Smith Jordan)

Shari Smith, with her typical beaming smile. (Courtesy of Dawn Smith Jordan)

Shari Smith's Last Will & Testament. (South Carolina Law Enforcement Division photo)

The Masonic Lodge in Saluda County, South Carolina, behind which Shari Smith's body was found after telephoned directions were given to the family by then-UNSUB Larry Gene Bell. (South Carolina Law Enforcement Division photo)

Shiloh Mobile Home Park on Old Percival Road in Richland County, South Carolina. The Helmick family's trailer was the first on the right. (South Carolina Law Enforcement Division photo)

Debra May Helmick, age nine. (Courtesy of Debra Helmick Johnson)

SLED lieutenant Jim Springs conducts a search at the Sheppard residence. (South Carolina Law Enforcement Division photo)

The bed and mattress cover in the guest room at the Sheppard residence used by Larry Gene Bell. (South Carolina Law Enforcement Division photo)

SLED agent Kenneth Habben collects hair and fiber evidence from the hall and doorway going into Bell's bedroom at the Sheppard residence. (South Carolina Law Enforcement Division photo)

The sheet of paper from Sharon Sheppard's pad on which she wrote notes for Larry Gene Bell when he was housesitting for her and her husband, Ellis. (South Carolina Law Enforcement Division photo)

Larry Gene Bell's parents' residence on Shull Island, Lake Murray. (South Carolina Law Enforcement Division photo)

This photograph of Larry Gene Bell was found in the attic of his parents' home after it was sold to new owners, who sent it to SLED photographer Rita Shuler. (Courtesy of Rita Shuler)

One of Larry Gene Bell's business cards. (Courtesy of Rita Shuler)

Mixed Seasonal Hardwood
Cord or ½ Cord
Stacked

Deliveries Daily

GENE'S WOODCHUCK
P.O. Box 1145
Lexington, SC 29072

GENE BELL
892-5165 Collect

Larry Gene Bell booking photo, taken the morning of his arrest. (Lexington County Sheriff's Department photo)

Shari's father, Bob Smith; John Douglas; and Sheriff James Metts at South Carolina Victims' Rights Week observance, May 2000. (South Carolina State Office of Victim Assistance photo)

SLED's Rita Shuler photographed the clothing and showed the pictures to Sherwood and Debra Helmick to spare them having to look at the actual items taken from the body. The parents positively identified Debra May's white pinstriped shorts and lavender T-shirt. Significantly, two pairs of panties had been on the body: one, a child's cotton underpants; the other, on top of the first, a bikini-style pair in an adult size, made of a silk-like material. Debra assured investigators that only the cotton panties belonged to her daughter and said she had never seen the adult pair, which added another troubling sexual dimension to the crime: The UNSUB had obviously played out some perverse fantasy with her. Based on our experience with other sexual offenders, we thought it likely that the adult-size panties probably belonged to another victim, and they might have made the killer feel less bad about attacking a child.

When the parents were shown the pink barrette, Debra said, "Yes, that's Debra May's. Around two o'clock that day, I washed her hair, brushed it, and put two pink barrettes in it. That's one of them."

Though the state of the body didn't allow for a definitive postmortem exam, Dr. Shaw determined that, as in Shari's case, suffocation was the most likely cause of death. They had to jump through some hoops to formally identify the body. Under the supervision of SLED fingerprint examiner David Caldwell, a comparison of footprints was made with those made at the hospital shortly after Debra May was born. Caldwell also was able to obtain a fingerprint card made at Hocking Technical College when the Helmicks lived in Ohio. SLED chemist Lieutenant Earl Wells examined hair samples from the body and at the crime scene with known hair samples from Debra May. He found they were consistent.

Analysis of the hair samples also showed residue of duct or masking tape on some of them. This was yet another link with the Smith case.

Since they had no access to Debra May's last dental records, which were in Chicago, Dr. Ted Allan Rathbun, a forensic anthropologist at the University of South Carolina, performed a craniofacial superimposition in which the skull of the deceased is superimposed by means of a video camera and monitor over a photograph of the individual the body is believed to belong to, to confirm identity. When the procedure was completed, Dr. Rathbun declared that the remains were those of Debra May Helmick within reasonable medical certainty.

When the news got out, and it got out quickly, the entire community was sent into a combination of sorrow and increased fear. The front page of the Saturday afternoon *Columbia Record* carried the banner headline CHILD'S BODY FOUND NEAR GILBERT. And even though the prominent subhead read, SHERIFF METTS WON'T CONFIRM IDENTITY OF GIRL UNTIL AUTOPSY PERFORMED, to the left of the story was a photograph of Debra May. The Sunday morning *State* gave the story equal prominence, with the nearly identical headline GIRL'S BODY FOUND NEAR GILBERT. Underneath was a photo showing the grim visages of Sheriffs Metts and Powell announcing the discovery. At the news conference they held, Metts said, "I urge all of you to use your best parenting skills possible. I don't want to frighten anybody, but as your sheriff it is my duty to tell you that you should exercise extra caution during these trying times."

The right-hand column of the paper was devoted to common-sense tips on how parents could protect their children.

Lexington County Sheriff's captain Bob Ford said his department's greatest challenge was investigating the cases while trying to prevent panic in the community and countering all the rumors circulating around. "The rumors are absolutely insidious," he told the Associated Press. "Our switchboard has been jammed to the point that I had to get operator assistance." The anxiety was heightened even more when authorities acknowledged they believed the killer was "homegrown."

Though the police composite sketches of the two kidnappers didn't look very much alike, at another news conference in the afternoon on Monday, June 24, Sheriff Metts stated, "We now believe the cases of Shari Faye Smith and Debra May Helmick are one and the same." He did not say what information led investigators to Debra's body. He also said that he did not believe the beating death of Marilee Whitten, a seventeen-year-old blue-eyed blonde, in Richland County, was related. Ron and I agreed. The guy we were looking for didn't have the chops for that kind of murder. There was also some strong evidence that she might have known her killer.

But for the first time in a public statement, Metts used the term "serial killer." In comparing the clear patterns in such previous cases as the Atlanta Child Murders and the killing of elderly women in Columbus, Georgia, he said, "Unlike those cases, these two kidnappings show no great common denominator: no obvious connecting thread. It is the lack of any apparent motive or connection that has hampered this investigation."

We certainly agreed with Metts that we were dealing with

a repeat killer who would not stop until he was caught. But what also troubled me was that the killer was not confining himself to a specific victim type. His fixation on Dawn after abducting Shari pointed to a very specific preference. The abduction and murder of Debra May told us that when the urge struck him, he would settle for any female victim, as long as she was weaker than him and unable to put up effective resistance. For example, people, even law enforcement personnel, are surprised when they see the same predatory offender targeting a child, a street person, and an elderly woman. They wouldn't seem to have anything in common in terms of victims of preference. And yet, from the offender's twisted perspective, they do. They are all relatively easy targets in that they are defenseless. For some killers, that is enough. Though I expected this UNSUB to continue targeting attractive females, we now knew that the age wasn't as important as how easy they would be to abduct and control. And if he couldn't find a pretty blond girl or young woman who met that criterion, he would go for whoever was available. But he would not stop.

Fear continued to permeate the community. As in Lexington, the sheriff's departments of the two adjoining counties were overwhelmed with calls and tips. While we always encourage the public to share whatever they see, hear, or think they know with law enforcement authorities, it is a simple fact that the ratio of useful information to useless or irrelevant detail is heavily weighted toward the unhelpful. One woman, who had been the twenty-fifth caller to the Richland County Sheriff's Department in an hour, said she had awakened from a dream with a vision of the man responsible for the deaths of Shari and Debra May, grabbed a pencil, and just started writing autonomically. She admitted she didn't understand what she had written, but knew it had something to do with the missing girls.

"If you would just send somebody out here to look at it, I'm sure you can tell what it means," she told the detective on the phone.

"No, ma'am. We're not going to send somebody out there," the detective replied as politely as he could.

"Okay, I'll bring it to you," she offered.

"No, please don't," the detective implored, thanking her for her concern and quickly hanging up.

By this point, four individuals had been arrested for either trying to extort ransom money from the Smiths or making purposely false reports.

RON AND I GOT A BRIEF RESPITE FROM THE PRESSURES OF THE CASE THAT SUNDAY, June 23, when Lewis McCarty picked us up from our motel and brought us out to his cabin on Lake Murray. It was a rustic wooden structure in a beautiful, peaceful setting, and it was relaxing for once just being able to take in the scenery rather than continually analyzing my surroundings for clues or proactive strategy ideas. McCarty would go out there, either alone or with friends, to hunt and fish. Ron also remembers it as the one break we got from the deep humid summer heat. Neither one of us was motivated to pick up a rifle or a fishing rod, so the three of us sat on the porch most of the afternoon, drinking McCarty's whiskey and shooting the breeze. In the short amount of time we'd been in South Carolina, Lewis had become not only a professional colleague, but a genuine friend.

For the first time since we'd been involved with the case,

everything seemed to slow down, and we could turn our minds to something other than pursuing the UNSUB. Still, I couldn't put out of my mind completely the memorial event we had planned for Shari's birthday on Tuesday, and we couldn't completely escape what was going on around us or what was coming out in the media.

"The watchword to this whole thing is helplessness," psychiatrist Dr. David C. Jacobs told Joyce W. Milkie in an interview for the *Times & Democrat* of Orangeburg, South Carolina.

"Reports have been received by the *Times & Democrat* and other media outlets telling of alleged kidnap attempts, sightings of the suspect, fears and suspicions," Milkie wrote. "Rumors of threats and concerns of parents have caused nursery schools to lock their doors, keeping children inside."

"It is a terrifying situation," Jacobs acknowledged, allowing that the "type of terror presented when you think of your own children taken from their yard is something people are just not used to here. And it is not an inappropriate type of response."

CHAPTER 12

On Monday, June 24, Sheriff Metts arranged for me to meet with several local media people to describe the event we were going to hold the next day. Without suggesting what they should write—journalists understandably don't take well to that kind of advice—I confided our own goals to them: to entice the UNSUB out into the open, to get him to come back to the gravesite at night to retrieve the koala bear, or at least to start calling again. I told them how a few years earlier, when I was working on the Tylenol poisoning case in Chicago, I had agreed to an interview with Bob Greene, the popular syndicated columnist of the *Chicago Tribune*, to describe how the FBI was pursuing the case. I told him about the youngest victim, twelve-year-old Mary Kellerman. He wrote a moving article focusing on Mary and when I read it, I hoped it would prompt the UNSUB to visit her grave, which we arranged to have surveilled.

As it turned out, we didn't get that UNSUB, although I still think the strategy was a good one, but while the surveillance was underway, someone else visited the grave right next to Mary's and confessed to the unsolved hit-and-run of another girl, and the police snatched him! You never know where your breaks are going to come.

By Tuesday the sheriff's departments of the three counties had revised their composite sketch to reflect input from both abductions. Though still described as medium height, twenty-eight to thirty-five years of age, and heavyset with a flabby build, the UNSUB was now said to have a dark beard and long-ish hair on the side, shaggy in front, whereas one of the previous sketches had had him clean-shaven and another had him balding. The sketch went out in all the regional newspapers.

On Tuesday afternoon, we held the memorial at the cemetery as I had suggested. A fair number of reporters were in attendance, as we had hoped. I stood back from the grave and the family, near the clutch of media, where I could scan the attendees to see if anyone looked like he could be our UNSUB. If so, sheriff's deputies, ostensibly there to control traffic, were ready to grab and detain him. My only concern was that the grave was so close to the road that if the UNSUB showed up, he could either stay in his car or watch from a distance.

Perhaps the most moving coverage of the event came from Teresa K. Weaver, a staff writer for the *Columbia Record*, published in the next day's edition under the headline COPING WITH THE PAIN. It began:

> *The slender blonde in dark sunglasses knelt gingerly at her sister's grave and silently fastened a 2-inch-tall stuffed koala bear to the artificial flowers.*

Afternoon traffic on U.S. 1 streamed by as the family slowly moved in and joined the girl, holding hands and listening as the father led them in a brief prayer.

Yesterday would have been Shari Smith's 18th birthday.

It was the first time the family had been able to return to the gravesite since the funeral, and Dawn was overcome by emotion. Tears streamed down her face as she placed the small koala on the pink flower arrangement. She'd told me beforehand that she felt manipulative acting out this scenario, which was preplanned rather than a spontaneous gesture, and as I watched her, I had to concede to myself that I was manipulating her, just as the UNSUB had been doing. Though the motivation was different, I knew it was still distressing to her.

Since there was no gravestone yet, we'd had a white wooden lectern constructed with Shari's picture laminated to the front. Several large flower arrangements flanked the burial plot. Numerous camera shutters snapped as the four family members joined hands around the grave and bowed their heads in prayer. Despite the fact that it was staged, the ceremony was almost unbearably moving, and I found myself choking up several times as I observed each family member's quiet and dignified grief, all the more difficult, I was sure, because it was on public display. Since I had been the one who urged them to stage this event, I hoped they were getting as much out of it emotionally as they were giving. And more than that, I hoped the UNSUB was watching and we could get him to react.

As part of the strategy to try to engage him, I wanted family members to speak to the media, to personalize their grief and pain. I hoped at the least that we would get the killer to call again and comment on things the family said to reporters. I knew it was too much to hope he would actually feel guilty in response, but it was worth a try to get any reaction from him.

I was gratified to see the article went into detail about what the Smiths had been asked, beginning with their abiding faith, which they acknowledged was the only thing getting them through the ordeal.

"That's the only way we cope," Bob Smith stated. "We believe."

We played up the birthday connection.

"It's even harder today, knowing that this is the day you gave birth and she's not here with you," Hilda said, "knowing she's not ever going to be here with you again." She mentioned that she and Bob had planned a pool party for Shari's birthday and as a surprise gift had bought a large poster of a koala bear.

Bob made an observation that I knew to be all too true from my many encounters with families that had lost loved ones to murder: "You know, the injury heals but the scar doesn't ever go away."

There were members of the public in attendance, and throughout the ceremony, I kept searching for any indication the UNSUB was present, anyone moving strangely or trying not to seem obvious. Metts's deputies took down license numbers of cars that slowed down as they passed, though I'm sure most of them were just curious to see what was going on.

When the event was finished, when the cameras were turned off and the reporters' notebooks put away, I could see the toll it had taken on every member of the family. They seemed shell-shocked, as if they didn't want to have to face anyone.

Dawn, who had had the major role, was particularly affected. She later told us, "I was really angry that I was having to do this koala thing and do all these other things to try to coax this man into reaching out to my family, because we thought that was the only way he would be caught. And so, while it was so upsetting on the inside, you wouldn't have seen it on the outside because that was my job. But then, of course, once those little assignments were done, we fell apart. My family fell apart when nobody was watching. I would go upstairs into my bedroom and just sob. But we had amazing friends and family, and people there to support us, to help us so we didn't go through it alone."

I wasn't happy that we had to put her or any of the others through this, but I genuinely admired the way she had conducted herself and told her so. Once someone in your family has been the victim of a violent crime, and murder, of course, is the very worst, a world of pain is opened up. Often the only way to get through it is to *go through it*. I knew that as much as they were going through now, they wouldn't really be able to properly grieve until Shari's killer was brought to justice. What we had done at the cemetery was certainly an effort in that direction.

DEBRA MAY'S FUNERAL WAS HELD THE NEXT EVENING AT THE WOODFIELD PARK Baptist Church, with burial at Memorial Gardens of Columbia. Her parents had postponed it by one day so it wouldn't fall on her little sister Becky's birthday. Police offers were stationed throughout the grounds and stopped and questioned anyone who seemed to them in any way suspicious. A sheriff's airplane circled overhead. We didn't know if the UNSUB would show up for the service—we still weren't sure if he had been in or around the huge number of people who had attended Shari's funeral—but we wanted to be prepared.

There were about three hundred people in the church. Six of Debra May's uncles, some of whom still lived in Ohio, served as pallbearers for her small casket, adorned with an arrangement of yellow daisies and pink and purple carnations. Among the mourners were the Smiths, who had never met the Helmicks, but had been praying for them and felt their loss acutely.

In his brief eulogy, the Reverend Max Pettyjohn acknowledged how everything felt as he addressed the congregation, "This is a very difficult time for all of us. We are afraid, angry, and confused. We are all sad and broken . . . We are afraid for our children. We don't feel safe in our own front yards. We distrust every stranger. We ask, 'When will it end?'"

After the ceremony, Ron and I accompanied Richland sheriff's deputies and SLED agents the eleven miles to Memorial Garden. Debra May's twenty-three-year-old uncle, Albert Lowe, read a poem at the gravesite and then the Helmicks picked up shovels and filled in the grave themselves. I surveyed the other people, looking for anyone who might fit the profile.

But whether he was there or not, I knew the UNSUB would read about the event and see the coverage on television, and I was sure that within a day or two, he would be back in touch with Dawn.

CHAPTER 13

With the burial of this sweet and lovable nine-year-old girl, Wednesday, June 26, was the saddest day of the entire investigation. The image of my two young daughters never left my mind. But this day also proved to be the most important.

While the Helmicks prepared to say goodbye to their Debra May, agents at the SLED laboratory in Columbia thought they might have a breakthrough in the examination of Shari's Last Will & Testament—the only real piece of physical evidence in the case except for the bodies and clothing of the two victims.

Employing the ESDA machine that can detect the impressions left by writing on previous pages in a pad, they had been able to reveal the almost microscopically slight impressions made from sheets of paper that had been higher up in the legal pad. One of the sheets appeared to have a grocery list, some of whose items could be made out. They also thought it contained a string of numbers. Under extremely close scrutiny, the investigators were able to make out nine numerals of a ten-number sequence: 205-837-13_8. In that pattern, it was most likely a telephone number.

Assuming this was a telephone number, the first three digits would be the area code—205 was the Alabama code—and 837 was a Huntsville exchange. Working with Southern Bell's security division, SLED agents went through all ten possible phone numbers in Huntsville, then cross-checked all the records to see if any of them had calls or were related in any way to the Columbia–Lexington County region.

They discovered that one of the ten phone number sequences had received multiple calls from a residential telephone number several weeks before Shari was kidnapped, about fifteen miles from the Smith home. This appeared to be the strongest lead yet, or could it be just one of those bizarre coincidences we often see in complex criminal investigations.

One of the authorities called the Huntsville number. The individual who answered sounded like a white male in his twenties or thirties. He didn't really sound like the UNSUB, but that person had altered his voice on the earlier calls, so it was a possibility. Had they hit pay dirt with this first call?

Rather than confront him straight out with whether he was involved with or knew anything about the two kidnappings and murders in South Carolina, the agent asked if he knew anyone who lived in the state.

Yes, he replied straight out. He said his parents lived near Lake Murray in the northeastern part of Saluda County. Their names were Ellis and Sharon Sheppard.

This man, their son, was called Joey and he was stationed at an army base in Huntsville. He was friendly and forthcoming. Agents fairly quickly concluded that he did not fit our profile, and he hadn't been in the Lexington-Saluda-Richland area anywhere near the time the two crimes occurred.

The next step was to check out what he had said about the other terminus of the multiple calls. Municipal real estate tax records showed that Ellis and Sharon Sheppard did, in fact, own a house in Saluda County, South Carolina.

Now it was time to pay the Sheppards a visit.

THE SAME EVENING AS DEBRA MAY'S FUNERAL, LEWIS MCCARTY DROVE TO THE Sheppard residence. He didn't know what to expect, so he brought several deputies with him. The pad of paper Shari's letter was written on appeared to have come from the Sheppard house, and McCarty had gone through all of the possible contingencies in his mind. If Ellis Sheppard was the killer, possibly with his wife as an enabler or even a compliant victim who knew about the crimes either before or after the fact, McCarty wanted to be ready.

But as soon as the door opened and he and as team were admitted into the house, he knew something was wrong; something didn't add up.

Ellis and Sharon Sheppard were in their fifties. They were friendly and hospitable, and seemed not at all threatened by the presence of law officers. They had been happily married for many years. The more McCarty gleaned from his conversation with them, the less they fit any part of our profile. Neither one had any of the background or characteristics we would have expected from the UNSUB. Just about the only thing that fit was that Ellis was an electrician. Just as significantly, when they were questioned about their lives and whereabouts over the past month, McCarty learned that at this point in their lives, they liked to travel, and they said they had been out of town when both abductions took place. Yes, they'd certainly heard about the horrible murders and they had great compassion for both families, but they really didn't know all of the details.

When McCarty asked them if they knew anything about the phone calls to the phone number written on the paper pad, they quickly acknowledged that it was their son Joey's number, that he was in the army in Huntsville, and that they called him frequently. The telephone number the ESDA machine had detected that led to a direct connection back to the Midlands of South Carolina had seemed like such a strong and compelling forensic lead that it just didn't make sense that it was a red herring. McCarty was experienced enough to know that most cases have false leads that don't go anywhere, but the disappointment was profound in feeling that they had come so close. They would investigate the Sheppards further, but McCarty and Metts both believed strongly in the validity of the profile; and, further, Ellis Sheppard just didn't seem like the kind of guy who could commit two heinous murders and be so calm and "normal."

The undersheriff wasn't giving up, though. Combining the profile and the composite witness descriptions, he asked if they happened to know anyone who sounded like a certain type of person he would describe. Then he went through the profile and physical description: white male in his thirties; portly, flabby, and of medium height; about 180 to 200 pounds; not very physically attractive; short, shaggy beard and hair; somewhat above-average intelligence but hadn't really done much with it; married but divorced, possibly with a child he doesn't see; currently living alone or with an older relative; unsuccessful military career and early discharge; worked in some blue-collar job, possibly involving electrical work and/or home repair; drove a several-years-old but well-maintained car; consumed and collected bondage and sadomasochistic-oriented pornography; a meticulous list maker and rigid thinker who wrote down everything he wanted to remember and who, if he was distracted from what he was saying, would start over at the beginning.

McCarty didn't mention one other aspect of our profile, that we believed the UNSUB had had previous run-ins with the law over sex crimes, or even just been accused of harassing women, because that was not something those who knew the offender would necessarily know, and McCarty didn't want that detail to throw them off if he was otherwise moving in the right direction.

Most significantly, McCarty said, this person's appearance would have changed noticeably in the last several weeks; he would seem more agitated and easily upset, and his behavior might appear more erratic; he could be drinking more or indulging in some kind of substance abuse; and he would be preoccupied by and seem overly interested in the coverage of the Smith and Helmick murders. These things would be obvious to anyone around him.

The Sheppards shared a look and just about simultaneously replied that the man Undersheriff McCarty was describing sounded exactly like Larry Gene Bell.

Bell was thirty-six years old, about five-foot-ten, somewhat overweight, and with reddish-brown hair. He had been working for Ellis as an electrician's assistant on and off since the early spring, often doing house wiring. The Sheppards didn't

like leaving their home vacant and unattended when they traveled. As good a worker and as meticulous and detail-oriented
as Gene, as he was known, was, he seemed like the perfect person to house-sit for them. His twelve-year-old son lived with his
ex-wife in another state, and Gene was living with his parents,
Margaret and Archie Bell, so staying at the Sheppards' house
for extended periods would not be a problem.

They always kept a legal pad near the phone in the kitchen
and before they left for their first trip, Sharon wrote down all
of the information that she thought Gene might need while
they were away. Of the several phone numbers they wrote
down for him in case of emergency, one was for their son, Joey,
in Huntsville, who would always know how to get in contact
with them.

The Sheppards remembered exactly when they had left for
the first time with Gene staying at the house because it was
Mother's Day, Sunday, May 12. Gene drove them to the airport,
and at the time he had a beard and mustache. When they returned home about three weeks later, on Monday, June 3, he
picked them up at the airport. They noticed that his beard was
much shorter, and Sharon Sheppard asked him why he had
shaved it the way he had.

He replied that he was getting ready for the hot summer
weather. And then, they said, he brought up the Shari Smith
kidnapping. And that was where the conversation remained
during the entire drive back to the house.

Bell spent that night with the Sheppards and inevitably, the
conversation kept returning to Shari Smith. Ellis said to Mc-
Carty that he remembered Gene asking him, "Do you think the

family would want to find the body so that they could make the funeral arrangements?"

"Well, since she was kidnapped, hopefully she is still alive," Ellis replied.

His wife mentioned something else she thought peculiar. When they had first met Gene, he had respectfully called her Mrs. Sheppard. As they got to know each other better, he started calling her Sharon. But when they returned home on June 3, she noted that he was calling her Shari. He had never done that before.

The next morning, Tuesday, June 4, he had gone to work with Ellis and then returned to his parents' home on Shull Island in Lake Murray, several miles away.

The day after that, one of the Sheppards' neighbors came by around 1:30 P.M. and told them that Shari Smith's body had been found behind the Masonic Lodge near the Saluda traffic circle. That was both heartrending for the Smith family and unnerving to Ellis and Sharon and their neighbor, since it was only about three miles from where they lived.

Gene returned to their house about a half hour later to drive them to the airport for the second leg of their travels. Sharon asked him, "Did you hear the news that the Smith girl's body has been found near the Saluda traffic circle?"

"No!" he responded, then added, "too bad."

She said that then that was all he wanted to talk about on the way to the airport. He repeated several times that he felt so bad for the family. Every time she or Ellis tried to change the subject, Gene would be right back at it, speculating about all the conceivable contingencies, what the killer might have done with Shari or to her body. It was as if he wanted them to go over all the possibilities with him. Sharon said that his obsessing over such a morbid subject was really getting on her nerves. She was relieved when he dropped them off.

IN WHAT SEEMED LIKE THE MIDDLE OF THE NIGHT, I THOUGHT I HEARD BANGING; yes, it was banging on the door. For a moment I thought I was back in Seattle, lying on the floor of my hotel room, unable to move. Then, as I awakened and my mind clicked into gear, I realized that back then I had heard nothing because I was unconscious. This time I definitely heard something. I glanced at the electric clock on the nightstand. It was a little after two A.M.

I kind of staggered out of bed, went to the door, and opened it. It was Ron Walker, standing there fully dressed.

Before I could say anything, he said, "Hey John, I just got a call from Lew McCarty. They've got a suspect and they want us down at the sheriff's office."

Did I hear correctly? I asked Ron to repeat it. As soon as it sunk in, I hurried to get dressed. Knowing I'd probably be wearing the same things for quite a while and knowing how hot it was likely to get again once the sun came up, I put on a white short-sleeve shirt and white slacks. When I caught a look at myself in the mirror, I thought I looked like either an ice cream vendor or a hospital orderly, but this was no time to worry about appearance. If this suspect McCarty had mentioned was a serious one, we had a lot of work to do.

THE SHEPPARDS AGREED TO A FORMAL INTERVIEW WITH THE SHERIFF'S DEPARTment detectives, and McCarty brought them to the office in the early morning hours of Thursday, June 27. Ron and I were already there, in Lewis McCarty's office and still somewhat bleary-eyed, starting to assimilate information on this Larry Gene Bell to determine how it correlated with our profile so we could advise on interrogation strategies and search warrant requests. We received regular updates on the interview.

When the Sheppards had returned from their latest trip that past Monday, June 24, Sharon related, Bell picked them up from the airport again. She noticed immediately that he looked thinner, as if he had lost about ten pounds since they last saw him. She also said his appearance wasn't as neat as usual, and he seemed "a little spacey."

On the drive back home, from the back seat behind him, she leaned forward, patted him on the shoulder, and said, "You look tired. Are you okay?"

"Well, no," he replied. "I'm just not myself."

Acknowledging that Gene had been spending a lot of his time the last several weeks tending to their house, Ellis said, "You need to get back home and eat your mama's cooking."

At their house, Bell packed up his clothing and organized his other belongings and said he would go home to his parents' house that night and be back to work with Ellis in the morning. The Sheppards thought this was somewhat strange. The last couple of times they'd been away, he'd simply left most of his things at their house, since they were coming and going. Bell knew they were planning to leave again on Friday and expected him to continue house-sitting, so they didn't see why he was clearing out.

Another thing stood out, based on how McCarty had described the profile. Despite the fact that they had grown impatient with Gene's persistence in wanting to talk about little else than the Shari Smith murder, they had been deeply troubled by such a horrible crime so close to their home and asked him to save the newspapers while they were away so they could catch up on what had happened while they were gone. What they hadn't expected was that he had cut out and organized all of the articles about the Smith and Helmick cases. He had them not only from local papers the *State* and the *Columbia Record*, but also from papers in other areas around the Carolinas.

When Sharon had seen the revised composite drawing in the papers, she said a chill ran through her: It certainly looked like it could be Gene. "Oh, my God," she said to Ellis, "could he have something to do with this horrible thing?"

Ellis told her no but told the investigators the thought wouldn't leave his mind. He went back to the newspaper reproduction of the police composite. It did seem to bear a certain resemblance to Larry Gene Bell.

Then another thought flashed through Ellis's mind. Living as far out in the country as they did, and so close to the lake, Ellis kept a loaded .38 pistol at home for protection. He recalled that he had told Gene about the gun in case he ever felt threatened while he was staying in their house alone. Some of the news stories speculated that Shari Smith was forced into her abductor's car at gunpoint. Ellis went to check on his handgun in the place where he kept it.

It wasn't there. He said this gave him an extremely weird feeling.

Troubled by the business over the gun, Ellis said he called Gene at his parents' house about eleven that night. Gene told him in a matter-of-fact manner that yes, he knew where the gun was. He had placed it under the mattress on the side of his bed closest to the wall. Ellis said okay, he would see him in the morning and hung up. Then he went to check out the bed Gene slept in. That was where the gun was, just as he'd described. Ellis picked it up and examined it. It had been fired and not cleaned afterward. It appeared to be jammed.

Also under the mattress was a copy of *Hustler* magazine, showing a beautiful blond woman in bondage in a cruciform position on the cover. Another aspect of the profile clicked into place.

By this time Sharon had gone to sleep and Ellis didn't want to wake her to tell her about the gun or the magazine. Still, he was trying to reason out how this could all be just coincidence; how maybe they had misinterpreted everything. But what about the gun being moved and fired and Gene saying nothing about it until he was asked? How did that work into a co-incidence? And the picture of the blonde all tied up? That was exactly what McCarty said the FBI expected to find. He and Sharon were both fine, upstanding people and everyone knew it. Could they possibly unwittingly have associated themselves with a vicious killer, and even entrusted their house to him? It all seemed unreal.

The morning after he picked them up from the airport, Gene had arrived at their house as usual, and as they were driving to the job Ellis commented that the composite drawing in the paper looked a little bit like him. What did he think about that?

"Well," he replied casually, "they did stop me twice in road-blocks they had set up, but they sent me on through. Other cars were being stopped, too."

Ellis said he tried to convince himself that this was a

logical explanation. He just couldn't believe the Larry Gene Bell he knew was capable of doing something like these horrible crimes.

After hearing the entire narrative of the Sheppards' return home this last time, of Bell's perplexing behavior and their own growing fears, investigators played them an excerpt of the UNSUB's last phone call to Dawn—the one in the first hour of Saturday morning when he had told Dawn that God wanted her to join Shari Faye and gave her directions to Debra May Helmick's body, in which he was no longer using an electronic pitch modulator.

Ellis and Sharon looked at each other and gasped. Sharon broke into tears.

Ellis said, "That's Larry Gene Bell. No doubt about it." He paused as he thought about all the implications of what he had just confirmed. "My God," he added. "He threw her body out around Bill's Grill." Apparently, Bell had disposed of Debra May's body not far from one of his favorite eating places.

CHAPTER 14

When Ron and I got to the sheriff's department in the early morning hours, Jim Metts was already there. He and McCarty started filling us in about Larry Gene Bell. Metts showed us a photograph his deputies had taken while they were surveilling Shari Smith's gravesite, which, as I mentioned, was close to the road. This particular photo showed a car registered to Bell on the road right near the grave, but the driver had not gotten out. This confirmed my belief that the killer would visit the grave, but he was also criminally sophisticated enough to realize the area was probably being watched so he couldn't take the chance of getting as up close and personal as he'd have liked.

The more the investigators learned about Mr. Bell, the more certain we were that he was our man.

As background, he was born on October 30, 1949, in Ralph, Alabama, southwest of Tuscaloosa. He was the fourth of five children, with three sisters and a brother. Ironically, his brother, James, was an attorney in Columbia. His father, Archie, was a mechanical engineer. The family moved around a lot, with Bell attending high school in both Columbia and then in Tupelo, Mississippi, where he graduated. From a yearbook photo, it was apparent that he played on Columbia's Eau Claire High School baseball team, nicknamed the Shamrocks, in the late 1960s. He had some training as an electrician and then moved back to Columbia, where he married a sixteen-year-old, tenth-grade girl. Notably, in terms of what was to happen, she had blond hair and blue eyes.

Bell joined the Marine Corps in 1970 with the intention of going to fight in Vietnam, but he didn't even last a year. He injured his knee when he accidentally shot himself while cleaning a firearm and was separated from the service. In 1971, he worked as a prison guard for the South Carolina Department of Corrections in Columbia. That job lasted a month. He and his wife moved the next year to Rock Hill, South Carolina, up near the North Carolina border and not far from Carowinds theme park, where Dawn would perform years later in the summers and where Shari had hoped to sing, too.

Ten years before the Smith and Helmick murders, in February 1975, Bell was arrested on assault and battery charges in Rock Hill after he approached a young woman in a shopping center parking lot and pressed her to go with him "to Charlotte and party."

When she refused, he pulled a knife, pointed it at her midsection, and tried to drag her into his green Volkswagen. She screamed and fought him, at which point he abandoned his effort, got back in his car, and drove away. A woman nearby heard the screams, rushed to a phone, and called the police. They were able to catch up with him a short distance from the shopping center. He pled guilty in May of that year, was sentenced to five years in prison, and was fined $1,000. The prison sentence was suspended on condition of payment of the fine and converted to probation. At this point in his life, he was employed as a reservations clerk for Eastern Airlines. He was still married and living with his wife and their two-year-old son. They would divorce the next year. At least twice after this, once while out on bond, Bell checked himself into psychiatric facilities—at the South Carolina State Hospital, a publicly funded psychiatric institution in Columbia, as well as the Columbia Veterans Administration hospital—for personality disorders of a "psycho-sexual nature."

This first sex-related crime on his rap sheet confirmed what we'd predicted about him: He had neither the strength, courage, nor emotional wherewithal to attack, control, and dominate a grown woman who was in a position to fight back. In that scenario, he would simply cut his losses and run. That was why he had focused on Shari Smith (requiring a firearm to control her); and then, when the urge grew strong in him again, on the even more vulnerable Debra May Helmick.

The next charge in his file only underscored this point.

In October 1975, just eight months after his previous offense, and five months after he pled guilty and got probation rather than jail time, he helped a woman to her feet after she had slipped and fallen in Columbia. He then said, "I am armed," showed her a handgun, and tried to force her into his car. They struggled and she managed to wrestle herself away from him. Again, having failed to capture his intended prey, he got back in his car and drove away.

Both of these women reacted in the best possible way.

Confronted with a terrifying situation like this, we advise potential victims to do everything possible to avoid getting into an offender's vehicle. Your odds of survival are far better if you try to fight him off and get away. Once you are in his car and under his control, as the Smith and Helmick cases tragically show, your options diminish dramatically. In a public space such as a street or shopping center parking lot, even offenders threatening victims at gunpoint will be hesitant to actually use the weapon, as it attracts immediate attention. This is not to say that there are no risks to resisting, and if the power dynamic between offender and victim is unbalanced, as it was with Debra May, resistance may not work. But someone like Bell understood, even if only on a visceral level, that once he had his victim in his car, he was in control, and his odds of successfully completing his crime rose exponentially. He was also sophisticated enough to understand his own limits and cowardice, so that if the victim was capable of resisting, it was better to drop the whole effort and move on.

In this second case, though, it didn't get him off the hook. Just as with his previous attempted abduction, he was identified and picked up by the police. It turned out the pistol he brandished was filled with blanks, but the woman who was his intended victim had no way of knowing that. In June 1976, he pleaded guilty to assault and battery in the case, his previous probation was revoked, and Circuit Court Judge Owens T. Cobb sentenced him to five additional years in prison and ordered that he receive psychiatric evaluation and counseling while incarcerated. He ended up serving only two in the Central Correctional Institute before being paroled, despite a psychiatric report that stated, "The chance of him repeating his acts is very high."

In October 1979, in Charlotte, North Carolina, Bell was convicted of making obscene telephone calls to a ten-year-old girl in Mecklenburg County from February through July of that year. This was totally in keeping with the type of individual we had profiled and would presage elements of his later crimes, such as his extended phone calls with the Smith family and his victimization of nine-year-old Debra May. The preteen girl was more on his level emotionally than someone his own age, and after Bell was picked up twice for physical encounters with women, the telephone gave him the protection that an in-person encounter could not. When the calls began, police gave the girl's mother a telephone recording device.

Although the obscene calls led to another arrest and guilty plea, Bell got no more jail time. Instead, he was given a two-year suspended sentence, with another five years of probation tacked on. From the standpoint of criminal evolution, he also learned to disguise his telephone voice.

After hours of assembling all of this information, the dossier was conveyed overnight to Eleventh Judicial Circuit Solicitor (the official designation of the district attorney, in this instance, for several counties) Donald V. "Donnie" Myers, who reviewed it, felt confident he had enough material, and presented it to Magistrate Judge LeRoy Stabler, who issued an arrest warrant for Bell.

Through a coordinated effort among the Lexington County Sheriff's Department, SLED, and the South Carolina Wildlife Department, a surveillance perimeter was established about a mile from the entrance to the driveway of Bell's parents' one-story, cedar-sided home in a cul-de-sac on the tip of Shull Island at Lake Murray. The officers were ready as daylight first appeared around 6:15 Thursday morning.

Around 7:30, Bell approached their roadblock. He was driving a late-1970s cream-gray Buick. An officer approached the car and asked the driver to identify himself.

"Larry Gene Bell," he replied. The officer asked to see his driver's license and requested that he step out of the car. He complied and calmly said, "This is about those two girls. Can I call my mama?"

He was immediately placed under arrest and read his Miranda rights. He was then handcuffed and placed in the back of a deputy's cruiser to be taken to the Lexington sheriff's office.

As the cruiser drove away, Colonel Butch Reynolds reached through the open window of Bell's Buick to turn off the ignition. He noticed an open folding knife with a double-edged blade on the passenger side of the front seat.

That morning, Metts, flanked by Richland County sheriff Frank Powell and Saluda County sheriff George Booth, held a brief news conference to relieve the public. "Late last night, and early this morning," he announced, "our task force developed crucial information that identified an individual that fits our profile to a tee." He didn't give the suspect's name, saying he expected to be able to report on an arrest later in the day. Just after Bell was picked up, Metts had called the Smiths and sent word to the Helmicks.

Before the Sheppards left the sheriff's department, they granted permission to search their house. Shortly after they arrived back home, SLED agents Kenneth Habben, James Springs, and Mickey Dawson arrived to conduct the search. Sharon Sheppard located the sheet of legal paper on which she had written the notes and telephone number for their son in Alabama. She turned it over to the agents, who also asked for samples of envelopes, notebooks, and pens from both the house and the Sheppards' car.

Sharon told the investigators that when she and Ellis had arrived home on June 4, she noticed a long blond hair stuck to the couch in the living room. "I just figured it was his girl-friend's," she said. "He had asked permission to bring her to the house while we were gone. I made some silly little remark to myself and plucked it up and threw it in the trash and didn't think any more about it until now."

When Habben went into the guest room, the bedroom Bell occupied, he found it predictably clean and orderly, the carpet recently vacuumed. The sheets on the bed had been freshly laundered. But underneath the sheets was a blue fitted mattress pad that Sharon said she had originally put on the bed. Unlike the top sheet and blanket, the mattress pad was wrinkled and stained. Among the stains were some that looked as if they could be urine, semen, and blood. Habben recalled that Shari's diabetes insipidus would cause frequent need to urinate if she didn't have access to her medication. Several red fibers were visible on the sheet, which Habben collected and placed in evidence bags. He then collected hair samples he found on the floor near the inner side of the door. One of the most significant discoveries in the bedroom, again consistent with our profile, was a bag containing seven pairs of women's underwear under some of Bell's own clothing in a dresser drawer, with several pairs similar to the silk-like bikini panties found on Debra May's body.

Investigators also found a pair of light blue shorts that matched the witness description of what the man who abducted Debra May Helmick was wearing. Among other items seized were a camera, photographs, audiocassette tapes, and a jump rope.

There was a business card in the bedroom from Loveless and Loveless, Inc./Topsoil, Sand, Gravel and Dirt Cheap, on Old Percival Road in Columbia. The company was owned by Bell's sister Diane and her husband, John, and it was directly across the road from the Shiloh Mobile Home Park where the Helmicks lived. It was later learned that Bell worked for the couple occasionally when they needed extra help.

The bathroom Bell used was across the hallway. There were four rugs on the floor, all with noticeable hairs on them. Habben rolled up each one individually and placed them in separate bags. He also collected apparent pubic hairs from the around the base of the toilet. The other agents found duct tape in the Sheppards' living room and in the blue pickup truck Bell had been using for work.

Bell had given the agents permission to search the 1978 Buick Riviera in which he was arrested. Habben took and bagged the knife that was still on the front seat. In the trunk there was a folded towel and bedspread. When Habben picked them up he saw a license plate in a standard glassine envelope, together with a registration card. The plates on the car read OCH 241. The plate in the trunk was DCE 604. It was in the name of Diane Loveless on Trenholm Road in Columbia, Bell's sister. The first letter, D, corresponded to what the witness had reported when Debra May was abducted. However, authorities believed a different car than Loveless's was used in the crime.

SLED photographer Rita Shuler and questioned document examiner Gaile Heath met with the Sheppards for them to take a close look at what the ESDA machine had produced with the Last Will & Testament. It became clear to the couple that Shari's letter had come from the pad in their home on which Sharon had written on previous pages.

Shuler asked her, "Did you ever suspect Larry of this while it was going on?"

She replied, "I didn't like the feelings I had when I saw the composite and Larry's obsession with all of it, so I told Ellis how I felt."

I've always felt that intuition can be a powerful force and Ellis swore to Shuler that he'd never question his wife's again.

CHAPTER 15

By the time Bell was booked at the sheriff's office, Ron and I had been working for hours on a strategy to conduct his interview and interrogation. I recalled the way I had advised the police in Adairsville, Georgia, in the Mary Frances Stoner murder case—the first thing I thought of when Ron had initially come into my office to tell me about Shari Smith's abduction.

After hearing my detailed profile of Mary Frances's killer, one of the officers on the phone call said, "You just described a guy we released as a suspect in the case," though he was still suspected in another crime. His name was Darrell Gene Devier, and perhaps most important, he worked as a tree trimmer and had been working for the local power company trimming branches on the Stoners' street about two weeks before Mary Frances's abduction.

Devier was a twenty-four-year-old white male, married and divorced twice, living with his first ex-wife. He had dropped out of school after eighth grade, despite IQ testing in the range of 100 to 110. He joined the army after his first divorce but had gone AWOL and was discharged after seven months. He drove a three-year-old, well-maintained Ford Pinto. He also was a strong suspect in the rape of a thirteen-year-old girl in Rome, Georgia, but had never been charged. In the Stoner case, he had been polygraphed with inconclusive results, which hadn't surprised me. I've never placed much faith in lie detector tests, except for law-abiding people. If you're cocky and have gotten away with serious crimes in the past, it's no harder to lie to a box than to a police interrogator.

What I suggested for Devier's interview was to have investigators from the local police and the FBI's Atlanta field office carry out the interrogation together to make it look serious and that the full weight of the government was involved in the case. Carry it out at night, I recommended, when it will be quieter and creepier, and when there won't be a natural break point for lunch or dinner. Stage the area with huge stacks of file folders on tables in front of him and write his name on each one, even if they're full of blank pages. And most important, without even mentioning it, place the bloody rock on a low table at a forty-five-degree angle from the suspect, so you can observe him turning his head to look at it. If he is guilty, I told them, this should create a high ass-pucker factor, and he won't be able to keep his eyes away from the rock.

He wasn't likely to confess, I said, because Georgia was a capital punishment state and even if he was simply sent to prison, he would know that other inmates, even murderers, don't like child molesters. I therefore told them that no matter how offensive or disgusting it might feel to the investigators, their best tactic would be to project blame onto the victim: imply that she enticed or seduced him in some way, then threatened to tell her parents or expose him to the police once she led him on to assault her. I felt this kind of face-saving scenario was the only thing that might work with him, given the confidence he would have gained after the polygraph.

Blunt force trauma and knife homicides tend to be pretty bloody, and it's difficult for the attacker not to get some of the victim's blood on him. I thought we could use this. If it looked like he was at all buying into this line, the interrogator should say something like:

> "We know you got blood on you, Darrell—on your hands, on your clothing, in your car. The question for us isn't, 'Did you do it.' We know you did. The question is, 'Why?' We think we know why, and we understand. All you have to do is tell us if we're right."

The interrogation went down just as I'd hoped it would. As soon as Devier saw the rock, he started perspiring and breathing heavily, his body language completely different from the previous interviews. The investigators followed the plan I'd set out, and eventually got him to admit to having sex with the girl, saying she threatened him afterward. They brought up the blood, and FBI special agent Bob Leary commented that they knew he didn't plan on killing her, because if he had, a smart guy like him would have used something more efficient than a rock. Ultimately, Devier confessed to murder and to the rape in Rome the previous year.

Darrell Gene Devier was tried for the rape and murder of Mary Frances Stoner, convicted, and sentenced to death.

Getting a confession for the Smith and Helmick cases was a tougher challenge, but I was hoping some of the same strategies might apply.

IN THE PARKING AREA BEHIND THE SHERIFF'S OFFICE, METTS HAD A TRAILER THE department had obtained in a drug raid. They used it as an auxiliary office. Ron and I suggested that it quickly be staged as a "task force" headquarters for the kidnappings and murders. Deputies grabbed crime scene photographs, composite police sketches, and maps of the area and pinned them up on the walls. I wanted photos of Shari and Debra May happy and smiling to contrast with the images of their dead bodies left in the woods to decay. As I'd advised the authorities to do in staging the Darrell Gene Devier interrogation, we worked with staff to stack the desks high with folders, some of them empty or unrelated, but they helped populate the scene. We suggested to Metts that when Bell was brought into the trailer, there should be several busy-looking cops sitting there, giving the impression of a tremendous amount of evidence amassed against the killer.

It wouldn't be easy to get a confession, I warned Metts and McCarty. Like Georgia, South Carolina was a capital punishment state, and in one of the phone calls with Dawn, the UNSUB had already expressed his fear of going to the electric chair. Even if he didn't get the death penalty, at the very least he'd be looking at many years or the rest of his life doing hard time as a child molester and killer, which he had to know would make him the lowest of the low in prison. None of these options were the optimum outcome for someone who values his own life and bodily integrity.

The best hope, I felt, would be to present some face-saving scenario, as we had for Devier—either shifting some of the blame onto the victims themselves, or getting Bell to explain himself away with some kind of insanity or diminished capacity defense. Accused individuals with no other way out sometimes will grasp hold of this tactic, even though, statistically, juries rarely go for it.

Once the scene staging in the "task force" trailer was complete, Bell was brought in, handcuffed. Sheriff Metts watched Bell's expression and said, "It was like a whitewash came over his face," as he looked around the trailer and focused on all of the evidence arrayed against him, taking in each piece. "It put him in the proper psychological perspective," the sheriff commented. Bell was Mirandized again and waived his rights to have an attorney present, agreeing to talk to the investigators. He would not, however, agree to give samples of his blood and saliva, which could have shown whether the semen on the mattress pad might have originated from someone with his blood type.

Lieutenant James Earl "Skeet" Perry from SLED and Lieutenant Al Davis from the sheriff's department took the first round of interviewing, while Ron and I waited in McCarty's office, receiving regular bulletins on the progress and sending in notes on what the investigators might try next. For one thing, I wanted them to keep hammering the point that every single bit of evidence pointed to Bell and no one else. They could be friendly with him, and even sympathetic, but they should not let him think for a moment that there was any way he could reasonably deny his involvement in the two abductions and murders.

As Bell was introduced to Lieutenants Perry and Davis, Perry asked him, "How you doing today?"

Bell replied sardonically, "Under the present condition, not so good." But he went on to reason with the detectives that he didn't think they should be holding him or even questioning him. "Am I being arrested?" he asked. "I'm not gonna have a chance to clear myself before you arrest me, 'cause that's kind of flimsy . . . something about the letter thing being taken out of their [the Sheppards'] house or something, or whatever it was. Gosh, that could be a whole bunch of people!"

"The arrest was effective when the arrest warrant was served on you," Perry explained. "The warrant is nothing but alleging. It does not say you are guilty of what's in the warrant."

But Bell persisted, "I don't think I ought to be arrested, especially on somebody's say-so that they identified my voice, which that could be a whole lot of people, and especially a legal pad or something like that. Anybody could have taken that, too."

"Gene, you're smart enough to know that the judge did not issue that warrant without sufficient probable cause in his mind and evidence to support it."

Bell held to an alibi that he was taking his mother to a doctor's appointment in Columbia during the time Shari disappeared.

"I know for a fact that Larry Gene Bell did not do that to these poor women," he insisted. "I'm not lying to you. I'll do everything I can to help you, but I can't confess for someone else. I'm sorry." Then, still speaking of himself in the third person, he said, "I don't want this Larry Gene Bell to be executed for something he didn't do."

Note his use of the word "women," though Debra May was a child and Shari a seventeen-year-old high school girl. Even as he denied abducting, assaulting, and killing them, it was as if he could only refer to them in a way that would make them age-appropriate for a relationship. He could not bring himself even to think of his victims as minors.

"If it was your sister's daughter and someone grabbed her, wouldn't you want someone to come forward to say what happened?" Davis asked.

"Son, bless your heart, it's time to get yourself straightened out with yourself and your God," Perry prodded. "Son, don't let this happen anymore."

"I don't want it to happen again," Bell replied. "But this fellow sitting right here did not do it."

"You know it happens to you, and you want to stop it so bad you don't know what in the world to do. It's destroying you," Perry asserted.

Davis tried a different tack. "Let's you and me try something different. Take this pad and pencil. Think real hard and relax. Think about what happened, and let that other person write what took place. Let it tell my friend Gene what took place."

But Bell continued to insist, "All I know for a fact is me sitting here—Larry Gene Bell—could not have done that bad a thing."

Meanwhile, deputies armed with a search warrant went to Bell's parents' home on Shull Island where he had been staying. The warrant, which made reference to what investigators expected to find based on our profile, was actually an extra procedural safeguard since the parents voluntarily consented to have their home searched. Apparently, they were well-liked and respected members of the community.

As we could have predicted, Bell's shoes were lined up perfectly under his bed, his desk was meticulously organized, and even the tools in the trunk of his three-year-old, well-maintained car were arranged just so. On his desk the deputies found a set of directions written out in precisely the same manner as the directions he'd given over the phone to the Smith and Helmick body dump sites. Just as we expected, they found more bondage and sadomasochistic pornography. Technicians retrieved blond hairs on his bed that later turned out to match Shari's. The commemorative duck decoy stamp that was on the envelope of Shari's Last Will & Testament matched a sheet in his desk drawer.

Back in the trailer, Bell parried back and forth with the investigators. When they played him portions of the taped telephone calls, he conceded that the voice sounded like him, and he even conceded that the officers "wouldn't have me here without evidence and stuff. I want to help y'all stop this. But if you're not sure about something, you can't confess for someone else."

Perry then outlined, "Well, we are going to prove that the letter came from the Sheppards' house . . . that the top sheet was torn off the yellow legal pad that Mrs. Sheppard left writing on, leaving impressions of numbers and letters through the pages . . . that this was the same pad that Shari wrote her 'Last Will & Testament' letter that was mailed to her family. No one could have had access to that pad but you. Only you had access to the Sheppards' house when they were gone."

By late in the afternoon, Bell still wouldn't confess to

anything and kept saying that he didn't think he should have been arrested. Perry called a halt to the interrogation session to give Bell time to sit and think about his situation. "You've jerked us around as you jerked that young lady around!" Perry shouted at him. "Don't tell me you don't remember. You probably are sick. It would take a sick, mentally ill person to do that."

After as many hours as this interrogation had dragged on, Metts and McCarty concluded that nothing more productive was going to come out of it. A little while later, Metts went back to the trailer and formally introduced himself to Bell. We thought this was important because in so much of his communication, the UNSUB had focused on Metts as the authority figure. Metts engaged in some conversation with Bell to see if he would offer anything else to the head man. After spending several minutes talking with Bell in the trailer, the sheriff led the suspect back into the main building.

Ron and I were still sitting in McCarty's office, waiting for the latest update on the interrogation when the sheriff escorted Bell in, accompanied by County Solicitor Donnie Myers. This was unexpected. I hadn't realized the sheriff intended for us to have direct contact with the suspect. It was also the first time either Ron or I had seen Bell close up. He was overweight and soft and reminded me of the Pillsbury Doughboy in the television commercials.

Metts said he was going to play some of the tapes of the telephone calls again, to which Bell responded, "I've heard all of them."

Undeterred, Metts said, "Oh, you have? Well, let's just start with this one."

All Bell could muster was, "I'm so nervous and scared. I'm not a criminal!"

"Why are you so nervous?" Metts asked. "What's done is done. You can't do anything about that. Talk to me, Gene."

Metts proceeded to roll one of the tapes. After a few seconds he stopped it, looked squarely at Bell, and underscored what Davis and Perry had already said to him. "That's you, Gene. I've already told you that we've got the evidence."

As the sheriff played another tape, Bell shook his head and said, "Naw, I can't believe that. That upsets me too much."

"Does it upset you, Gene?" Metts came back. "You know it's you on these tapes. You know your voice, right? You would have to agree with me that sounds like Gene on these tapes, doesn't it?"

Bell replied that it did sound somewhat like him, but that he hadn't heard his voice recorded enough to really know. He also suggested that whoever was calling could have been disguising his voice, which we thought was an interesting observation. "Yeah, put it like that," he declared with what sounded like a forced laugh. "Yes, sir."

Most of the interrogation had focused on Shari Smith, but Metts thought he might be able to get to Bell by bringing up the other equally heinous crime, the one he'd committed after telling Dawn he was either going to turn himself in or kill himself. Metts said he could understand how anyone could be turned on by a beautiful young woman like Shari Smith, but that didn't explain Debra May Helmick. "One thing I'm totally baffled by," Metts said. "Why the nine-year-old girl? The defenseless, helpless nine-year-old girl? Help me on that. Ease my mind. You've got to feel guilty about that one, Gene. You've got to feel guilty."

With his voice quivering, Bell responded, "When I think about it, a nine-year-old girl. I heard it on the news. When you tell me that, I can't believe I did that. It's like God strike me dead for doing something like that to either the nine-year-old girl or the other girl. But I can't see me doing that. I can't relate to that, not really either one of them."

Then, for the first time, Myers motioned to Ron and me, sitting silently on the sofa observing. He said to Bell, in his Carolina accent, "Do you know who these boys are? These boys are from the F-B-I," accentuating each letter for dramatic effect. "You know, they did a profile and it fit you right down to a tee! Now, these boys want to talk to you for a little bit." Metts directed him to a white sofa against the wall and told him to sit. Then he and Myers both left the room, leaving us alone with Bell.

Not knowing we would get this opportunity, I hadn't prepared anything or discussed it with Ron. But I was not going to let it pass without trying to get something out of Bell. I sat on the edge of the coffee table directly in front of him. Ron stood near him, looking stern. I was still wearing the white shirt and practically matching white slacks I'd put on at the motel early in the morning. Had I known we'd get this chance, I might have opted for a different getup. In addition to looking like an ice cream vendor, I thought it was the kind of outfit superstar singer Harry Belafonte might have worn. But in this context, especially in the room with white walls and the white sofa, I think I looked kind of clinical, and the entire scene was sort of otherworldly.

I started out by methodically detailing some of the background on our serial killer study. In the process, I tried to make it clear that we understood perfectly the motivation of the individual responsible for these homicides; that it wouldn't be possible for him to put anything over on us. He looked fairly intimidated to begin with, so I tried to up the ass-pucker factor even further, telling him that in my and Special Agent Walker's analysis, we believed he may have been denying the crimes in his interview with investigators because he was trying to repress thoughts that he didn't feel good about.

"Going into the penitentiaries and interviewing all of these subjects," I elaborated, "one of the things we've found is that the truth almost never gets out about the background of the person. And generally, when a crime like this happens, it's like a nightmare to the person who commits it. They're going through so many precipitating stressors in their life—financial problems, marital problems, problems on the job, or problems with family or a girlfriend. There are compulsions in your body and mind that you may not be aware of. People can have blackouts and dark sides to their personalities."

As I was saying this, Bell nodded as if he recognized and had all or most of these problems.

I continued, "The problem for us, Larry, is that when you go to court, your attorney probably isn't going to want you to take the stand, and you'll never have the opportunity to explain yourself. All they'll know about you is the bad side of you, nothing good about you; just that you're a cold-blooded killer. And as I say, we've found that very often when people do this kind of thing, it is like a nightmare to them, and when they 'wake up' the next morning, they can't believe they've actually committed this crime."

Bell continued nodding his head subtly in apparent agreement.

I didn't ask him outright at that point if he had committed the abductions and murders, because if I phrased it that way, we were certain to get a denial. He had already built up that emotional armor in the interrogation this morning and afternoon, so if we were going to get into his head, it had to be via the "side door." Instead of confronting him directly, I leaned in close to him and in a slow, quiet voice, I said, "When did you first start feeling bad about the crime, Larry?" Without trying to give away any physical cues, Ron and I both remained silent and held our breaths.

After a couple of silent beats, Bell replied, "When I saw a photograph and read a newspaper article about the family praying in the cemetery on Shari's birthday."

Bingo. He had to be referring to the moving story that had appeared in the *Columbia Record* about the ceremony we staged with the hope that the UNSUB would visit Shari's gravesite and maybe even try to take the tiny koala bear with him. I still think that would have happened if the ESDA analysis of the Last Will & Testament hadn't led to him when it did. As much as you want to catch an UNSUB as soon as possible, before he can do any more human damage, you have to be willing to play the long game. In this case, that meant going through with the cemetery ceremony, as painful as it was for Dawn and the rest of the family, with the hope that it would pay dividends somewhere down the line. As far as I was concerned, those dividends just came rolling in.

I said, "How do you feel about it now? Larry, as you're sitting here now, did you do this thing? Could you have done it?" We had learned from our serial predator research that it was always best to stay away from accusatory or inflammatory words like *kill* or *murder.*

He stared down at the floor and when he looked up he had tears in his eyes. "All I know," he said hesitatingly, "is that the Larry Gene Bell sitting here couldn't have done such a thing. But there's a bad Larry Gene Bell that could have."

I knew this was as close as we would ever get to a confession. But there was one more act to play that evening. When Metts had gone to fetch Bell from the trailer, before he handed him off to Ron and me, Bell asked if he could speak with the Smith family. Seizing on this request, Donnie Myers thought if Bell was confronted face-to-face with Shari's parents and siblings, we might get a more spontaneous reaction from him. Perhaps he would be overcome and beg for forgiveness, which would be another form of admission. I knew this would be tough on the family, especially Dawn, whom we'd already subjected to more than an individual should have to bear, but I agreed with Myers that this might be productive.

When Metts called the Smiths with this request and explained the strategy behind it, Hilda and Dawn apprehensively agreed. Bob and Robert weren't home at the time and Metts wanted to seize the moment. He sent a deputy and patrol car to pick up mother and daughter and bring them to the office. In retrospect, it was probably more effective to include only the women since Bell was intimidated by men and had established a telephone relationship with Shari's mother and sister.

"I remember Mom and me riding in complete silence," Dawn recalled. "There was nothing to be said. I think we were so exhausted, we were spent every way you can imagine. And I don't know that we could even allow ourselves to believe it was actually going to be over, because it felt like it would never end, that he would never be caught."

It was close to seven P.M. when they arrived at the sheriff's department. The timing worked out well; Ron and I had gotten everything we thought we could out of Bell.

Before the officers brought him back into Metts's office, Ron, Myers, and I prepared the two women for what to expect and how to act and react. I related the comment that while the good Larry Gene Bell could never have done these horrible things, the bad Larry Gene Bell could have. We said we wanted to see if coming face-to-face with Shari's mother and sister would move him beyond what he had said to us. I told them that whoever got the chance should tell Bell straight out that she recognized his voice.

We got them seated and somewhat settled before Bell was brought in. It was apparent that both women were tense and nervous. I was hoping they could just get through this latest exercise, which must have been one of the most painful experiences of their lives.

When the deputies brought in the handcuffed Bell, they placed him in a chair only a few feet from Hilda and Dawn. The officers stood nearby and watched him carefully in case he made any sudden moves.

Sheriff Metts asked him to say something so the Smiths could hear his voice. Bell said a few words and then, it was as if he had taken over. Despite his position, he started speaking as if he were in charge or holding court, just as he had on the phone calls. "Thank y'all for coming," he began with forced humility. "Sheriff Metts said that the evidence is here, but this person sitting here, this Larry Gene Bell, I could not have done this ungodly thing. Right now, I don't know how to explain it. I know it's touched a lot of people and destroyed a lot of lives. When I click on that reason, I'll let your family know."

Even though he was, at the moment, terrified for himself, he was still carrying on as if he was objectively analyzing what had happened and was taking Hilda and Dawn into his confidence. As he began to talk, Dawn told me afterward, she knew this was the guy, and it was the most fearful realization. She said it suddenly hit her that she was sitting in the room with this man who did so much to her family.

She confronted him, just as we'd asked her to. "I recognize your voice!" she asserted. "I know that it's you. I talked on the phone with you. Do you recognize my voice?"

"I recognize your face from TV and the picture in the paper," Bell replied. Then he went on to elaborate, "It's just the bad side of me that caused all this horrible destruction in people's lives: your sister and that little girl. It's just something in me."

But Dawn wasn't letting him off the hook. "You honestly can't think back and remember my voice, because you know we talked? Do you remember what you called me on the phone?"

"I guess just Dawn," he said innocently.

"How about the middle initial?" she asked, recalling when he referred to her as "Dawn E."

"No. I requested that your family be here. I'm trying to put you to some kind of rest with why. They have the evidence against me. I feel terrible about this if this was directly the result of something bad in me. If God chooses that I end up going to court and being put to death, that's just something I have to do."

This was a pretty sick individual sitting before us here, but also a rational one. I could see that he was already composing his multiple personality defense and looking for sympathy, as if he had no control over this bad side of himself, if, in fact, that was who had abducted and killed these girls—something he claimed not to actually know.

"Well, why would you have wanted to hurt me?" Dawn challenged. She had taken the lead, sparing her mother much of the confrontation.

Bell continued with his poor, innocent, confused guise. "I don't want to hurt you. I don't even know you." Recall that in the phone calls, he had asserted that he was a personal friend of the Smith family. "The person sitting here, Dawn, is not a violent person. I wish I could answer your questions now. If I come up with the answers, and I know I can do that, I'll tell you everything I remember about it. If I was sure this person here was capable of controlling what happened to your sister, I would confess in a minute. I feel guilty about something. When I picked up the paper a couple of days ago, I felt like I was directly or indirectly responsible for something like that and, Dawn, that's when I felt that somehow, I was drawn close to your family . . . as being a part of your family . . . if I was responsible for taking away part of your family. It just horrifies me that I can do something like that, Dawn. I hope you believe me. I have soul searched all day, and I'm glad that you came."

I wasn't surprised that he was repeating many of the ideas we had talked about during the interview. What did surprise me was that in spite of everything and in front of everyone, it was as if he was making a play for Dawn. This guy was a total narcissist, which became ever more apparent as the dialogue continued.

"You said in one conversation that you and my sister had become one," Dawn said. "Do you think that might have anything to do with that feeling of being a part of our family?" What was apparent to me at that moment was that Dawn herself had become a profiler of sorts, analyzing what the offender said and laying it out for him, probing, looking for any clue to what could have led him to destroy her family, yet giving him a sense that she actually cared about his feelings.

You can coach people, put them through years of education and training, and not get them to the level of proficiency in dealing with someone like Bell that this previously sheltered young college student was demonstrating. It was as if Dawn had an innate understanding of how to read the master manipulator before her and pivot the content and tone of her statements in a way that neither yielded her position nor pushed him too far so that he'd shut down. Suffering as I knew she was, the level of composure she was maintaining while sitting across from the man who had violently taken, tortured, and murdered her sister was truly impressive and more than anyone could have hoped for.

He didn't answer right away, as if he either didn't know what to say or was contemplating some deep and profound response. Finally, he said, "I can't answer that now, Dawn. The main reason I want your family here is maybe we can hit on something that would help me explain. I didn't want to talk to you on the phone 'cause I had to sit there for hours today and listen to them darn horrible phone calls. It wasn't helping me. It was hurting me."

"But you had listened to them today, and you hear that is you and your voice."

"I would say that ninety percent of it sounded muffled. But Dawn, the other part of it would have to be . . . unless it's a mighty darn good imitation."

"Talking to me now, can you tell that was me talking on those tapes?" Dawn countered.

"Your voice sounds different now than on the tape, but, Dawn, whatever caused this, I truly hope this won't destroy y'all's lives." He must have picked this up right from Shari's Last Will & Testament. "This is gonna destroy my family, too, but hopefully they'll be strong enough to go on with their lives. There's bad in me, but I can't say the devil put it there, 'cause I say my prayers every night and every morning." In other words, whatever happened wasn't his fault because he communicated regularly with God. Did he have the audacity to actually be blaming God for his actions? The contrast between Bell's self-serving statements concerning the almighty and the pure faith embodied by the women sitting across from him could not have been starker.

"Well," Dawn went on, "you have recognized that could be your voice?"

"Oh, yeah. Like I said, ninety percent of it was muffled, but the rest was." He turned to Hilda. "Like I told your daughter, Mrs. Smith, if I'm directly responsible for this crime, I do apologize if I've brought tragedy into your lives and tragedy to myself. Your daughter can explain everything else that I've said. I don't know what to say to you. I just can't believe I've done those horrible things."

"Did you know our daughter?" Hilda asked. I was interested to see how Bell would respond. The UNSUB had claimed to be a friend of the family, and he was talking to the two women as if he were on highly familiar terms with them, making it seem as if they shared a tragedy that someone else or some other force had visited on them all.

"No, and I don't know your family," he replied. "Maybe on down the road I'll have that breaking point that I can come up with the answers for you."

"Nothing you can say or do can bring Shari back," Hilda said.

"No, and if I could honestly say today that I did this, I would tell you right now."

"I know definitely that it is you on the tapes, no question in my mind. I talked to you, and you talked to me, and there definitely couldn't be a mistake there. We just want to know the truth, nothing else."

"When I can come up with the truth, I'll tell y'all all of that."

Suddenly, I had a mental flash, and I didn't know if it was something that had occurred to Metts, McCarty, or Walker. What if Dawn or Hilda was armed? I didn't know them well enough to know if that was a possibility. Were they checked out when they were picked up at their house or when they arrived at the sheriff's department? I didn't remember anyone saying anything about doing this. From that moment on, I was literally sitting on the edge of my chair, practically bouncing on the balls of my feet, ready to grab a gun and disarm either of them if one started reaching into her purse. I knew what I'd want to do in a situation like this if it was my child who'd been murdered, and I knew from experience that a lot of other parents felt the same way. If they wanted to, this would have been the perfect opportunity to take this guy out, and no jury in the world would have convicted them.

Fortunately, neither Dawn nor Hilda had tried to smuggle a weapon into the sheriff's office. They had more restraint and faith in the system than I might have had. But Ron did check afterward, and they hadn't been searched.

Hilda looked straight at Bell and what she said next, whether I had the urge to kill him or not, I knew I never would have been able to bring myself to say if I was in her place. "Even though I sit this close and look at you and know you're the man that called my house, I don't hate you. There is not enough room in my heart for more pain." She later wrote that it was only by the grace of God that she was able to tell him that.

Dawn recalled her own state of mind. "I was done playing roles and I had no more kindness at that moment. And yet here's my mom showing all this amazing grace and kindness to this man, which later became such an incredible example to me, how to come to closure."

Dawn spoke up again, and it was clear she was on message, as we had primed her. "You said you didn't know me. Maybe I look so much like Shari looked, maybe you can possibly remember something from that."

"If I put that picture of her up beside you, y'all don't look alike." Then he added, "In my personal opinion."

This had gone on long enough. Metts stood and indicated to Hilda and Dawn that they could leave. As the sheriff was escorting them out of the office, Bell, continuing his manipulation, said, "If I remember down the line, can we conference again, and tell you what I know?"

Metts kept them moving so they didn't have to answer as Bell called after them, "Thank you very much. God bless us all."

CHAPTER 16

Late in the day, a weary-looking Sheriff Metts held another news conference with the other two sheriffs, addressing more than thirty reporters and about a hundred citizens who had gathered and waited patiently in the department's small public lobby. This time Metts announced the arrest of the subject and gave his name.

"We do not anticipate any additional arrests," he said. "As far as I'm concerned, the matter with Shari Faye Smith is now ended." He said he hoped the arrest "will put the minds of our community at rest."

It had been twenty-eight days—four weeks exactly—since Shari's abduction, and fourteen days since Debra May's.

Teresa K. Weaver reported the story in the *Columbia Record*, quoting seventeen-year-old Robin Hutta, a friend of Shari's at Lexington High, as saying she felt "a lot better" and "more safe" after the arrest. "I've been staying in the house and not doing anything alone—I haven't been myself since this started."

The article concluded, "Miss Hutta said she thinks the abductions have permanently changed her lifestyle.

"'I don't know when I'll feel comfortable out there again.'"

In another story, Weaver reported, "Sources also said the suspect had already pinpointed his next victim, a young blond woman who works at Columbia Metropolitan Airport."

"It's scary to think he was out here checking things out," one woman who worked at the airport was quoted as saying. Her desk was in a spot prominently visible from the main airport entrance.

Another employee, according to Weaver, "said she saw a man at the terminal sometime Wednesday that she thought resembled a composite drawing of the 'serial killer' suspect. When she saw the suspect's photograph in news reports after the arrest, she said she became even more convinced it was the man she had seen."

This story emerged from an apparent call by the same UNSUB to a telephone tip line the previous weekend, stating when and where he would strike again—another two-week interval after the Smith and Helmick kidnappings. Whether this was actually Larry Gene Bell, we weren't sure. But as a result, the sheriff's departments and SLED agents were desperate to find the guy before Friday, June 28.

Bell finally met with an attorney close to midnight. Jack B. Swerling, a New Jersey–born, thirty-eight-year-old, six-foot-five, three-hundred-pound mountain of a man known as one of the best criminal defense counsels in the area, had been retained by Bell's family. Even the prosecutors who went up against him had a tremendous amount of respect for him. Swerling announced that his new client "denies any knowledge of the cases and charges, and says he is innocent."

As we sat in Sheriff Metts's office reflecting on the day's events, we agreed that it was all of the investigative elements coming together that had led to the solution—the optimum way for any major investigation to be handled. Those responsible for the investigative, forensic, and behavioral elements had all worked together and supported each other's pieces of the overall mission. In the grim ledger of murder investigation, that made this case both a tragedy and a triumph. In hunting down the killer of these two beautiful and innocent souls cruelly taken from this life and their adoring family and friends, we had stopped a serial killer before he could extend his violent criminal career.

If we hadn't gotten the brilliant work from the specialists at SLED analyzing Shari's Last Will & Testament using the ESDA device, followed up by meticulous investigative work and supported by a detailed psychological, behavioral profile, we still think the event we staged on Shari's birthday with Dawn and the family might well have brought Larry Gene Bell out. Fortunately, though, we never had to test that theory.

As it was, without the science and technology, we would not have had the lead on the phone number that was traced to Huntsville, Alabama. Without the follow-up detective work of Lew McCarty and his team, we would not have had the lead to Ellis and Sharon Sheppard. Without the profile, the Sheppards would not have led the investigation to Larry Gene Bell. And without a well-staged interrogation setting and Sheriff Metts's investigators spending an entire day wearing Bell down with the compelling evidence against him, I would not have been able to apply my extensive experience interviewing incarcerated violent predators to employ the psychological approach most likely to get him as close as we did to an admission of the crimes.

So, we all concluded, Shari's final letter, written in her own hand, under the most horrible and terrifying of circumstances, led to the solution to her own murder and that of an innocent and precious little girl she had never even met. And we all agreed that that was an emotionally and spiritually fulfilling way to close the case.

THE DAY AFTER BELL'S ARREST, DAWN WENT BACK TO HER APARTMENT IN CHAR-lotte. The following day, Bell was moved from the Lexington County Jail to the Central Correctional Institution (CCI) in Columbia. Ironically, the Lexington County Jail was one of the institutions where Bob Smith conducted his prison ministry, and officials were concerned that some of the inmates who knew and admired Smith would take their revenge on Bell. Lexington Sheriff's Department captain Bob Ford said, "His being in our jail could possibly pose a great security risk."

In CCI he was placed in a cell on death row, not because he had been convicted of a capital crime, but again because prison authorities determined it was the area where they could keep him safest from the contempt and wrath of other inmates.

At the SLED laboratory, technicians went over the evidence collected from the Bell and Sheppard residences and the two vehicles used by Bell. Chemist Bob Carpenter employed a laser light to examine and analyze the blue mattress pad from the guest bedroom in the Sheppard house. Under the laser, reddish fibers stood out. When viewed under a microscope using polarized light, the red fibers matched fibers found in the shorts Shari was wearing when abducted. Chemist Earl Wells microscopically compared head and pubic hair exemplars from Shari with hairs found in the Sheppard guest bedroom and bathroom. They were consistent, and some showed indication of being forcibly removed. This could be from brushing, contact with duct tape, or other causes.

Serologist Ira Jeffcoat analyzed a small, dried sample of Shari's menstrual blood, taken from the crotch of a pair of her pantyhose still in the clothes hamper, and compared it to two apparent blood spots found on a pair of shoes from Bell's bedroom. One of them tested positive as human blood and was the same Type A as Shari's blood. Three of the stains on the blue mattress pad were identified as semen and urine.

Investigators interviewed several individuals who testified to Bell's post-offense behavior and, like the Sheppards, they confirmed what we had predicted in the profile regarding change of physical appearance and obsession with the crimes. Sammy Collins was a neighbor of Bell's parents a few lots down on Lake Murray. He told detectives that on the morning of June 1, the day after Shari disappeared, Bell had told him he was staying at a friend's house while he and his wife were on vacation. "Then he started spouting off, 'A good friend of mine's daughter was kidnapped yesterday afternoon. Have you heard about it—the Smith kidnapping? She was a real pretty girl. I called the Smiths' house last night, and guess who answered the phone? Sheriff Metts.'

"I told him I hadn't heard anything about it. He walked over closer to us and handed us a bag of peaches, and came out with the statement, 'She's dead now.' That's when I noticed he was clean-shaven. I had never seen him without a beard until that morning."

IN THE DAYS FOLLOWING BELL'S ARREST, THE INEVITABLE STORIES STARTED COMing out about what a nice, quiet guy he seemed to be, how helpful he was to neighbors, and how no one who knew him suspected he was capable of such terrible things. I have heard these kinds of reactions so often in my career that I can write the script myself. The point is, serial killers and violent predators, whatever is going on inside, do not look or act like monsters in everyday life. If they did, it would be much easier to identify and catch them. Their advantage is that we tend to look right through them.

A former colleague of Bell's at the Eastern Airlines reservation desk told reporter John Monk of the *Charlotte Observer*:

> *"He was always smiling and laughing. He was the most likable guy you ever knew. Then to see his picture on TV and hear them say he did these horrible crimes, it's like somebody kicked you right in the stomach. It just shocked me. I can't believe it's the same person. It's like he was a Dr. Jekyll and Mr. Hyde."*

One neighbor of Mr. and Mrs. Bell on Old Orchard Road said that when she and her son and daughter moved into the area about a year before, Bell was the first person to welcome them and offer to lend a hand with whatever they needed.

A story by Jef Feeley in the *Columbia Record* read:

> *"Neighbors described Bell as a helpful man who never gave them any cause for concern or suspicion.*
>
> *"And one Shull Island resident said he and Bell fished together often.*
>
> *"'I would go fishing with him at night a lot. And I still trust him,' said the man, who did not want to be named.*

'I would still go fishing with him right now on the dock. He was a good guy.'"

Someone who had carpooled to Eau Claire High School with Bell and one of his sisters described him as "a quiet guy who never really had much of anything to say." No one else from the high school had much in the way of memories of him other than he didn't get into fights, he wasn't very outgoing, he didn't "stick out," he didn't get very good grades, and he was "a very nice, quiet, reserved person."

The son of the woman Bell had welcomed into the neighborhood told reporters for the *State*, "This was quite a surprise. I just think they don't have the right guy. It just doesn't seem like it's possible that he could do something like this."

Bell's sister told reporters, "If he says he's innocent, if he says he didn't do it—well, he never gave us a reason to think he'd lie. He was always coming around to ask if there was any way he could help us. I'd trust him with my life."

Though the three county sheriff's departments had worked together and were still trying to sort out jurisdictional issues so that a full array of charges could properly be mounted against Bell, Richland County sheriff Frank Powell issued a statement: "The Helmick case must stand on its own and separated from the Shari Smith kidnapping-murder investigation." He said he expected the investigation of the Helmick case to be completed within two weeks. "We're going from ground zero to building our case," Powell said.

The jurisdictional questions were ones that plague many murder investigations and prosecutions. When a victim is known to be abducted in one state, county, or municipality and then the body is found in another, a determination has to be made as to where the killing actually took place so that the most serious charges can be filed in that jurisdiction.

Within a couple of days of the arrest, the other, less benign, side of Bell began to emerge. In addition to what we already knew about his two arrests for assaulting women, and the obscene phone calls to the preteen girl, the details of the psychiatric report from the state-run William S. Hall Psychiatric Institute in Columbia, of which we only had a snippet the day of the arrest, were fleshed out. It stated in part:

> *"Patient has a lifelong pattern of sexual deviation manifested by aggressive attacks on females. It is felt that the chance of repeating these attacks is very high. Our recommendations are that the patient be placed in a controlled setting for a long period of time, preferably one where psychiatric help is available."*

Bell had at least enough self-awareness to tell a staff member at the facility, "I feel uncontrollable urges to attack females and want help before I really hurt someone."

This, certainly, is a highly significant statement, and a large part of the preparation for his trial was how comments like this would be unpacked. The defense would want to claim that this proved he was operating under the influence of a mental illness so severe that he was compelled to assault women and, being aware that his problem could lead to real harm to innocent people, desperately wanted help to be cured.

The defense would interpret it as a means to explain away Bell's previous charges by claiming that though he had committed these crimes, he really didn't want to. It was akin to the phenomenon we've noticed many times in our work when a diagnosis of multiple personality disorder (MPD) pops up postarrest as a way to mitigate a murder charge. This is not to say that MPD doesn't exist as a known psychiatric condition, it is just that it is virtually always first identified when the subject is a young child, and almost always a result of physical and/or sexual abuse within that child's home environment. When I see it emerge as a diagnosis for the first time in a man who has just been arrested or put on trial for murder, I am always suspicious.

The question in Bell's case would hinge on the meaning of his use of the word "uncontrollable," and what exactly it signifies. There was never any question in my mind that Larry Gene Bell had a mental illness, as I would say just about every violent predator does. But in all of my years of behavioral analysis and criminal investigation, I have almost never seen someone whose urges to harm others were actually uncontrollable.

A rare exception and example of someone who really was compelled would be Richard Trenton Chase, a diagnosed paranoid schizophrenic with severe hypochondria, who murdered six victims in the space of a month in the Sacramento, California, area in 1977. In addition to having sex with some of the corpses, Chase drank their blood, which was his motivation for the murders. He thought he needed it to stay alive and keep his heart beating. Like many serial killers, he had escalated from less serious crimes, but in Chase's case that amounted to killing rabbits for their blood. When he was institutionalized, he caught several birds, killed them by breaking their necks, and drank their blood. He also stole syringes to extract blood from therapy dogs, when that was the only source available. Not that

I've tried it, but I can say from extensive research on aberrant personalities that it is extremely difficult to drink undiluted blood without throwing up; you really have to be compelled by something to even make the attempt. When Bob Ressler interviewed him in prison, Chase spoke of his mortal fear of Nazis and UFOs, and while admitting that he had killed, insisted that anyone would do the same thing if that's what he needed to stay alive. The year after he was incarcerated, Chase died by suicide the day after Christmas by swallowing several weeks' worth of the antidepressants he had been saving up for this purpose. He was thirty years old.

In my mind, this is clearly not the kind of compulsion that Larry Gene Bell was under. Unlike someone like Chase, Bell didn't do anything desperate. Both the Smith and Helmick abductions and murders, though high risk for the perpetrator, were well planned and efficiently carried out. He did what he wanted with both victims and seemed to get just as much satisfaction out of the manipulation, domination, and control he exercised through his voice-disguised calls to the Smith family and reporter Charlie Keyes, and the cat-and-mouse fear he instilled in the Midlands community. Though he talked repeatedly about either killing himself or turning himself in, it was clear he would do neither, but would continue abducting and murdering young women and girls as long as he remained free.

So, I would argue that rather than Bell being under an uncontrollable compulsion, he abducted, assaulted, and murdered his victims because it was the one element in his otherwise ordinary, uneventful, and largely unsuccessful life that gave him satisfaction, a sense of accomplishment, and sexual fulfillment.

He made the choice.

PART 3

IN PURSUIT OF JUSTICE

CHAPTER 17

Ron and I flew back home to Virginia. There were plenty of other cases awaiting our attention in Quantico. Unlike local detectives, we weren't often able to stay with a case from beginning to end; there were just too many to deal with. So we tried to keep abreast of developments and come back in if and when we could be of most use to local police or prosecutors.

As the prosecutors in the various counties began preparing their cases against Bell, investigators across the region did what all good law enforcement agencies do: They looked for possible linkages to other unsolved cases.

Police in Charlotte, North Carolina, considered Bell to be a suspect in the disappearance of twenty-six-year-old Sandee Elaine Cornett, an insurance adjuster and part-time model who had been missing for more than seven months. She had been last seen on November 18, 1984, wearing a blue jogging suit, and may have been abducted while running near her home. When police examined the house after her fiancé couldn't get in touch with her, they found the television on and the contents of her purse dumped out on her bed, including her checkbook, but nothing except for the clothes she was wearing and what she was known to be carrying with her, like her ATM card, was missing. This also brought up the possibility that she was abducted at home. She could have returned from running or, neighbors said, she often wore that kind of outfit around the house.

In considering victimology, the fact that she was very attractive was one consideration for the Charlotte police. Even more tantalizing was that detectives established Sandee had met Bell at a party at her home a few years before through a boyfriend who had worked with him at Eastern Airlines. Police established that at the time of her disappearance, Bell lived about four miles away from her in the Mint Hill neighborhood and, according to Division of Motor Vehicles records, moved away just weeks after she vanished.

"We're looking at that guy," Charlotte police captain Wade Stroud said. "We don't know at this point if there is a connection, but we're trying to establish his whereabouts when [Sandee Cornett] disappeared. We know that he was an acquaintance; how close, we don't know. We know he had been to her house and was a friend of some of her friends. But we don't have anything to link him with her at the time she disappeared. This is something we are trying to establish." Investigators were looking into the hairs found in Bell's bedroom to see if any matched up with Sandee's.

In the days immediately following her disappearance, her bank card was used three times by a man and woman who tried to withdraw $1,000. This didn't sound to us like part of Bell's

M.O. Criminal enterprise, or crimes committed for money or profit, did not seem to be part of his motivation.

In September 1985, acting on a tip, officers of the North Carolina State Bureau of Investigation and Charlotte PD went down to the sandpit owned by Bell's sister Diane and brother-in-law John Loveless, where Bell had occasionally worked. Joined by SLED and Lexington County agents, they dug around the area, looking for the bodies of Sandee Cornett and two other missing women. They came up empty.

Twenty-one-year-old Denise Newsome Porch, the manager of the Yorktown Apartments complex in Charlotte, had disappeared on July 31, 1975, and no trace of her had turned up since then. At the time she went missing, Bell lived about three hundred yards away. Like Bell's known victims, Denise was a pretty blonde. She had been married for a year when she disappeared.

Five and a half years later, on December 18, 1980, another pretty girl, seventeen-year-old Beth Marie Hagen, was found strangled with an electrical cord in the woods near Mint Hill, the same area where Bell was living when Sandee Cornett went missing. His apartment was about a mile from where Beth's body was found in Mecklenburg County. One Mecklenburg County police officer later noted that Beth looked a lot like Shari Smith.

Porch, Hagan, and Cornett all fit the profile of Bell's known victim of preference: attractive and outgoing young women with long hair. Bell lived close to Porch, often stayed in a house close to Cornett's, and had lived close to where Hagen's body was found. All three were presumed to have been abducted at gun- or knifepoint during daylight, as Shari Smith had been.

Bell himself wasn't at all reticent talking about these

cases—at least not initially. While being transported from CCI to the Richland County Courthouse for a hearing regarding charges filed against him for kidnapping Debra May Helmick, he said to Lieutenant Michael Temple, "I want you to make arrangements for officers from Charlotte, North Carolina, to come see me. I want to tell them some things about a missing girl named Sandee."

Temple advised him that he was potentially making statements against his own interest, but when Bell went on anyway, he decided to let him continue talking without either encouraging or discouraging him. Bell continued, "On Monday, God is going to reveal to me where Sandee Cornett's body is." He said that when authorities found the body, her hands would be folded in a praying position, as he had gone on about Shari Smith. He also mentioned two other women who had disappeared in the Charlotte area but didn't give any names.

Temple informed Richland County's district attorney, Fifth Judicial Circuit solicitor James C. Anders, who in turn contacted Bell's attorney, Jack Swerling. "After learning of this, I immediately advised his attorney that he might want to confer with his client," Anders said. He then sent the case to the Charlotte-Mecklenburg Police Department to investigate.

Swerling stated publicly that Bell "completely denies any knowledge of the Cornett case." Neither, he added, did Bell know anything about the other Charlotte cases. He no doubt could already see how difficult it was going to be to work with a client who was too egotistical and narcissistic to shut up, whether he had anything useful to say or not.

In preparation for the court case or cases against Bell, Ron and I had already concluded through psycholinguistic analysis that the calls describing the body dump sites for both Shari and Debra May were from the same caller. On a more scientific level, FBI technical analysts established that the voiceprints on the tapes all matched one another and Larry Gene Bell, though as Columbia FBI Special Agent Donald Haydon pointed out, they were not admissible in court like fingerprints and were mainly used to help police identify a suspect. Several other people, including some who had worked with Bell at Eastern Airlines, also identified his voice on the tapes.

There was still a mystery surrounding the car Bell had been driving when he kidnapped Shari, and there was a presumption that the DCE 604 license plate found in the trunk of his car—which had been on the vehicle he used when he grabbed Debra May—was also on the car in which Shari was carried away. A woman driving near the Smith home on Platt Springs Road who thought she had seen the suspect lean over to talk to a blond woman in the passenger seat shortly after the time of the abduction had described a cranberry-colored, late-model American car. On Wednesday, July 4, Sheriff Metts's officers and SLED agents impounded a cranberry-colored 1984 Buick Regal from a car dealership in nearby Camden. The previous December, the car had been rented to someone with a Kershaw County address and had been reported stolen in April. It was later found abandoned in the parking lot of a Sheraton hotel two days before Bell was arrested. If this was the vehicle Bell had used in the Smith abduction, it showed his criminal sophistication in changing cars for the next crime and spoke against him having acted under an uncontrollable impulse caused by mental illness. The Richland County Sheriff's Department also put out an alert for the silver-gray 1980 Pontiac Grand Prix they

believed was used in the Helmick case. Tire tracks found near
the Helmick trailer home were consistent with certain General
Motors models of Pontiacs and Buicks.

"Anyone having any knowledge of Bell having this kind
of car in his possession on June 14, or anyone who may have
loaned Bell such a car, is asked to give us a call," said Sheriff
Powell. "If we find out later on that someone loaned Bell that
car and didn't tell us, it may be necessary to possibly bring
charges [for] obstruction of justice."

Solicitor Donnie Myers announced that he was waiting for
further tests to be completed but hoped and intended to try
both the Smith and Helmick cases himself, regardless of final
results that might determine where Shari had actually died.
"As far as I'm concerned, there's no difference because I'm solicitor for both Lexington and Saluda Counties," he said.

On July 2, Richland County authorities formally charged
Bell with Debra May Helmick's kidnapping. Part of the evidence supporting the charge came from the eyewitness testimony of Ricky Morgan, the neighbor who had seen the bearded
stranger approach and grab Debra May, observed the car with
the license plate beginning with a D, and ran to get her father,
Sherwood. It was Morgan who had worked with the sheriff's
department sketch artist on the composite of the suspect.

ON THE AFTERNOON OF SUNDAY, JULY 14, CHARLOTTE INVESTIGATOR LAWRENCE
Walker went to CCI to interview Bell. "I will dedicate one hundred and ten percent cooperation," Bell assured him.

For the next eleven or so hours, that is exactly what Bell
tried to persuade Walker he was doing. Walker could hardly
get a word in edgewise. Switching between first and third per-

son, Bell told Walker about his visions from God. Walker noted that he seemed to greatly enjoy having an audience. Without admitting that he had killed her, he described how he made sure Shari had water to drink and again mentioned the crossed hands of both Shari and Debra May. He said that after Shari died, he cleaned up everything, placed it in a green dumpster, and then went back to the Sheppards' house for a long, cold shower. He talked for quite awhile about the Cornett murder and the other two unsolved cases in North Carolina, and how God had sent him a vision of how the crimes might have happened. But for all the verbiage and performance, Bell never offered a confession or gave Walker anything solid to act on. I wasn't sure at that point what to believe, but I've often said that false confessions are easy, while true confessions are difficult.

Shortly after this, the Charlotte and Mecklenburg PDs also started investigating Bell for two additional cold cases: the kidnapping and murders of ten-year-old Amanda Ray and five-year-old Neely Smith. Amanda disappeared from her home on July 18, 1979. Her body was discovered the next day in the northern part of Mecklenburg County. Neely disappeared February 18, 1981. Her skeletal remains were found April 12 of that year. Both girls were abducted during daylight hours, just like Shari and Debra May. Perhaps we hadn't caught Bell as early in his murderous career as we had hoped. But after talking to him in prison, Mecklenburg police concluded he didn't know anything that was not public knowledge.

"We talked to him, and he didn't tell us anything that was in any way connected to our cases," said Assistant Chief R. B. Dixon. "Our investigation has led us to stop looking at him as a prime suspect." He added, though, that due to the similarities between Amanda and Neely's abductions and Debra May's, "He had lived in Charlotte when our two girls vanished. It all fit. We had to check him out," and, "As far as we're concerned, his name will go in the inactive files in the cases. We've checked out hundreds of suspects. His name will be added to theirs." Bell still remained a suspect in the Cornett disappearance.

Prosecutors Anders and Myers and the sheriffs of Lexington, Saluda, and Richland Counties worked together for several weeks trying to sort out the jurisdictional issues in charging Bell with murder. The kidnapping charges were no problem, since it was clear where each girl was abducted. But under South Carolina law, if it is not clear from the investigation and physical evidence where a murder actually took place, it is presumed to have occurred in the jurisdiction where the body was found, and that is where the charges are brought. There was tension between Myers and Anders for a while that spilled out into the media, as Anders was ready to try Bell in his jurisdiction for kidnapping but not murder, while Myers felt that trying him only for kidnapping would threaten any murder charges.

"If Solicitor Anders is in such a hurry to go ahead and try Bell on the kidnapping charge—which charge might jeopardize a later trial on a murder charge—he should go ahead and try him for the murder in Richland County," Myers stated.

Newspaper articles also suggested that part of the conflict might have been that Anders was a Democrat and Myers was a Republican, and several editorials called for the state attorney general to get involved and settle the dispute, possibly by convening a state grand jury. Eventually, toward the end of July, the hairs found in Bell's bedroom—the guest bedroom in the Sheppard home—that lab analysis confirmed were consis-

tent with Shari's convinced all parties that she had been killed
in Saluda County. This ended the legal maneuvering, and the
jurisdictional dispute was settled so that the kidnapping and
murder charges were combined so the Smith case would be
tried in Saluda County. Debra May Helmick was abducted in
Richland County, but was found in Lexington County, so it was
agreed that was where the trial for her kidnapping and murder would take place. This suited Myers, whose circuit included
both counties. Myers said he and Anders would work together
as needed.

The formal charge in the Smith case was brought against
Bell on Tuesday, July 23, 1985.

On Friday, August 2, Bell was charged with the Helmick
murder in Lexington County, where the kidnapping charge
was transferred so that it could be merged with the murder
charge. Though the two medical examiners had not been able
to determine with certainty how either Shari or Debra May
died because of the condition of the bodies when found, both
examiners concluded that the deaths were not accidental,
natural, or suicides, but rather homicides, which simply means
that the deaths of these two human beings were caused by
the act of another human being. Since Bell had been shown to
have abducted both victims, it meant murder charges could be
brought even though the precise manner of death could not be
proven.

On Monday, August 12, a grand jury in Saluda County presented a true bill of indictment for the kidnapping and murder
of Sharon Faye Smith and served notice that if the defendant
was convicted, this would be a death penalty–eligible case.
State law specified that capital punishment could be imposed

in murder cases with aggravating circumstances. Kidnapping and sexual assault were two of those circumstances. Others included torture, armed robbery, burglary, and the killing of a law officer.

Myers said the "gruesome circumstances" of Shari's murder and the condition of her remains were what convinced him to go for capital punishment. "I decided to seek the death penalty the day I saw the body," he said. Under South Carolina law, if a jury reaches a guilty verdict in a capital case, it then votes on whether to impose the death penalty. The vote must be unanimous, or execution is taken off the table.

In recognition of the cooperation between the various sheriff's departments, the solicitors' offices, SLED, and the FBI that led to a successful investigative outcome, the *State* ran an editorial advocating that this kind of collaboration be formalized with the creation of a special strike force for serious crimes. "In such cases," the editorial concluded, "a well-coordinated strike force could speed up the process of apprehension. And it might save a life."

Bell was brought to Circuit Court for a bond hearing and placed in the back of the courtroom while Judge Hubert E. Long instructed a pool of potential jurors for other cases. While the judge was speaking, Bell shouted out, "I'd like to legally request and ask that the Smith and Helmick families be allowed to put their friends on the jury that tries me. I am totally innocent of kidnapping Sharon Faye Smith and Debra May Helmick, and it will be proven without a doubt." Those in the courtroom looked stunned by the outburst. He may have been trying to show that he was crazy to mitigate his sentence if convicted, but I'm sure the one who was really going crazy at this display was Jack Swerling.

Predictably, Bell continued to want all the attention focused on him. "And when this hearing is over," he said as officers took him out of the courtroom in handcuffs and leg chains, "I'd like an hour to speak to the press." As the marshals dragged him out, he shouted, "My constitutional rights have been violated!"

When Judge Long completed his business with the jury pool, Bell was brought back into the courtroom and Swerling immediately moved that the hearing be closed to the public and media so that pretrial publicity wouldn't get in the way of a fair trial. "In the twelve years I've been practicing law," Swerling said, "I've never seen the amount of publicity this case has generated, nor have I seen the amount of talking and fear in the community."

"I don't like gag orders and that sort of thing," Long replied in denying the motion. "We're living in America."

The judge then denied bail. Interestingly, Bell said he had decided he didn't want bond anyway. Jack Swerling stated that while his client wished to reserve the right to request bail at a later date, "Mr. Bell wishes to say that while he maintains his innocence he does not want to apply for bond at this time because he is fearful for his own life."

Due to Bell's mental history, Donnie Myers moved to have Bell sent to the state hospital for a fifteen-day psychiatric evaluation. Swerling objected since, he said, the defense had not yet decided whether to claim insanity during the trial. Myers countered that it was important to have the matter settled ahead of time one way or the other so that the trial could go forward without that becoming an issue. Judge Long agreed to this and turned down Swerling's request for a protective order to guarantee that anything Bell told the psychiatrists would not be admissible in court.

A trial date for the Smith kidnapping and murder was set for November 11. In the meantime, Bell was examined by a team of mental health professionals from the South Carolina State Hospital. Together, after a series of tests, they concluded and reported to the court that Larry Gene Bell knew right from wrong at the time Shari Smith and Debra May Helmick were abducted and murdered and was mentally competent to stand trial and assist in his own defense.

At Donnie Myers's request, I flew back down to South Carolina at the end of October, accompanied by Special Agent Jeffrey Higginbotham from the Legal Training Unit, to consult on case strategy. Higginbotham had been working with us to figure out how to establish criminal personality profiling as a standard subject for expert witness testimony and felt this trial, which would be so highly publicized, would be a good way to introduce the profiling process. He wanted it to set a precedent for future requests from the law enforcement and judicial communities.

The prosecution team had two aims for my testimony. First, they felt the statements Bell had made to me when Ron and I spoke with him at the sheriff's office were crucial to their case, since that was as close as we'd come to an outright confession. Second, Myers wanted to force the defense to raise the subject of the profile, which trial rules would not allow the prosecution to introduce on their own. But by having me testify, Myers could question me in a general way and have the defense bring up the profile in cross-examination. He believed strongly that the release of the highly accurate profile would be damaging to the defense case.

Myers had been interested in how we had advised prosecutor Jack Mallard in the Wayne Williams trial for some of the Atlanta child murders. I suggested that if Bell took the witness stand, which I thought he would, the aim should be to try to strip him of his flamboyant and crazy veneer and let the jury see him for what he really was: a sick but methodical killer who knew exactly what he was doing. Myers was confident he could do this.

While I was down in Columbia, I was formally served with a subpoena to appear at the trial, which I gladly accepted.

CHAPTER 18

ury selection for the kidnapping and murder of Shari Smith began on November 4, 1985. Knowing what a challenge it was going to be to seat an impartial twelve-person jury, court officials put together a pool of 175 potential jurors—three times the normal pool. Judge John Hamilton Smith (no relation to Shari) ruled from the psychiatric report that Larry Gene Bell was competent to stand trial.

"He was able to answer questions and relate to us," Dr. John C. Dunlap told Judge Smith. "There was no time when I saw him or any of my coworkers saw him that we thought he was psychotic."

Defense attorney Swerling questioned him on whether it was possible for an individual with a history of psychiatric issues to have been psychotic in the past but appear more normal when interviewed in the present. "You are aware that there is a history of mental illness," the defense attorney said.

"I am aware that he has been examined for psychiatric reasons," Dunlap replied. "The diagnosis that was made then probably went along with the picture that they saw at that time. The picture that they saw at that time was probably accurate."

On Monday, November 11, the day the trial was scheduled to begin, Jack Swerling moved for a change of venue based on the enormous amount of publicity the case had garnered and the consequent difficulty in assuring that jurors were not influenced by that. There is a difference between knowing about a case and feeling you can't judge the facts fairly during a trial, but this is a potential knife edge every judge has to evaluate each time there is a high-profile prosecution. Judge Smith responded that he would first try to draw a jury there in Saluda County.

The county, with a population of about 17,000, was largely rural. The town of Saluda, where the courthouse was, had about 7,500 residents. It was a quiet and hospitable place with very little crime. Myers knew the area and people well enough to believe that even though they all would have heard about the case and formed some sort of opinion, they would all either be open to whatever was brought out in the trial or honest enough to say they couldn't be. More than anything else, residents told reporters they were mainly concerned about the crush of media that would descend on them and how difficult it was going to be to find a parking place anywhere near the courthouse.

On the morning of the trial, the courtroom was protected by seven SLED agents and four Saluda County deputies. SLED agents also swept the building for bombs. When Bell was brought in, wearing a light-brown suit, his beard was closely cropped, and he appeared to have lost about twenty-five pounds. His mother was among those present in the courtroom. The Smith family was not.

After two full days, only twenty-three members of the jury pool had been fully questioned, and of those, only six had been seated. Judge Smith was clearly not satisfied with the pace of jury selection or the prospect of assembling a full jury and two or three alternates.

On Wednesday morning he surprised many in the courtroom when he announced, "Larry Gene Bell will not be tried in Saluda. After the last two days, I am convinced there is probability that Mr. Bell could not receive a fair trial in the small town and community of Saluda County." I thought this was a wise decision. The last thing any of us would have wanted was a guilty verdict overturned on appeal due to pretrial publicity and the inference of jury bias.

The following Monday, November 18, Judge Smith announced that the Bell trial for the kidnapping and murder of Shari Smith would be moved about a hundred miles away, to the Berkeley County Courthouse in Moncks Corner, just north of Charleston. He set the new date as January 27. "That is where I found some open court dates and it is out of the range of the Columbia television stations," he explained.

Edith Padgett, the clerk of the Saluda County court, estimated that it would cost about $10,000 to move the trial. County officials were quick to reassure the public that even if trial expenses went over the allotted budget, they didn't anticipate a need for a tax increase, but this was just one more example of how the actions of Larry Gene Bell upset the normal routine and way of life in the Midlands area.

As the year came to a close, another possible sign was Sheriff Metts's report that almost every category of serious and violent crime had risen in the past year, the first year it had gone

up since 1979. He attributed some of the rise to the early release of a number of prisoners, but also said that the murders of
Shari and Debra May had probably made citizens more aware
of crime and, therefore, they were reporting it more often.

For me, just as when I often go by places—streets, woods,
schoolyards, wherever—they remind me of crime scenes or
body dump sites, it's impossible to go through a major holiday
without thinking about all the families who are having experiences different from mine because one of their loved ones has
been taken away by someone. It still brings tears to my eyes to
recall a support group meeting for survivors of homicide victims Mark and I attended in which the speaker talked about
sprinkling red, white, and blue foil stars on her daughter's
grave for Independence Day and a small wreath in front of the
headstone for Christmas. As Bob Smith observed on Shari's
eighteenth birthday, time does heal wounds, but the scar remains forever.

I'm sure it was a difficult Christmas for the Smith and
Helmick families—their first without a daughter and sister.
Dawn Smith said that Hilda and Bob didn't even want to cel-
ebrate, but she and Robert felt an obligation to do it in their
sister's memory. They placed the snowman ornaments with
Dawn, Shari, and Robert's names on the tree, but couldn't bring
themselves to put up the Christmas stockings that traditionally had been hung on the fireplace mantel. How would it
be to put up three stockings when only two would be filled?
As Dawn later wrote, "The first Christmas without Shari was
dreadful," and, "As we opened the gifts on Christmas Eve, the
usual laughter was replaced with tears of grief."

The Smiths' heartache was compounded by having to go

over every detail with the prosecution team and the knowledge that Donnie Myers wanted all four of them to attend the trial every single day, so that the jury would be constantly aware of them and the missing member of their family.

In a pretrial hearing, Judge Smith ordered Bell to record the typed telephone transcripts of some of the conversations with the Smiths and Charlie Keyes so they could be compared in court with the actual recordings of the offender. Swerling argued that this violated the defendant's Fifth Amendment right against self-incrimination and said the state was "actually trying to get a person to incriminate himself by repeating phrases that are incriminating." Judge Smith disagreed.

After a delay caused by Jack Swerling having a severe case of bronchitis, court was finally called into session Monday, February 10, 1986. Knowing I would be called to testify, I had kept up on the developments, receiving reports from Lewis McCarty and Donnie Myers' office every couple of days. It was a rainy morning as expectant spectators began lining up outside the courthouse around seven, hoping to get a seat inside. Most had no personal connection with the case or participants, but just wanted to see the man they were told had terrorized an entire region. One couple had a granddaughter who wouldn't come out of the house during the terror. They wanted to see what it was all about. Another woman said, "I'm just fascinated with the case. It's so weird. I wanted to see a person who could kill someone's daughter and then call them and tell them that he feels like part of their family." Several journalists likened the crowd to those seeking tickets to a hit Broadway play, a rock concert, or a championship sporting event. Those in line tried to monitor and control anyone trying to break in, and at one point a shoving match erupted between two women.

For security, Bell was transported the short distance from the jail to the courthouse in a police patrol car. As soon as he emerged from the car—wearing a brown Lacoste sweater with its signature green alligator logo over a white shirt, tan slacks, and sneakers, his beard neatly trimmed—he shouted to the clutch of reporters standing outside, "I am Larry Gene Bell. I am not guilty!" In the middle of his chest, a homemade paper button clipped to his shirt read, "I am the victim. Larry Gene Bell. I am innocent."

When Bell entered the high-ceilinged courtroom, the Smiths were already seated. They were being put up by the state at the Holiday Inn in Charleston. It was the first time Bob and Robert had seen him in person and the first time for Hilda and Dawn since that late afternoon in Sheriff Metts's office. They each glanced at him and then quickly looked away. Dawn remembers him having a smirk on his face as he was led in.

Once he was sure he had everyone's attention, Bell stated loudly, "I am innocent and will not get a fair trial!"

A little later, as Judge Smith was explaining the laws concerning death penalty trials and the definition of aggravating and mitigating circumstances, Bell rose to his feet and said, "Why in the hell am I being held at the gates of hell when Sheriff Metts knows that Gene Bell is innocent?" The judge told him to sit down and rejected a motion from Swerling for a mistrial based on the outburst having tainted the jury panel.

With that, jury selection got underway.

When Bell arrived at the courthouse for the second day

of jury selection, he addressed the waiting media, "My silent friends, whatever the legal outcome of the trial, I pray daily that the Smith family, the Helmick family, and the Bell family can constructively go on with their lives." Not only was he in court for his life, he seemed to be *holding court* with the press.

Once inside the courtroom, after apologizing for the previous day's disturbance, Bell grabbed a microphone and proclaimed, "Your Honor, for the record, I'd like to state that Gene Bell is not a vicious, mean, dangerous individual and anyone that can say that otherwise doesn't know me personally!"

A few minutes later, after another juror was accepted by both sides and led out of the courtroom, Bell stood up again and in a sobbing voice said, "I can't take this anymore! Gene Bell is not responsible. I didn't do this, and you all are trying to give me the death penalty or life imprisonment. It's not right!"

Predictably, Judge Smith ordered the defendant to sit down and be quiet or he would be removed from the courtroom during the jury selection. "These outbursts are not beneficial to you," he told Bell.

Swerling told the judge that his client was not communicating with him and his co-counsel Elizabeth Levy, and was not assisting in his own defense. Bell sat quietly for the rest of the day.

Two juror candidates were excused when they said they were unalterably opposed to the death penalty. Another woman said she had no opinion on the death penalty, "except it's not used enough. We need to dispose of people who kill innocent children." She was also excused, as was a man who opined that Bell was guilty and didn't deserve a trial.

Sheriff's deputies were dispatched to a twenty-four-hour watch on Jack Swerling's house because of death threats. "Representing someone like Larry Gene Bell keeps the system honest," he later told *The National Law Journal*. "Making sure Mr. Bell receives all his rights protects all of our rights."

CHAPTER 19

On Wednesday morning, Bell had another message for the phalanx of reporters and television cameras. "Common sense, questionable. Has Gene Bell already been tried? Has the state been poisoned? Justice: boom!" The media had already begun to eagerly await these pronouncements.

By the afternoon, a seven-woman, five-man jury had been empaneled and sworn in, evenly divided between Black and white. The selection had gone much faster than predicted, largely because it turned out the local residents really didn't know that much about the Midlands case in advance.

AFTER OPENING STATEMENTS FROM EACH SIDE, SHARI'S BOYFRIEND, RICHARD Lawson, was called to the witness stand by the prosecution. He related the events of the fateful Friday afternoon: how he and Shari met up at the shopping center, how they went to the pool party with Shari's friend Brenda Boozer, and that he drove both girls back to the shopping center to pick up their cars. Brenda followed Richard to the stand and confirmed Richard's narrative.

Next, Bob Smith told of seeing Shari's car at the head of the driveway, then going down to look for her when she didn't come directly back to the house and the panic he felt when he couldn't find her. He testified to calling the sheriff's office, of the early-morning phone call promising a letter from Shari, and then being brought to the post office by deputies to sign for and officially accept the letter that turned out to be Shari's Last Will & Testament. He told of several other phone calls from the same unknown subject.

Myers asked him if he knew Larry Gene Bell and if he was, as the caller had said, a "friend of the family."

"No, sir."

"Did you even know he existed on May 31 or June 1 of 1985?"

"No, sir."

Swerling said he had no questions for Mr. Smith, which was wise. There is absolutely no advantage for a defense attorney in trying to impeach a grieving father.

John Ballinger, a local businessman who happened to be passing the Smith driveway at the critical time, described the car that had stopped next to the mailbox where Shari was standing.

Terri Butler, a homemaker with two children who lived nearby, described the driver and the car that almost ran into hers before swerving to the side of the road. She said the entire episode was brief, only a few seconds but, "I looked into his eyes, and he looked into mine." Just before that, she had seen Shari's blue Chevette pull up to the driveway. She had helped the sheriff's office create the first composite sketch.

"Would you point him out?" asked Assistant Solicitor Knox McMahon.

"He's sitting right there with a white shirt on," she said, indicating Bell.

"Any doubt in your mind, Mrs. Butler?"

"No."

"Anything different about him today than when you saw him on the afternoon of May 31, 1985?"

"He has a beard, and his hair is combed down."

When it was Swerling's turn to cross-examine, he said, "So this identification you made was on the basis of a split-second look, wasn't it?"

"I don't know how long I seen him," Butler replied, "but I seen him."

Bell's parents' neighbor Sammy Collins described talking to Bell on Saturday morning, June 1, and how interested he seemed to be in the Smith kidnapping. He also described how Bell's appearance changed between June 1 and 22.

Hilda Smith was the next witness. She related her own experiences on that Friday. Then Myers took her through the series of phone calls: how the caller first wanted to speak to her, and then focused on Dawn. Myers homed in on the second call—the first to be recorded.

"Your Honor," he said, "at this time we'd like to offer that tape into evidence."

The jurors, court officers, and attorneys were instructed to put on wireless headphones to hear the tapes. Swerling didn't bother challenging the relevance or validity of the thirty or so law enforcement officers and telephone company technicians who set up the recording device and traced the calls—a tactic the prosecution anticipated he might employ to question the legitimacy of the recordings. It would have just bogged down the trial and annoyed the jurors, all with no benefit to the defense. The media had access to written transcripts showing how Hilda had beseeched the caller about Shari's health:

> *"I think you know how I feel being Shari's mother, and*
> *how much I love her. Can you tell me is she all right*
> *physically without her medicine?"*

The recording went on with the other voice telling her to have an ambulance ready and to tell Sheriff Metts to stop looking in Lexington County and instead focus on Saluda County. This was the call in which the UNSUB declared,

> *"I want to tell you one thing: Shari is now a part of me,*
> *physically, mentally, emotionally, spiritually; our*
> *souls are one now."*

Though Bob Smith had testified that "We held out [hope] to the end that she was alive," when Ron and I first heard this recording, we pretty much knew that Shari had been killed. You didn't have to be a profiler to recognize the satisfaction this guy was deriving from being able to manipulate, dominate, and control the terrified family.

Myers asked Hilda if the voice on the tape was the same as the one from the first call. She affirmed that it was. The playing of tapes continued. By the fifth recording Myers had played, Shari's mother could no longer hold back her tears.

After the final tape, Myers jumped ahead to the June 27

meeting with Bell in Sheriff Metts's office. "Had you ever seen his face before that day?" he asked.

"No, I had not," Hilda responded.

"When you talked to Larry Gene Bell that day, how did the voice compare with the person's voice that made those telephone calls?"

"I had heard that voice over and over, even when I tried to go to sleep at night. I couldn't cut that voice off, but it didn't have a face. When I heard Larry Gene Bell talk, then I had a face that went with that voice I had been hearing over and over again. Larry Gene Bell was the voice, and he had been caught."

Swerling was smart enough not to challenge the mother of the victim. All he asked on cross was, "There is no question that you did not know and had never seen Larry Gene Bell before, is that correct?"

"I did not know him and had never seen him."

"Thank you, Mrs. Smith. That is all I'm going to ask you."

Dawn followed her mother to the witness stand and Myers continued with the tapes. The first was the June 6 call, so Dawn had to endure listening to:

> *"I tied her up to the bedpost with the electrical cord. She*
> *didn't struggle or cry or anything. I took duct tape*
> *and wrapped it around her head and suffocated her."*

The call went on:

> *"I gave her the choice to shoot her, give her a drug*
> *overdose, or suffocate her . . . She said she knew she*
> *was going to be an angel."*

This was also the call where he said:

> *"This thing got out of hand, and all I wanted to do was*
> *make love to Dawn. I've been watching her for a*
> *couple of weeks . . ."*
> "To who?"
> *"I'm sorry; to Shari."*

The implication that he hadn't intended to kill Shari had been quickly belied when he kidnapped and murdered Debra May Helmick. Had he just wanted to make love to this nine-year-old, too? Had he not intended to kill her? Had things just gotten out of hand again? He did exactly what he clearly intended and what he wanted with, and to, her.

After Myers played the one recording from the afternoon of Saturday, June 8—the one following Shari's funeral—he asked, "Now Dawn, in this tape he said he was going to kill himself, again, and they would find pictures in a plastic bag on his body. Did he kill himself and did you ever find the pictures he was talking about?"

"No."

Then the prosecutor revisited the encounter in the sheriff's office. After establishing that she had not seen Bell before that afternoon, he asked, "How did the voice that you heard coming out of Larry Gene Bell's mouth that Thursday compare with the voice on the telephone calls you all were receiving?"

"It was the same voice."

"Any doubt in your mind?"

"No, sir. None."

One piece of evidence Judge Smith would not let the jury hear was the caller saying to Dawn:

"Okay, you know God wants you to join Shari Faye. This month, next month, this year, next year. You can't be protected all the time. You know about the Helmick girl."

Judge Smith had decided that the June 22 recording was too prejudicial and would damage the defendant's legal presumption of innocence. Swerling had wanted the judge to go further and not let the jury hear Hilda and Dawn's voices on the recordings because the natural juror sympathy toward them would be redirected as anger against Bell. Judge Smith turned down that motion. Swerling further tried to convince the judge that Bell had carried on the conversation with us all in Metts's office without benefit of counsel. But it was clear from the record that Bell had voluntarily waved his Miranda rights and, in fact, was eager to talk and requested that the Smith family be brought to him. At that time, Metts had told him flat-out that an attorney would advise him not to talk, but he clearly wanted to anyway. In a session held outside the jury's hearing, Metts testified that Bell's brother, an attorney, was waiting in the lobby at the time, but Bell said repeatedly that he did not want to see his brother.

Even without the excluded tape, I thought the evidence already presented would be impossible for the jury to ignore. My main concern at this point was that they would think Bell's bizarre and narcissistic behavior was due to uncontrollable mental illness. Again, I acknowledge that he had a degree of mental illness, but it was nowhere near beyond his ability to control himself, nor did it prevent him from knowing the difference between right and wrong. What most "normal" people have trouble understanding is that sociopaths like Bell do comprehend the difference between right and wrong, but they come to consider their desires and sense of their own omnipotence as higher values that, in their minds, overrule standard morality.

WIS-TV reporter Charlie Keyes testified about the call to him in which the caller promised to turn himself in, an event that, like so many of the UNSUB's other promises, was not fulfilled.

Toward the end of the day, Judy Hill, who worked as a cashier at the Grand Central Station truck stop on Interstate 77 where the June 6 call originated, identified Bell as having come in that day for coffee and change for the telephone. She watched as he went through the lobby, saw that the pay phone there was in use, then walked off toward another pay phone in the parking lot.

What you're trying to do as a prosecutor with all of these witnesses is to make your version of the narrative unimpeachable to the jury. You want each juror to think that if even this one part of your story is accurate, then the defendant must be the one who committed the crime, and when you add this piece of testimony to all the others, how could they all be wrong?

Dr. Joel Sexton, who had viewed Shari's body where it was found and performed the autopsy, also testified the same day as Hilda and Dawn. Based on his physical findings and the fact that no rigor mortis was present, he concluded that Shari had been dead at least two days. "Decomposition was present," he explained. "Flies had laid eggs, and maggots and beetles were present. This is the normal process in nature of destroying a dead carcass found in the wilderness." As raw as this sounds, it was what the killer would have known would happen when he placed Shari's body in that environment, making specific findings about manner of death difficult to come by. It was either due to smothering and/or strangulation, or from severe dehydration due to her medical condition. In any case, her kidnapping and being held against her will were the proximate causes of her death in the legal sense, so the person who kidnapped her was directly responsible for her death.

Dr. Sexton went on to explain to the jury that because of the severe decomposition, it was impossible to determine whether Shari had been raped. On that point the jury could make up its own mind based on Bell saying in one phone call that he had "made love" to her three times. As horrible as it is to contemplate, that determination was almost beside the point.

CHAPTER 20

On Friday, February 14, when it was his turn on the stand, Ellis Sheppard described the couple's house-sitting arrangement with Bell and confirmed that he had employed him as an electrician's assistant for the six months preceding the arrest. He said that he and his wife returned home temporarily from their scheduled nine-week trip to check on the progress of a job in Saluda County that Bell was working on. And while he was driving the couple back from the airport, he initiated a detailed conversation about the Shari Smith disappearance. "He [Bell] asked me if I thought the family would want to have the body back."

Sheppard said he replied that he hoped the girl was still alive, upon which Bell responded, "But if she's not, do you think they'd want the body back?"

The .38 pistol that Sheppard had shown Bell was introduced into evidence after Sheppard described finding it dirty and jammed, in a different location from where he had left it.

He identified the voice on the tapes as Bell's, even with the pitch modulation device. "I was mad," Sheppard said. "I knew it was Mr. Bell's voice on [the recordings]. There was no doubt in my mind."

"And whose voice did you hear on that tape telling people what he did to Shari Smith?" Myers asked, driving home the horror of this to the jury.

"It was Mr. Bell's voice. It was no other."

In her own testimony, Sharon Ellis confirmed everything her husband had said. Both described Bell as a good worker, but "weird" and "strange." They said he was a compulsive note-taker who wrote out step-by-step instructions for just about any task he had to accomplish, and that he would revise those instructions repeatedly.

SLED questioned-document examiner Marvin "Mickey" Dawson described the working of the ESDA machine, based on a technique developed at Scotland Yard in London, and how it could discern indented markings from several pages above the sheet of paper in question, and how Shari's Last Will & Testament was conclusively linked to the legal pad on which Sharon Sheppard had left instructions for Bell.

Using a photo chart, Dawson also explained, "I compared the known handwriting of Sharon Faye Smith to the handwriting in the Last Will & Testament and positively identified it as Shari's handwriting."

Swerling tried to have the document removed from the evidence the jury could take into the jury room during deliberations, arguing that Shari's messages to her family and boyfriend had little to do with the case itself, but could inflame the jurors against the defendant. Judge Smith immediately denied the motion, noting that the document was the single most im-

portant piece of evidence, without which the murder might not
have been solved.

Larry Gene Bell, attired this day in a white shirt, a vest,
green slacks, and a green tie, took the witness stand without
the jury present. He complained that he had allowed the search
of his car and home—his parents actually allowed the search,
since it was their home—without knowing he could consult
an attorney first, and that Sheriff Metts talked him out of demanding one, since "a lawyer would only tell me to shut up."

Metts had told him it would save time if he just agreed to
sign the forms, but also said that if he didn't, they would obtain
a search warrant, which, in fact, they did for the house. So, as
far as I was concerned, the question was moot.

Once Bell was in the witness box, it was like his performances on the telephone calls. He was in his element and
comfort zone. He refused to sit, instead standing as if trying
to dominate the courtroom, claiming that was the way it was
done in nineteenth-century England.

"We're not playing games here, unless you think Shari
Smith's life was a joke and my life is a joke," he accused Myers.
"Let's try to act a little professional here." One of the things
that bothered me most was the way he had taken to tying his
life with Shari's, as if they were both victims of the same ad-
versary.

Judge Smith told him repeatedly to stick to the point of the
questioning, such as when he veered off to complain that the
sheriff's department had not returned his wallet, which contained eighty or ninety dollars, to him.

"You'll have to limit your comments to the matter at hand,"
Smith informed him.

In response to the judge's admonition he replied, "I can appreciate that, but I hope you can appreciate my situation."

As Saturday's court session opened, and just after Bell reached the defense table, he stood to complain about how SLED agents had taken a pen away from him, saying it could be used as a weapon. Judge Smith explained that the move was standard security procedure when a defendant is brought in and out of the courtroom without handcuffs.

"Sir, I do not accept your apology!" he shouted. "That may be the reason, but I do not accept it."

"I wasn't apologizing to you," the judge responded.

With the court's attention focused on him, Bell seemed to pick up where he'd left off on Friday. "I have been standing at the gates of hell for over seven months," he said. "It can't come close to what the Smith and Helmick families are going through. I am standing at the gates of hell, and they are in hell. Let's get this over with and get on with our lives." Judge Smith had already ruled that the prosecution couldn't bring up the Helmick case because it would be prejudicial, but Bell did it anyway. He then told the judge that the transcripts of the interrogation and the session in Metts's office should not be believed because important things were left out. "A blind man can see that false witnesses and false testimony have been given against me."

A little later, after Metts contradicted Bell's testimony and stepped down from the witness box on his way out of the courtroom, Bell extended his hand to shake Metts's. The sheriff merely glared at him and continued on his way.

At another point, Swerling turned to Bell and asked harshly, "Do you have to wave to everybody?"

"I'm only showing respect for the law," he replied. Just another manifestation of his yen for manipulation, domination, and control.

"What do you think you are," the defense attorney demanded, clearly irritated, "a maître d'?"

With the jury still not present, Smith prepared to rule on whether what Bell had told the Charlotte police officers about Shari Smith while they were questioning him about the Sandee Cornett disappearance would be admissible.

Swerling characterized the interview as "eleven hours of gibberish." When he questioned investigator Lawrence Walker about Bell's assertions of visions from God, trying to underscore the mental illness angle, he posed, "Didn't you think it was a little bizarre? Didn't you wonder about his visions from God?"

Walker replied, as we have seen ourselves in the Bureau, that attributing a fact to a vision or message from God is often a suspect's means of admitting he was involved without coming right out and stating it, another variation on the face-saving scenario. "It is not uncommon in my experience as a police officer for someone to tell you they've had a vision. It's a way for them to get something off their mind."

"Do you think he was acting in an unusual manner?" Swerling asked.

"Yes, sir. At times throughout the interview, Larry Bell did act in an unusual manner, and I will emphasize the word *act*."

Pressing his point, Swerling brought in psychiatrist Dr. Harold Morgan, who had been hired by the defense and reviewed the transcripts of the interview. He said that Bell was in no position to waive his right to have an attorney present

because he was "psychotic" at the time and "He was so obviously out of his mind he couldn't give informed consent. He
was out of touch with reality."

Morgan testified that he interviewed Bell on July 16, two
days after the Charlotte police had, and found him in a manic
state. "He was expressing delusions that he had certain powers
and was in contact with God. He was rambling. It was clear to
me he was out of his mind."

This is where those in my line of work often find ourselves
at odds with psychiatrists and other mental health professionals. They tend to focus on these rambling statements that
sound illogical to the normal ear, while we tend to look at the
degree of planning, organization, and efficient execution that
go into a violent crime, as well as how much the offender can
recall and relate in a reasonably coherent manner.

Judge Smith ruled that while Bell's statements were rambling, they didn't indicate that he had lost contact with reality or that he failed to understand his constitutional right. The
judge decided that what Bell said relative to Shari Smith could
be introduced, which would also include passing references
to Debra May Helmick, but nothing about the Sandee Cornett
case.

Much of the Saturday session then involved the forensic
findings from the Bell and Sheppard houses, and the mattress cover from the Sheppards' guest bedroom. SLED forensic
chemists testified that the hair, blood, and urine stains on the
carpet were consistent with Shari's type, based on hairs taken
from her hairbrush and blood from her pantyhose. Her blood
type from the sample also matched blood drops on a pair of
Bell's sneakers.

The experts said they could not confirm whether any of the stains came from Bell, since he had refused to give samples of his blood, urine, and saliva. In a mixed ruling, Judge Smith decreed that the prosecution could tell the jury that the defendant had refused to give samples of his blood and urine for comparison with the mattress cover stains, but they could not mention that he had disobeyed a court order to give hair or voice samples. Regarding his voice, Smith reasoned that since the jurors had heard the tapes, they could make up their own minds.

So far, those in the courtroom had heard a number of Bell's outbursts. The jury, on the other hand, had been out of the room for all of them.

On the morning of Monday, February 17, Myers rested the prosecution. By the conclusion of its case, Myers had called dozens of witnesses and introduced fifty-nine pieces of evidence, including photos, charts, maps, the handgun, rope, duct tape, pens, envelopes and the duck decoy stamps found in Bell's bedroom, the yellow legal pad, the telephone recordings, and, of course, the crucial Last Will & Testament.

Now it was the defense's turn to try to at least sow reasonable doubt that Larry Gene Bell was the killer, or show that he was so far out of his mind when he kidnapped, held, and murdered Shari Smith that he was removed from reality and unaware of the difference between right and wrong. Those of us in law enforcement considered that a pretty tall order.

CHAPTER 21

Monday afternoon, the defense opened its case, beginning with testimony from three mental health experts. The first, clinical social worker Susan Appenzeller, testified that Bell had broken most of his appointments when he was an outpatient at the William S. Hall Psychiatric Institute. Also, in his first interview there, he told the diagnostic team that his mother was dead, which was not true.

Dr. Lucius Pressley, a psychiatrist at Hall, testified that in 1976 Bell was diagnosed as a sadistic sexual deviant. Pressley asserted, and our research has certainly confirmed this, that sexual sadism "is among the most difficult problems to treat," due to the pleasure and positive reinforcement of his own urges that the individual derives from the deviant act.

Even though this testimony was offered in his defense, Bell turned to the press section and commented, "If y'all believe that, Mona Lisa is a man."

Dr. Robert Sabalis, a psychologist with the department of family medicine at the University of South Carolina School of

Medicine, said he had examined Bell at Hall in 1975 and found him to have a below-average IQ of 88 and showing "potential early signs of psychosis." When he was cross-examined, Dr. Sabalis conceded that the condition would not be considered legal insanity.

The jurors would be able to make their own assessments soon enough: Bell took the witness stand next. It's generally a big risk for the defense counsel to put a client on the stand, subject to cross-examination and contradiction. But Swerling was playing the best card he had, hoping to show the jury that Bell was irrational, if not outright bonkers. When Bell took the stand, again on his feet with his hands clasped behind his back rather than seated, Swerling opened by asking, "How old are you?"

"Silence is golden," Bell replied.

"I didn't ask you that," Swerling snapped. "I asked how old you are."

"Thirty-seven," Bell finally allowed. Not exactly an auspicious start if you want to show your client is crazy, as opposed to just an annoying smart-ass. Bell then asked to meet privately with Swerling, and after the meeting had gone on for twenty-five minutes, came back and apologized for the delay. But of course, it wasn't that clear-cut.

"I'll start tomorrow. I'm confused, but I'll be one hundred and ten percent better." Then Bell turned to the press section and said, "I'm so confused. Ain't we having fun?"

"I can't take much more of this," Myers muttered. "I think I'm going crazy."

"I'm confused. I can't comment any further," was all Swerling had to offer.

Smith adjourned court for the day.

THE FOLLOWING MORNING, TUESDAY, FEBRUARY 18, BELL TOOK THE WITNESS BOX in front of the jury for the first time. It was standing room only in the courtroom. He complained that he'd given officers an alibi when he was arrested, but that they'd never checked it out. Making himself once again into the victim, he insisted, "I pleaded with them to check my alibi. I've been misled, naive, and stupid to depend on them." He never mentioned what that alibi was.

He testified that he had seen many psychiatrists and mental health professionals in his life, summarizing as he turned toward the jury with, "Food for thought. Gifted, dumb, or a fruitcake? You pick one." He explained, "I've been poisoned. You wouldn't believe how many doctors I've talked to in my lifetime. I've listened to doctors say I'm a fruitcake all my life."

He denied deep mental or emotional problems, insisting, "I do not have a mental illness. But you could never convince the doctors of that. I've talked with them all my life and told them over and over again there's nothing wrong with me. They've never listened."

When Swerling tried to delve into his family background, Bell countered, "You're covering everything. You're not going to leave any secrets. I don't care. That's the way my whole life's been—everything twisted and turned around."

Bell shifted a query about his junior high school years into a complaint about his current living conditions at CCI. "When I was unjustly thrown into the gates of hell, my weight dropped because of the heat and the food. But I didn't complain. I knew my day would come." The day he was referring to was when he would come to court to refute "the one-sided coin presented against me." Mixing metaphors was the least of his issues.

Jurors didn't seem to know where he was going when he

described himself as "a loner, an individualist, and a leader," then went into a monologue about his and his older brother's sports prowess in high school. From there he spouted Bible passages, recited some of the words to "Amazing Grace," then abruptly declared that he was going to "rip the door off the prosecution's case. The stuff they've brought up doesn't relate to the case. Justice not likely. Things blown out of proportion."

At the lunch break, Bell said to Myers, "You're the best!"

"Not yet," the prosecutor replied, "I'm still waiting to get you on the witness stand."

During the afternoon session, Bell admitted that he had pled guilty to assaulting a woman in Rock Hill and trying to force her into his car at knifepoint but claimed the plea was against his better judgment, made because his attorney and family members told him he was guilty.

THE PREVIOUS DAY, I HAD FLOWN DOWN TO SOUTH CAROLINA. MYERS PLANNED TO call me as a reply witness, after all the others had had their say. He called the FBI's Columbia field office, and they relayed the request to me at the Academy. He and I talked about my intended testimony several times on the phone beforehand, figuring there was a good chance the mental health experts presented by each side would effectively cancel each other out in the jurors' minds. I, on the other hand, could speak about Bell's organizational capabilities and the degree of planning and criminal sophistication that went into his crimes—not the kind of thing that a hallucinatory or hopelessly delusional mental patient could pull off.

After dinner, I met with Myers and his team at my motel. I asked Myers how the Smiths were holding up, particularly Dawn and Hilda. He said that they were staying strong and seemed to be doing as well as could be expected under the circumstances. I then asked if Bell was still focusing his attention on Dawn and Myers said that he certainly was. She definitely looked uncomfortable when he gazed at her, and whenever possible, her brother Robert tried to position himself to block Bell's view.

I warned Myers to expect an outburst from Bell in court as soon as he found out I was on the witness list for the next day. He would be discerning enough to understand my utility to the prosecution, and he would do his best to show that he was both irrational and in charge. Those two goals might seem contradictory, but with his inflated sense of self, I felt Bell would try to neutralize my testimony, as well as that of the prosecution's mental health experts, while at the same time continuing to stroke his own ego.

The morning of Tuesday, February 25, which was my first opportunity to watch the trial firsthand rather than simply receiving reports and updates, Bell was back on the stand, and again refused to sit. He said he chose to stand "because unfortunately, there are no chairs at the gates of hell, and if you sit, you sit on the cold floor or on a hard bed." I had never heard the gates of hell described as cold, but whatever.

Swerling asked, "What are the gates of hell?"

"One step away from being there." He said he had seen Shari Smith die in one of his visions but insisted he was not involved in her kidnapping or death, or any other crime of which he was suspected. He couldn't say who killed Shari "because I don't want to be in trouble, legally and in the eyes of the law."

When pressed about these visions, he uttered a phrase that would become a hallmark of his testimony: "Silence is golden."

He explained that this was in deference to the Smith family, who had already suffered enough. He said he had accommodated the psychiatrists who examined him because "It's important to cooperate with the doctors. After all, that could save a person from the electric chair and get a person a 'guilty but mentally ill' verdict. All things are possible." His act was going pretty much as I'd anticipated.

If you took Bell at his word, which was admittedly a dicey proposition, it seemed he was in direct conflict with Swerling, who was giving his client enough leeway to establish serious mental illness, while Bell himself was contending he was perfectly sane. He also probably didn't endear himself much to the jury when he announced that he had all of their names, home addresses, and personal information.

Finally exasperated by Bell's nonsense and nonresponsiveness, Judge Smith called a recess, sent the jury out, and warned the defense, "All right, Mr. Swerling, Mr. Bell has been on the stand for approximately six hours or longer. This is certainly enough time for the jury to be able to observe his demeanor in answering the questions. I have noticed that Mr. Bell understands the questions that he is asked and that his answers are lucid. Mr. Swerling, if you do not choose to limit your client in his responses to the questions you ask, then I am going to do so. If not, we may be here for the next three weeks."

"I'm ready for that!" Bell replied brightly.

When the jury returned to the courtroom, Bell finally detailed his alibi for the time when Shari was abducted, but not without protest. "You want me to give away my solid concrete alibi?" he asked Swerling. "I was trying to save that as my ace in the hole."

Prodded, he said that he was taking his mother to the podiatrist in Columbia, and then he did detail everything, in the truest sense of the word. In the compulsive manner that we had profiled, he described meeting her at the Lexington County post office at 1:15 and getting behind the wheel of her car. Then he went through every street name, traffic light, stop sign, and other landmarks along the way to the doctor's office. They left the office at 2:50 and went to Krystal's restaurant on Elmwood Avenue, where he ordered a hamburger and where he said a man behind the counter knew him. They left Krystal's at 3:30 and drove back to the Lexington post office to pick up his car, arriving at four o'clock.

"Guess who drove up and parked two spaces away?" he said, addressing the jurors directly. "It was the honorable James R. Metts, sheriff of Lexington County. When he drove up, Mama came out of the post office and met him in front of it. They must have talked for ten minutes!" He added that if Metts, who was not in the courtroom, didn't recall the encounter, then he must be suffering from amnesia.

Bell had the rest of the day detailed as well: He drove back to his parents' house at Lake Murray, then to the Sheppards' house—where he watched the University of South Carolina–Florida State baseball championship game until midnight—and then back to his parents' house, where he went to bed. This all meant that he had had nothing to do with Shari Smith's abduction.

Now, let's imagine for a moment that the prosecution didn't have all the physical evidence it presented from both Bell's parents' house and the Sheppards', the witness descriptions of the suspect and car, or the identification of the sadistic caller's voice as Bell's by not only Shari's family but also by people who knew Bell. In my experience, accused murderers—particularly those facing the death penalty—don't hold on to a legitimate alibi as an "ace in the hole." Recall that Bell had been locked up for some eight months at that point, on the receiving end of threats and taunts from the rest of the population at CCI so that he was already living on death row for his own protection. If he could have proven that he was someplace else at the time of Shari Smith's abduction, he would have crowed about it in exhausting detail from the moment he was brought to the sheriff's office. And you can bet that a skilled and experienced defense attorney like Jack Swerling would have worked to validate every point, likely rendering a trial unnecessary, but certainly having witnesses lined up to support the alibi if need be—and I have to believe Bell's mother would have gladly testified to save her son's life. But the defense had no one. The supposed alibi was just another means for Bell to enjoy time as the center of attention on the stand, manipulating the judicial process by getting to have his say even though everyone knew it was bunk.

Though Judge Smith had prohibited the prosecution from bringing in either the Helmick case or the disappearance of Sandee Cornett, Bell mentioned them himself in his testimony. He said he was shopping at Bush River Mall at the time Debra May was kidnapped, but after he heard about the abduction, he had a vision of what had happened, which he described in detail. Yet when Swerling probed about his failed marriage and the son he didn't see, Bell became choked up and said, "I'm going to be 'silence is golden' on that." He was very much choosing what he did and did not want to talk about.

CHAPTER 22

Myers got his turn at cross-examination in the afternoon, but the responses weren't that different from what Swerling had obtained. The visible difference was that for some reason Bell decided to sit down this time rather than stand. When questioned about his dreams, Bell clarified that they were visions and upbraided the prosecutor: "Apparently you didn't do your homework last night. I said yesterday that silence was golden, my friend. You are crossing a line from business to personal things. Maybe you are deaf."

"Do you know how Miss Smith was abducted?" Myers asked.

"Silence is golden," came the reply.

"I know you understand the questions, Mr. Bell," Judge Smith broke in. "Just answer the questions; then you can explain." He clarified for the jurors that his statement was not an opinion on the defendant's mental state, merely an evaluation that he did understand the questions being put to him.

"Silence is still golden, my friend," Bell replied. He looked at Myers and noted, "You're still the honorable solicitor to me."

When Myers pressed him about why he told one of his parents' neighbors that he knew Shari had been taken from her home in Red Bank and that someone had called her family, Bell answered, "I feel sure that my mother told me about the kidnapping. When we heard about it that morning, naturally we were concerned. We watched the morning news and saw it."

Then, significantly, I thought, even though Bell was loathe to talk about his personal life, Myers got him to admit that the only times he sought mental health help was after each of the incidents for which he'd been arrested. "You've never been to see a psychiatrist or psychologist except when you've been charged with a crime."

"Yes," Bell responded.

Myers's introduction of statements Bell had made about the case to the Charlotte detectives during his interview with them elicited a cavalcade of his stock phrases:

"I'm not going to incriminate myself."

"Ain't we having fun?"

"Silence is golden."

Bell complained to the judge that Myers was trying to trick him into confessing to the Smith murder. "You can't confuse me," he charged. "I don't know why you're wasting the court's valuable time. Saluda County is already in the red."

Since Bell had introduced the topic of his visions of the Helmick case, Myers asked him about the visions. "Silence is golden, my friend," Bell reprised. "I'm not going to confess to something I didn't do. We're going to wrap this up. Give me liberty or give me death!" I knew what my choice for him would have been.

Bell's performance got even more bizarre from there. He

said he wouldn't speak about his God-given visions because the families of the dead girls were in the courtroom.

"I've asked them to step outside," Myers said. "Would you tell us about these visions now?"

"I want to close all the loopholes," Bell assured him. "But this could reach the wrong ears. I respect the members of the press. They have a job to do. I don't want to give the person responsible a head start. No siree, buddy boy!"

This last statement was addressed right at the media section. So was a subsequent statement—a license plate number that he said was connected to the case. When they later checked it out with the state highway department, it belonged to Jack Swerling's car.

Myers asked if he remembered telling officers that he saw Shari Smith at the Lexington post office the afternoon of her abduction.

"Silence is golden," he said again. "I'm not crossing over into that line anymore; not again, buddy boy."

After Bell left the stand, Swerling played the tape of the interrogation in the trailer behind the sheriff's office to show that Bell had cooperated with investigators, that they had suggested he was suffering from mental illness, and that perhaps they hadn't made him fully aware that he was entitled to have an attorney present. At various times while the court listened to the long recording, Bell laughed, cried, cracked his knuckles, and looked bored.

Dr. Thomas R. Scott, a psychologist who had examined Bell at the VA hospital in Columbia in 1976, and then again after he was arrested for the two murders, labeled him a paranoid schizophrenic and "seriously disturbed fellow" who was "most probably" mentally ill at the time of the crimes and therefore had no control over his impulses to attack women. He said of such people, "In one area of their life they could be crazy as a bat, but in another area they could function well."

"But he would know that it was wrong to kidnap a seventeen-year-old girl and leave her rotting in the woods, would he not, Doctor?" Assistant Solicitor Knox McMahon asked during cross-examination.

"I'm sure he would," Dr. Scott replied. "But I don't think it's fair to say he would understand. When you have a serious thinking disorder like this, your understanding is not working too well, either."

McMahon asked if Bell was sadistic as he repeatedly called and taunted the Smith family.

"I've heard the tapes. It did not sound like he was being sadistic to me. He sounded like someone atoning for what he's done. It sounded like a misguided attempt to try to make everything all right," the psychologist said. Though the jurors hadn't been allowed to hear this part of the tape, Scott's statement was confounding to me, given as how Bell had told Dawn:

> *"Okay, you know God wants you to join Shari Faye.*
> *This month, next month, this year, next year. You*
> *can't be protected all the time. You know about the*
> *Helmick girl."*

How threatening the sister of the girl he'd abducted, sexually assaulted, tortured, and murdered could be interpreted as an attempt at atonement seemed a leap of logic that was unfathomable to me. It also speaks to the importance of evaluating what an offender does and says in totality. As I learned from our prison interviews, there are no throwaway statements. Everything they say and do reveals an aspect of their makeup.

On Wednesday, another psychologist, Dr. Diane Follingstad, testified about the eleven hours she had spent interviewing Bell after his arrest. She related that he told her he had a split personality—the bad Larry Gene Bell versus the good Larry Gene Bell—though she saw no evidence of multiple personality disorder. As I said before and have observed many times, when MPD is asserted in an adult defendant for the first time, it is almost always after an arrest.

On the other hand, Dr. Follingstad diagnosed Bell as a manic depressive who also showed signs of schizophrenia and paranoia. Clearly, this was another one of the defense's tactics to show that Bell was mentally ill. But my question was, and always has been, how does this diagnosis make someone unable to prevent himself from kidnapping and murdering women and girls, but still capable of planning his crimes and taking sophisticated steps to avoid detection?

Rather than having two personalities, as Bell suggested, the psychologist referred to the times when Bell committed his crimes as "psychotic episodes."

"He tries to face what happened, but the bad side would never let him admit to it." She said the tests that were administered after the arrest indicated hallucinations, illogical thought patterns, and loss of touch with reality. "He told me such things as that he had the power of suggestion and could get other people to do what he wanted. He also told me that he could move things with his mind and that God sent him special messages."

Okay, fine. Assume he had hallucinations, lost touch with reality, had the power of suggestion over other people as well as telekinetic ability, and received special messages from God. How does any of this compel him to abduct and kill people? And assuming for the sake of argument that the abductions of Shari Smith and Debra May Helmick occurred during psychotic episodes, despite all of the rational thought that went into them—switching license plates, for example, and taking his victims to places where he had total control of the environment—did all of the manipulative and sadistic phone calls to the Smiths take place during psychotic episodes, too? How was he able to be lucid enough to pick obscure pay phones, making sure not to leave any prints or other trace evidence behind, in the midst of such episodes? You can't have it both ways. It struck me as a little too precise to thread the needle as to what Bell could control—and when—and what he couldn't. So he could be perfectly controlled at work, among people who considered him a friend, but then not when he got it in his head to go kidnap and kill someone?

The standard for a verdict of guilty but mentally ill in South Carolina, a lower standard than legally insane, was that the defendant "cannot conform his behavior to the law." Bell was, by many standards, a nut case, but I had seen no evidence to indicate that he couldn't conform his behavior to the law *if and when he chose.*

On Friday morning, Swerling, clearly exasperated with his client, called for a halt to the trial based on Bell not being able to mentally follow and process the proceedings. "He right now won't talk to me," the defense attorney stated. "I asked him if he was going to consult with me, if he was going to assist me. He did not answer in any intelligent way."

Around noon, Judge Smith suspended testimony and excused the jury so that Bell could be examined again to see if Swerling's claim had merit. After the examination, the psychological experts reported back to the court late in the afternoon.

Dr. John C. Dunlap, who had testified before Judge Smith in the November pretrial hearing, said Bell's behavior was bizarre and his dialogue full of clichés, but that it was intentional. Dunlap said, "He thought he had powers that other people didn't have, that he could control people; that he was a child of God, and that silence was golden, and that that is food for thought. That is not a psychiatric disease; it's an attempt to control the interview." He called Bell a narcissistic personality with histrionic tendencies he believed was willing to be caught so he could bask in the attention and credit. He added that Bell probably also believed he could outsmart and outmaneuver investigators and prosecutors if he was arrested and brought to trial.

Dr. Jeffrey McKee agreed with Dunlap and said he believed that Bell had tried to manipulate the testing to appear more mentally unstable than he actually was. "I believe that he has the capacity to consult effectively with his attorney but has simply chosen not to."

Defense psychiatrist Dr. Harold Morgan thought Bell had deteriorated dramatically during the trial, and Dr. Diane Follingstad thought Bell was acting strangely. "He mentioned several times that he is going to marry Dawn Smith today and, in fact, invited us to the wedding and would understand if we could not make it." That does sound strange, until you put it in the context of Bell's overall sexual fantasies about both Smith sisters. Several times in court he came on to Follingstad ("Off the record, you're beautiful. I love blondes, in a professional sense.") and defense co-counsel Elizabeth Levy, caressing her cheek.

Bell also mentioned that his murder trial related to plugging national security leaks, and he was expecting President Ronald Reagan to come to South Carolina to set him free.

Before ruling on the defense motion, Judge Smith called Bell back to the stand. He picked up the Bible used for swearing in witnesses.

"State your name," Swerling directed.

"My name is Larry Gene Bell."

"What if I told you not to talk about Dawn Smith?"

Instead of answering, Bell started thumbing through the Bible. Swerling repeated the question.

Still not answering, Bell looked out into the courtroom and said nonsensically, "Food for thought: Like I stated earlier, it's on the record. If you believe this is true, you will believe what I say following: Mona Lisa is a man and silence is golden, my friend." He stood up, stepped down from the stand and walked toward the defense table.

Swerling tried to get him to come back, ordering, "Larry, take the stand."

He kept walking.

"Larry, get back on the stand!"

Bell stopped, looked back at his attorney, and said, "I put my life in your hands. Treat it as your own." Then he sat down, adding only, "I'm tired and let's get this over with."

Myers rose to his feet. "Your Honor, this is nothing but a show!"

"I object to the solicitor's remarks that this is a show," Swerling was quick to counter.

Shortly after four o'clock Friday afternoon, Judge Smith ruled, "I feel the defendant is fit to stand trial . . . and therefore order these proceedings to resume."

The most accurate mental picture, I thought, was presented the next day. Dr. Gloria Green, a psychiatrist practicing in Oklahoma City who had been on the evaluation team at the Hall Psychiatric Institute in 1976, concluded that Bell was largely faking mental illness to get a more favorable legal outcome to his case. "We felt he did not belong back in society," she testified. "We felt he had no conscience. He did know right from wrong, and he could control himself when he chose to do so, but he had no remorse or sorrow about anything. Because of that, in combination with poor impulse control, we felt the man did not need to be out in society until he had lived in some controlled environment." She allowed as how treatment for such character disorders was seldom effective, but "if there was any hope of finding one shred of conscience in the man, he was entitled to it." She further stated, "When some of the charges against him had been dropped, he acted up again," becoming less confused and more aggressive, showing that he could calibrate his own behavior to suit the situation.

MY TURN ON THE STAND AS A REPLY WITNESS DIDN'T COME UNTIL THE FOLLOWING day, Saturday, February 22, given all that had taken place in the courtroom on Friday. Myers began by qualifying me, having me outline my experience and education, the research and interviews we did with incarcerated repeat murderers and violent predators, and what I did as manager of the FBI's criminal profiling program. The jury seemed to be paying close attention.

Then he transitioned into the substance of my testimony, asking me how Bell appeared to me when we were all together in Metts's office and what had transpired between Bell and Ron Walker and me when we had him alone in McCarty's office.

"He was very lucid, very rational, very articulate, and was interested in talking to law enforcement," I observed.

On cross-examination, Swerling asked, "During any of this time did he confess guilt?"

"He confessed guilt by saying that the bad side of Larry Gene Bell may have done this crime," I said.

On re-direct, Myers asked, "Did you have a plan before he was interviewed for the officers to present this question to him about the good and bad side to give him an out?"

"Yes, sir. We call it a face-saving scenario for providing an excuse for the subject to express his involvement in a crime."

"Did you and the officers bring this up, the 'face-saving scenario,' about was it the other side?"

"Yes, we did."

"Did he take the bait?"

"Yes, sir."

"Your Honor," Myers said, "the state rests."

As I had thought about and Myers and I had previously discussed, all of these conflicting professional views had to put an intellectual burden on the jurors, who were all laypersons, not psychiatrists, psychologists, or social workers. In the end, though, a jury trial is about having a group of one's peers evaluate all the evidence and decide which story makes the most sense. We certainly felt the Bell trial had provided that, both to the question of whether he was guilty of committing the crimes in question and, if so, whether he was mentally capable of preventing himself from doing it. I had essentially been brought down to Moncks Corner to be the last word on the subject and I was satisfied that I'd done what I set out to do.

WHEN JUDGE SMITH HAD DISMISSED THE JURY FOR THE EVENING, AND JUST BEfore he adjourned court, he addressed the two lead attorneys. "You two have been exemplary in regard to the trial in this case and to your kindness to me. It has been a long trial, and I think that the slight amount of friction in the air at times just shows what good lawyers both of you are."

As court was letting out, Metts came over to me and asked if I'd ever been to a Beaufort Stew party. I allowed as not only had I not been to one, I had no idea what it was. "Well, you're going to one tonight," he said.

He picked me up at the motel after I'd had a chance to wash up and change and we drove out to this huge, impressive house. It belonged to one of his officers, who had apparently married into a very wealthy local family. There had to be at least a hundred people there, most of them with some connection to the sheriff's department or other parts of the law enforcement community. There was beer on tap, fried chicken, and all kinds of side dishes. The center of attention was this enormous boiling kettle. Apparently, you throw in crabs and shrimp and any other kind of local fish or seafood you have on hand, plus sausage, potatoes, ears of corn, and several different kinds of seasoning. My impression was that each "chef" or local area had its own particular recipe, but this one was pretty memorable.

Even more memorable was the fact that just about everyone from the trial was there: Metts and McCarty, Donnie Myers and his team of lawyers and investigators, Jack Swerling, and even the judge! I hadn't seen anything like this up north, especially with the trial not yet completed. But after all of the confrontation and adversarial arguments, I was struck by how cordial everyone was to everyone else and how well they all got along. Jack Swerling, who all along had been trying to convince the jury that Bell was suffering from severe mental illness, told me what a good witness he thought I'd been in trying to convince the jury otherwise. In turn, others on the prosecution side were complimenting Swerling on what a good job he'd been doing with such a difficult and uncooperative client, and how he'd maintained his integrity and professional dignity in spite of Bell's antics.

I told Swerling that his accent gave him away as someone who came from the New York City area, just like me. He smiled and said he grew up in Belleville, New Jersey, went to Clemson Law School, and stayed in the area afterward. He seemed to know just about everyone in the state. We also realized we shared something else—both of us had wanted to be veterinarians growing up and spent summers working on farms.

The gathering gave me a new perspective on how you could do your best to win in the courtroom where the stakes were literally life and death, but then come together as a community on the outside.

I STAYED AROUND FOR THE FINAL ARGUMENTS AND VERDICT, KNOWING I WOULD have to leave right afterward to get back to Quantico. I was hoping I'd have some private time with Dawn and the other Smiths, but we couldn't arrange it around the trial hours in the time I had down there.

Sunday morning, final arguments began. Knox McMahon was the first up for the prosecution. He went methodically through the evidence: the various eyewitnesses; the telephone calls to the Smith family and to Charlie Keyes; the numerous witnesses who identified Bell's voice on the taped calls; the forensic findings on the Last Will & Testament; the hair, fibers, and bloodstains on the mattress cover and Bell's shoes; the duct tape residue found on Shari's body; and the recordings of the interrogation and confrontation with Hilda and Dawn.

When Donnie Myers then rose to give his final summation to the jury, he reminded the jurors of the more than forty witnesses presented and asserted that rather than having a clouded mind, Bell kidnapped and killed Shari Smith with malice in his heart.

"Need we even talk about Shari's Last Will & Testament and the Sheppard document, the evidence that broke the case? The telephone number was on that pad. Who was the only one in that house, the only one with a key? Who was the pad left for? The Last Will & Testament being written on the same pad?

"And what did Larry Gene Bell tell the officers while he was in CCI? 'I thought I threw that pad away.' Does that convince you beyond a reasonable doubt?"

Myers suggested that someone as "out of touch with reality" as Bell was portrayed to be by the defense could not have been as precise as the caller was when describing what he had done to Shari and where he had left her.

"Do we have someone who is out of his mind, out of touch

with reality, no control, or do we have someone who gets sick pleasure out of taking girls, killing them, and then calling their families? The question is simple," Myers offered, his voice rising, "could Larry Gene Bell follow the law, or would Larry Gene Bell follow the law? Who is the real Larry Gene Bell? You know the answer. Use your common sense."

He reminded the jurors that Bell had only sought psychiatric help when he was arrested or convicted of assaulting women and asserted that a verdict of guilty but mentally ill would be a reward for this tactic. "Is he crazy? Out of control? Or is he sadistic? Cold? You decide. Listen to the phone calls, and what they tell you, and the interviews when he finally said that was his voice, but it must have been the bad Larry Gene Bell, not the good one, and the FBI agent who said it was a face-saving way to admit it.

"When I sit down, you are not going to hear any more from the state on behalf of Shari Smith as to guilt or innocence. We will have rested, as she is resting. She is in a cemetery, and this trial is about who put her there. And if the state has not proved to your satisfaction beyond a reasonable doubt that Larry Gene Bell did it, find him not guilty and let him go. You are the judges of the facts. Your verdict should ring out loud, the real Larry Gene Bell, and for whom the bell tolls—for Larry Gene Bell or for Shari Smith. Speak the truth."

In his summation, Jack Swerling conceded that the state had proved beyond a reasonable doubt that Bell had kidnapped Shari. Pacing the courtroom, making eye contact with each juror in turn, he said, "I wouldn't insult your intelligence. I didn't come here to blow any smoke that would keep you from seeing the truth . . . They got the right guy. They got Mr. Bell for the abduction. Mr. Bell's voice is on those tapes. Now, as far as the murder, I don't know. Was Mr. Bell's revelation on that tape the result of what really happened or was it the ravings of a lunatic who is out of his mind and didn't know what was happening?"

Swerling went on to explain the types of guilty verdicts open to them. "If your verdicts be guilty to the kidnapping, which I submit it should be, and murder, which is up to you, then I do ask for a verdict that speaks the truth that Larry Gene Bell is guilty, but he is mentally ill. He is still responsible for his act under that verdict."

I was not surprised that Swerling didn't ask the jury to return a verdict of not guilty by reason of insanity because it had been pretty well established, I thought, that Bell knew right from wrong, the crucial test. Instead, Swerling made a strong case for guilty of kidnapping but mentally ill, which was his tactic for precluding a death penalty–eligible verdict and sentence. He said, "It seems to me the state of South Carolina is asking us to bury our heads in the sand and go back to the sixteenth century, when people with mental problems were treated like everybody else.

"How many rational people who have abducted someone and who may have caused a death would call so the call could be traced?" Swerling posed. I didn't get the logic of that, since Bell made all of his calls from random locations and made sure he was long gone by the time authorities arrived, leaving no evidence behind.

Though Bell had been quiet and controlled during Myers's remarks, toward the end of the defense summation, when Swerling told jurors they had observed a "wacked-out man on the witness stand," he stood up and said to the judge, "Mr. Smith, today is the Sabbath and I think legally and in the eyes of God it's my turn to take the witness stand."

"Sit down, Mr. Bell," Judge Smith responded.

He sat down and was quiet for about three minutes, then stood up and interrupted Swerling again. "Mr. Smith," he said, "I've heard enough! Today is the Sabbath. The time for work is done and now it's time to play. It's been too long for Sergeant Lust and Sergeant Rust. It's time for some R and R. I'm asking Dawn Smith to marry Gene Bell!"

Judge Smith ordered him taken out of the court for the remainder of final arguments and didn't bring him back until he gave the jury its final instructions. As he walked back to the defense table, Bell suddenly veered toward Dawn, who was sitting in the area behind the prosecution table. Both Bob Smith and several of Sheriff Metts's deputies leapt to their feet, but court bailiffs got to Bell first and forced him back where he belonged.

CHAPTER 23

I t didn't take the jury long to decide what to make of the eleven days of testimony. On Sunday, February 23, after just fifty-five minutes of deliberation, they returned their verdict: In the case of *State of South Carolina v. Larry Gene Bell*: as to count one, guilty of kidnapping; as to count two, guilty of murder in the first degree of Sharon Faye Smith.

Dispensing with his previous antics, Bell listened to the verdict announcement without comment or visible reaction. Judge Smith announced that the sentencing phase of the trial would begin Tuesday morning.

"We hoped the jury would find him guilty but mentally ill," Swerling told reporters outside the courthouse. "But I believe in the system. I've never argued with a jury verdict."

As he was led out of the courthouse, someone in the clutch of reporters asked Bell how he felt.

"Silence is golden, my friend," he responded.

The penalty phase would be Bell's last chance to avoid a

death sentence, and whether he meant to or not, he did just about everything possible to display his bizarre behavior.

Jurors got to hear the recording of him threatening Dawn on the phone and giving directions to Debra May Helmick's body.

The prosecution put Dawn and the other women Bell had been convicted of assaulting on the stand. Dawn said that because of the telephone threat, she had had to remain at her parents' house under twenty-four-hour police protection until her sister's killer was caught. Bell stared at Dawn continuously and waved to her as she stepped down. She never gave him so much as a glance.

When it was his turn, during his forty-five minutes on the witness stand, Bell refused to answer Swerling's direct questions about his life, saying they were "personal matters." Instead, he complained, "I'm fighting for my life here, but I haven't had any time for pleasures. I'm way overdue." He asserted that his guilty verdict was not valid because it was sinful that it was rendered on a Sunday. Then he repeated some of his other mantras. "I'm tired, cold, and hungry, and it's time to go home. I want to take one other person with me. Dawn, will you marry me, my singing angel? Look into my eyes, my holy angel. It's guaranteed that if you'll accept my hand in holy matrimony." I wasn't sure what was guaranteed, but he said again, "Will you marry me? Now is the time to keep silence."

Robert Smith, who had been positioning himself in court to block Bell's view of his sister and glared at him every time he stared at Dawn from the witness stand, looked like he was about to jump up and rip Bell's throat out, but he restrained himself.

"Why did you do this terrible thing to Shari Smith?" Myers asked in cross-examination.

"I didn't," he replied. "I'm not responsible. I'm not answering that question again."

When Myers was finished with him, Bell asked Judge Smith if he could make a statement to the jury. "If you say this is a sin, then I'm definitely guilty," Bell began. "From the top of my head to the tips of my feet, I'm lusting for Dawn Elizabeth Smith. I'd like to take her hand in holy matrimony. That's the only thing I'm guilty of. That has a lot to do with the trial." By informal count, it was the third time he had proposed to Dawn in the courtroom. She later said the experience was "gut-wrenching."

Several of Bell's neighbors testified to what a nice, friendly guy he was. Defense co-counsel Elizabeth Levy asked seventeen-year-old Melissa Johnston if she was ever afraid of him.

"He never gave me any reason to be," the high school student replied. "Gene was a lot of fun to be with."

A reservations clerk who had worked with Bell in Charlotte said, "If I ever had to say someone was like a brother to me, he was." She said he had helped her through a tough divorce and helped her around the house.

I understood why these character witnesses were called, but in a very real sense I thought they proved the very point the defense had been trying to deny: that, like so many serial killers we've studied, Larry Gene Bell was completely capable of controlling his manner and actions and only acted out when he chose to.

The defense called several prison guards who testified to Bell's generally quiet and courteous behavior at CCI, suggesting that he always followed the rules and could be rehabilitated in prison. I, on the other hand, thought of our friend and colleague forensic psychologist Dr. Stanton Samenow's observation that it is difficult to rehabilitate someone who has not been *habilitated* in the first place.

Mereth Beale, now nineteen, whom Bell had harassed with obscene phone calls when she was ten, testified, "On the phone, he said some very nasty things. They were mostly suggestions of sex that he would like to perform on me and have done. Lots of oral sex was mentioned." Beale and her mother both stated that the most terrifying aspect of the ordeal was that the caller always seemed to know when they arrived home and sometimes said he was coming over.

In addition to the Smith family, Sherwood Carl Helmick was in court for most of the trial. For the sentencing phase, both of Debra May's parents were there. Once this trial was over, they would await the ordeal they hoped would give their daughter whatever earthly justice there was.

Bell's sister Diane Loveless testified that he had been depressed before and after the Smith murder and told her he might be questioned about it because of his prior record, but she said she was shocked and appalled when he was charged.

Their father, Archie, said he had noticed changes in his son's behavior in the spring of 1985. "He got real moody. He was restless. When I addressed him, it was like he was out in left field. He acted like he didn't hear me."

Bell's mother, Margaret, testified that she was horrified to learn of his alleged crimes and had no idea her son was the killer until he was arrested. She thought his previous problems had been cured by his earlier prison sentence and therapy. She didn't know he had been fired from his job at Eastern Airlines, even though he came to live with them at that point, or that he had been convicted for making obscene phone calls. "So much I have learned in this courtroom, through newspapers and from what people have said," she noted through her tears. Talking about his depression and inability to keep a job after he moved in with her and Archie in 1983, she said, "Looking back, I should have picked up on it. If I'd known what I do today, I would have. I didn't think it was anything this serious. You know, if we'd known, we'd have tried to do something."

Altogether, Swerling called twenty witnesses in the sentencing phase.

For their part, the Smith family wept as Myers read Shari's Last Will & Testament aloud. Several jurors and law enforcement officers were also in tears. "She said some good would come out of writing that letter," the prosecutor stated. "She was right. If she had never written it, we would have never had her kidnapper and killer in this courtroom today."

Pacing back and forth, Myers turned Bell's surname into a leitmotif as he narrated, "In 1975, when he attacked that woman in Rock Hill, that sadistic bell was ringing. In Columbia, when he tried to grab that USC student, that horrible bell sounded again. It has to stop! Let your verdict ring out for justice. Let it sound out that sweet clear name of Shari Smith. Stop that terrible bell from ever ringing again!"

He admonished the jurors not to heed the defense's call for mercy. "Mercy? You tell me mercy? How did her head and face look when he wrapped the tape around it, strand after strand? Did he give her mercy?"

Swerling countered with his own plea. "The only issue left to decide is whether you will put Larry Gene Bell to death or wait for God to do it in His own time. I submit to you that you should leave it in His hands. He said that vengeance was His and not jurors'."

After arguing that our society does not put sick people to death, he concluded, "We are a society that strives to preserve life . . . This has been a tragedy. All I ask is for you not to compound this tragedy."

The jurors began deliberating a little before noon on Thursday, February 27, as wind-driven rain pelted the courthouse. Twelve minutes in, they asked Judge Smith if and when Bell would be eligible for parole if they sentenced him to life imprisonment. Smith answered that under South Carolina law, they were not allowed to consider that question.

It took them a little more than two hours to decide Larry Gene Bell's sentence.

"We the jury in the above-entitled case, having found beyond a reasonable doubt that a murder was committed while in the commission of the statutory aggravating circumstance of kidnapping, now recommend to the court that the defendant, Larry Gene Bell, be sentenced to death for the murder of Sharon Faye Smith."

Bell, wearing a white shirt, beige slacks and vest, and a brown tie, sat silently as the verdict was read, turning to glance at the clock on the back wall of the courtroom. It read 2:14. Bob and Hilda Smith hugged. Dawn and Robert smiled at each other. Sherwood Helmick glared at Bell. Myers had assured him there would be no plea bargaining for his daughter's killer.

When asked if he had anything to say before sentencing, Bell uncharacteristically replied, "Uh, no sir, sure don't."

Judge Smith set the execution date for May 15, but he knew that was only a formality. By state law, all capital sentences were automatically appealed to the Supreme Court of South Carolina. "All right then," he said to the court officers, "you can take him away."

Outside the building Myers observed, "We couldn't be happier with the jury's verdict. It's always tough in a death penalty case for twelve people to all vote for the death penalty." He said this trial was "the hardest case I've ever had to prosecute. This one has been the toughest one we've ever been involved in because of the emotions involved."

Both prosecution and defense attorneys complimented the jury for their cooperation and attentiveness during what was a difficult and often grueling three-week trial. While Swerling expressed disappointment with the verdict and sentence, he told reporters, "This was a bad case. A young girl was abducted and killed. The jury resolved it against us. I can't find fault with that."

IN JULY 1986, LESS THAN SIX MONTHS AFTER THE HARROWING ORDEAL OF THE trial, Dawn Smith, with great hesitation and trepidation over whether she was doing the right thing for herself, her sister, and her family, entered the Miss South Carolina pageant in Greenville, after competing in Miss Columbia (in which she did not place) and Miss Liberty (which she won). She had decided that Larry Gene Bell was not going to prevent her from fulfilling her own destiny as he had for her sister. She was not going to allow him another victory. Also, she and Shari grew up watching every pageant on television together, and Shari had been the one who suggested Dawn enter the competitions in the first place. Dawn's voice teacher at Columbia College and her roommate Julie also encouraged her. If she won or placed in the Miss South Carolina pageant, the scholarship money she would receive would be enough to pursue her musical education after college.

For the Saturday night final, she sang the aria "Ah! Je veux vivre" from Charles Gounod's 1867 opera, *Roméo et Juliette*. Dawn explained her choice, "It's Juliette at her fifteenth birthday and she's talking about how happy she is to be alive, how excited she is and she's just in love with life. That's how I feel when I'm performing."

Her courage, poise, and natural but hard-worked talent saw her through. At the end of the competition, she was crowned Miss South Carolina, with a full schedule of appearances around the state. Her aunt, Sue Smith, had been Miss South Carolina twenty years earlier, when Dawn was a baby.

In September, Dawn traveled to Atlantic City, New Jersey, for the first time to represent her state in the Miss America pageant. She won a talent trophy accompanying herself on the piano as she sang "I'll Be Home," and tied in the preliminary swimsuit competition. She made it through each round and into the finals, where she was named second runner-up.

CHAPTER 24

The *Columbia Record*'s Jef Feeley interviewed Debra Helmick the summer after the Smith trial, as she and her husband, Sherwood, were waiting for the trial of Debra May's killer. When she heard either of her surviving children yelling outside, she said, "I run a little too fast to see what's happening. I guess it's a natural reaction, but it takes on more meaning for me now."

She said her son, Woody, had seen Bell in court "and told us he's the man that took Debby. He was right there. He got the best look at the man." She said Woody was still having nightmares about the kidnapping. "He wakes up screaming sometimes." She added that he wouldn't go out of the house without his sister Becky and wouldn't go to the bathroom at night by himself out of fear that the bad man would come back to get him.

I have seen a wide variety of reactions from homicide families to their loved ones' killers during my career. Everyone has his or her own way of dealing with about the worst trauma anyone ever has to face. Judging no one, I think my own reaction would be more similar to that of Debra May's aunt, Margaret Helmick, than Hilda Smith's. Margaret told Feeley, "I hate his guts. I'd just like to have my hands around his throat and watch the last breath go out of his body."

Debra said she and Sherwood would be in no mood to put up with Bell's antics at the next trial. "If I were Larry Gene Bell, I'd stay where I was supposed to sit and not come over to us," she warned. "I know Sherwood has told the SLED agents that if he comes over to us like he came over to the Smiths, he'd defend himself."

In a related article, Feeley described the intense hardships the Helmicks had suffered through since the murder. He detailed how, in the year since the murder, Sherwood had lost his job, started drinking heavily, and suffered a nervous breakdown requiring hospitalization. After he lost his job with the construction company, the family was forced to move into his brother's cramped mobile home.

"He'd sit and stare at Debby's picture for hours," Margaret was quoted as saying. "He just let all of this get to him. He couldn't even work. The bills have just piled up."

Once he was treated, Sherwood secured a job working with his brother hanging drywall while Debra worked part-time as a waitress. They were hoping to move back into a home of their own.

In an effort typical for many small-town communities, predating today's GoFundMe accounts, residents of Richland and Lexington Counties established a Helmick Family Fund to help them get back on their feet. Ammie Murray, the fund's chairperson, told Feeley, "Debra Helmick is not the only victim here.

Her family still suffers every day, and soon they have to face her trial. They shouldn't have to worry about whether they have a roof over their heads, too."

Donnie Myers also worked with their creditors to give them more time to resolve their past-due bills. Within three weeks, the fund had collected enough for the Helmicks to pay off some of their debts, buy a car, and have money to live on for the time being.

IN DECEMBER 1986, IT WAS CONFIRMED THAT THE TRIAL FOR THE HELMICK MUR- der would begin February 23, 1987, about a year after the first trial. Judge Lawrence E. Richter of Charleston was later ap- pointed to preside. The trial was delayed until March so he could get up to speed on the legal issues involved with the case. Like the Smith trial, this one would take place outside the Mid- lands, in Pickens County.

Having studied the first trial, Judge Richter ordered that a room in the courthouse be equipped with speakers so that if Bell "acted up" he could be taken there and still listen to trial proceedings. Richter had already agreed that the jury should be sequestered.

The jury pool assembled in March numbered 175 residents, the largest ever drawn in the county. Some taxpayers com- plained about the projected cost of the trial, arguing that the money could be better spent on roads or prisons, since Bell was already scheduled to be executed.

Myers retorted, "Anyone who complains about the cost of prosecuting this case should go up and tell Mr. and Mrs. Helmick that their daughter's life isn't worth the money it will cost to convict that man who killed her." He also had another reason for pursuing the second case. He knew there were any number of ways a capital case could be overturned, either on the state or federal level, on the long road of appeals that every death sentence verdict entails. He wanted to make it that much more difficult for Bell to escape justice.

Around the same time, a North Carolina man, forty-one-year-old Fred Coffey, was charged with the July 1979 murder of ten-year-old Amanda Ray, one of the cases for which Bell had been investigated. Police were also considering Coffey in the Neely Smith case.

On March 23, 1987, Larry Gene Bell formally pleaded not guilty to the charges that he kidnapped and murdered Debra May Helmick. The second quest for justice was now underway.

CHAPTER 25

Security was tight in the small Pickens County Courthouse as the Helmick trial began. Ten SLED agents were assigned to the building, which, as with the previous trial, was expected to draw standing-room-only crowds of spectators. Color-coded metal shirt or collar tabs were handed out to journalists and potential jurors so they could be quickly identified. Everyone had to pass through a metal detector.

Even in this small, Piedmont-region town, when the 175 potential jurors were asked if they knew anything about the murders, almost everyone stood up. Seventeen people said they knew enough that they had already formed an opinion. From there, the pool was soon whittled down to 108. Unlike in the Smith trial, Bell sat quietly during jury selection. He even refrained from talking to reporters as five SLED agents surrounded him and led him through the courthouse's rear entrance. He wore a gray three-piece suit with a white shirt, brown tie, and gray sneakers. Inside, he hugged both of his parents before sitting down at the defense table.

By Wednesday, March 25, the jury, consisting of nine women and three men, had been picked. Among those chosen were a Clemson University professor, a homemaker, and a physician. As the selection neared completion, Bell was observed leafing through a pamphlet titled "Is There Life after Death?"

With the jury seated, Donnie Myers began, "All these events will revolve around June 1985. On June 14, 1985, a nine-year-old little girl was playing near her trailer with her three-year-old brother. As stated in the indictment, Larry Gene Bell kidnapped this little girl, took her away from her home and family, and carried her into Lexington County. There he committed the most heinous crime known to mankind: murder. Debra May Helmick's body was found eight days later, on June 22, 1985, in Lexington County. These facts won't be very pretty, but we have to present what the case shows. You are the twelve judges of the facts. The judge is the judge of the law. Combine that together and render a verdict that speaks the truth."

After opening statements, the prosecution began with Sherwood Helmick describing coming home from work and seeing his children playing outside. He went inside to change his clothes and eat lunch, and never saw his daughter alive again.

His wife, Debra, then personalized their little girl. "She was my oldest daughter, blond hair and blue eyes. She was a straight-A student and wanted to be a school principal." She described washing Debra May's hair and how she dressed her before leaving for work. Then she described what no parent should ever have to go through: when her mother-in-law came to get her at work and told her that her daughter had been taken from their own front yard. She went on, "After her body was found, officers brought us pictures of the clothing from the body and the pink barrette found at the scene. The pink barrette was one of the ones I put in Debra's hair that afternoon, and the shorts with the snaps and the lavender T-shirt were Debra May's. The cotton panties were Debra May's, but the silk bikini panties were not."

The prosecution introduced the seven pairs of similar panties found in a dresser drawer in Bell's bedroom, along with several rolls of duct tape and rope found in a storage shed behind the house and in the pickup truck Bell was using. Myers had Ken Habben, the SLED agent who had searched Bell's room, drape the seven pairs of panties on the railing of the jury box. "We are saying Miss Helmick was found wearing silk underwear that are identical to those Bell had," Myers told the media after court on Thursday.

Habben also identified other items marked as evidence, including the DCE-604 license plate found in Bell's trunk, corresponding to the "D" Ricky Morgan had observed. There was also the white bag from the closet of the bedroom with a starter pistol, a .22-caliber bullet, four five-foot lengths of rope, and the knife that was on the seat of Bell's car when he was arrested.

Ricky Morgan testified about seeing a man drive up, get out of his two-door silver Pontiac Grand Prix or Chevrolet Monte Carlo, leaving the door open, and approach Debra May and Woody Helmick. "Next thing I observed, the man walked over like he was trying to go to their house. I thought he was a friend. The man reached down and grabbed Debra up around the waist and began running to the car. She was screaming and kicking. I could see one of her feet hitting the top of the car." When he was asked whether the man was present in the courtroom, Morgan pointed to Bell. "There's no doubt at all in my mind, that's the man." As soon as he saw Bell's photograph on television after his arrest, Morgan said he knew it was the man who had taken Debra May.

On cross-examination, Swerling asked, "He wasn't doing anything to conceal himself, was he?" suggesting Bell must have been mentally ill to be that obvious.

When Dawn—now identified by much of the media as "the reigning Miss South Carolina"—was called to the witness stand after the jurors had listened to the relevant telephone recordings through headphones, she described the call that provided the directions to Debra May's body. She said she had no doubt the voice she heard on the calls was that of Larry Gene Bell. Swerling did not try to impeach her recollection.

Lexington County Sheriff's Department colonel Butch Reynolds testified that the phone calls with directions to each victim's decomposed body both began with the phrase "Listen carefully," and were apparently from the same individual.

Hilda Smith wept on the stand as she recalled her conversations with the caller.

Before testimony began, Swerling had objected to calling either Hilda or Dawn, arguing that evidence of previous crimes is generally not allowed due to the legal presumption of innocence. Myers pointed out the similarity of the two crimes and argued that the telephone call giving directions to the body was crucial evidence and tied both cases together. Judge Richter agreed.

Lamar "Chip" Priester, a former SLED chemist, stated that clumps of Debra May's hair bore residue of electrical or duct tape. One was attached to a pink plastic barrette. Given Debra Helmick's earlier testimony about washing her daughter's hair, the tape residue had to have appeared after the girl was taken. The barrette also was consistent with the mother's testimony.

Swerling only chose to cross-examine two of the twenty-four witnesses the state presented.

On Friday, it was the defense's turn, but Swerling rested without calling any witnesses or introducing any evidence. "Your Honor, Mr. Bell will not offer a defense in this case," he announced. "The defense rests."

In his closing argument to the jury, Swerling said, "I'm not even asking you not to find him guilty. That may surprise some of you. Our strategy is not to offer a defense of what he did, but to offer an explanation of why he did it. Why would I get up and defend what happened? That's not right. There's no defense for that. My job is to protect Larry Gene Bell and see that he gets every legal right he's entitled to and do it in a dignified manner. I concluded this morning that there's only one verdict in this case you could come back with, so as his attorney I am not offering a defense as to what happened in this case, but we advise you that down the road we are going to tell you why it happened. Follow your conscience and do what is right."

After the summations and final instructions, the jurors retired to consider the verdict. Not long thereafter, the judge and the attorneys were summoned from a restaurant where they had gone for lunch. It had taken the jury about an hour to come to a decision. They returned to the courtroom at about 1:45 Friday afternoon with a verdict of guilty in the kidnapping and first-degree murder of Debra May Helmick. Hilda and Bob

Smith sat directly behind Debra and Sherwood Helmick. As the verdict was read, Bob leaned forward and squeezed Sherwood's shoulder.

Bell showed no emotion. Swerling had told him the previous evening that there was no chance of a not-guilty verdict. The fact that he was able to control himself throughout this trial, in direct opposition to his behavior during the Smith trial, showed once again that his outbursts were selective and that he absolutely knew what he was doing. Swerling later explained, "I believe Mr. Bell is now composed. I hope he stays that way." *So, he had a psychotic episode for the entire three weeks of the first trial?*

Larry Gene Bell was led out of the courtroom and allowed to finish the large deluxe pizza he had ordered for the lunch that was interrupted by the jury's return.

IN THE PENALTY PHASE ON MONDAY, MARCH 30, THE STATE CALLED SIX WIT-nesses, including psychiatrist Dr. John C. Dunlap, who once again labeled Bell a sexual sadist. "I examined Bell after his arrest and arrived at an opinion that Bell knew legal right and legal wrong, and he realized the consequences of criminal acts. He might not be able to control his thoughts, but he certainly can control his acts. He does what he wants, when he wants, to whomever he picks out to satisfy himself. The big thing was his lack of any feeling of remorse or regret for what he had done." Myers quoted this last statement in his closing remarks.

Interestingly, Dunlap's assessment virtually mirrors evaluative statements in a probation report from June 1976 assessing Bell's state then. It said, in part, "It is felt by the staff that the defendant apparently feels no guilt or remorse for his actions, blames his present situation on others, and represents a significant danger to others." It was correct and, sadly, prophetic in 1976, and equally applicable ten years later. To me, it is one of the most important points in our consideration of the criminal mind. In evaluating mental illness and culpability in violent offenders, people often confuse the inability to feel empathy or concern for another human being, or guilt or remorse for anything the offender has done to them, with the inability to control one's actions.

Myers concluded his questioning of Dunlap by asking, "Assuming on June 14, out at Shiloh Trailer Park in Richland County, a nine-year-old girl, Debra May Helmick, was playing in her yard about four o'clock in the afternoon. If there had been a police officer standing by, would Mr. Bell have taken the child?"

"No. He was certainly aware that what he was doing was illegal, immoral, and he would be arrested promptly." In law enforcement, we refer to that as the doctrine of "the policeman at the elbow," meaning if an individual would still commit the crime in front of a uniformed officer, he is clearly out of his mind. If not, he has some ability to control himself.

Another prosecution witness, Mary Jane New, who was a waitress at Mr. George's Restaurant near Lake Murray that Bell frequented, said she had trusted him completely and considered him a friend. She related how his parents, Margaret and Archie, had come into the restaurant on the evening of May 31, 1985, and asked her to call him and see if he would like to join them for dinner at Mr. George's. He told her he was watching the University of South Carolina in the College World Series on television. It was an exciting game, with the score tied at 0. She called back later at Archie's behest to find out the score. Bell recounted what had happened in the first five innings of the game. At that time, Shari Smith was either tied up with electrical cord and lying on the mattress cover in the Sheppards' guest room, terrified and awaiting her fate, or Bell had already killed her.

New said she had discussed fears for her own safety with Bell, who agreed to check her house each night. "I trusted him," she said. "If not for him, I would have been scared to go home."

Some might wonder at how someone so vicious could also appear to be so nurturing, or vice versa. This doesn't surprise me at all. It is part of the thrill for this type of predator that he feels the power of life and death; that he can save or kill at will. In both cases, he feels in possession of the other person, that through his intervention she belongs to him.

The jury listened to six telephone recordings, among them the one in which Bell described to Dawn how he had killed Shari. Swerling objected to the playing of the recordings, reasoning that Bell had already been sentenced for that crime and therefore this would constitute double jeopardy. Myers argued that the tapes demonstrated Bell's character as "mean and vicious" rather than psychotic.

The final prosecution witness in the penalty phase was Dawn, who described the call that had led to Debra May.

"Did you get any more phone calls from this person after the one giving directions to Debra May's body?" Myers asked her.

"No. That was the last one we received."

"And please tell the court again what else he said to you during that call."

"He told me that I would be next."

AS IN THE SMITH TRIAL, I WAS BROUGHT IN AS A REPLY WITNESS. AGAIN, I FLEW down the day before my scheduled testimony. I met briefly with Donnie Myers when I got to Pickens, but we were both pretty confident about what I was going to say, so a long strategy session wasn't necessary. I had not been personally involved with the Helmicks the way I had been with the Smiths. They had not had to be recruited to draw their daughter's killer out, so I didn't have a relationship with Debra, Sherwood, or their children. Still, the victim here was closer in age and description to my own two girls than Shari had been, and I felt both a sense of connection and need for completion in participating in this trial. Even though we'd gotten a conviction in the Smith case, I felt we had to get this one over the finish line with a similar guilty verdict if justice was going to be achieved for Debra May.

In the prosecution's presentation, several of Bell's former victims described what he had done or tried to do to them. Dale Howell described how Bell had pulled up in a green Volkswagen as she was walking home from the grocery store and asked her if she wanted a ride. When she declined, she said, "He grabbed me and stuck a knife to my stomach. But I screamed and scared him."

Speaking about the 1976 conviction, former Fifth Circuit Solicitor Ronald A. Barrett related how Bell asked a female UNC student "for directions. And when she could not give him any, he pointed a gun at her and threatened to shoot her. He then grabbed her and pulled her to his car." Fortunately, she was able to break free and run away.

Swerling also produced the familiar array of psychiatrists and psychologists. Dr. Edwin Harris, a psychologist who treated Bell in Charlotte in 1979, said according to his tests, Bell had a problem dealing with women. "He thought of women as objects to be used in a sexual way," he noted, adding, "I saw him as very psychologically conflicted, disturbed, and mentally ill." He said that Bell had not comfortably integrated the male and female sides of his personality. That may well have been true, but what does that have to do with the compulsion to rape and kill? Under cross-examination Harris conceded that Bell still would have known and understood the difference between right and wrong.

Dr. Lucius Pressley again characterized Bell as a sexual sadist who could not control his impulses. And Dr. Robert Sabalis called him a "borderline psychotic," though not schizophrenic, saying, "Mr. Bell saw a lot of conflict between good and evil and devils and gods" on the Rorschach inkblot test. This probably shows the difference between what psychologists do and what we do because I don't see a correlation between that and the ability to control oneself not to kidnap and methodically kill another person.

Though I wasn't allowed to testify about the profile itself, since that is not considered actual evidence of a crime, I was called to the stand again, this time for my evaluation of Bell when I observed and conversed with him in the sheriff's department. I said that although he was certainly odd, he seemed mentally sound and understanding of what was happening.

"He appeared neat, orderly," I stated. "He seemed somewhat gregarious and logical. He appeared to be enjoying the attention he was getting."

Again, I explained my approach. "We provided him with a proper face-saving scenario, to sort of give him a way out. He told me that he was responsible for these deaths, but it was not the Larry Gene Bell sitting here before me, it was the bad Larry Gene Bell. As far as I'm concerned, it was very effective because he admitted he was involved in the homicide."

THE JURY RETIRED TO CONSIDER THE SENTENCE AT 11:39 A.M. ON THURSDAY, April 2. They concluded their deliberations sixty-seven minutes later, and everyone returned to the courtroom. After handing the verdict slip to Judge Richter, the clerk read out loud, "We the jury, in the above-entitled case, having found beyond a reasonable doubt that a murder was committed while in the commission of the statutory aggravating circumstances of kidnapping, recommend to the court that the defendant, Larry Gene Bell, be sentenced to death for the murder of Debra May Helmick."

But for the name of the victim, it was the exact wording of the Smith jury's decision. It was the first time a jury in Pickens County had imposed the death penalty since the U.S. Supreme Court reinstated it in 1976.

Satisfied with the verdict and the sentence, I said goodbye to Myers, Metts, McCarty, and their teams and flew back to Virginia. Not only was our case load continuing to grow, but I had now been given a couple of additional manpower slots, so I had new agent profilers recently assigned to the Behavioral Science Unit to train.

CHAPTER 26

Following the sentencing, Bell was taken to Pickens County Jail, and from there back to CCI in Columbia. He had twice been condemned to death, but now the byzantine appeals process had begun.

As he sat in prison, police and prosecutors in Charlotte started looking at him more closely again in connection with the still-unsolved disappearance of Sandee Elaine Cornett around two and a half years earlier. Revisiting the interview they had done with him, investigators said Bell gave them accurate details of the money that had been withdrawn from Cornett's bank account after she disappeared, and he told officer Larry Walker, State Bureau of Investigation agent Steve Wilson, and Mecklenburg County police captain Chris Owens that her abductor was someone like him, though not him.

Walker reported, "There were some of the things that he told us we did not know about in reference to our case that we went back and verified." Bell detailed that the offender had originally gone to burglarize the home but saw Cornett there with her fiancé. He waited for the fiancé to leave, and then knocked on the door. At first frightened, she recognized him and let him in when he said he was driving through the neighborhood and decided to stop in for a drink. He then bound and strangled her.

These details could certainly fit with Bell's M.O., though he denied through his lawyers that he was involved. "He's always maintained an innocent posture on that," Swerling commented. The Charlotte PD said it had no other suspects in the case.

IN SPITE OF EVERYTHING THEY'D BEEN THROUGH, BOB SMITH CONTINUED HIS prison ministry and served as a chaplain for the Lexington County Jail. Dawn appeared regularly with him and on her own. He also held a weekly Bible study at a boys' correctional school, and Hilda ministered at a woman's prison. Together, Bob and Hilda joined the board of Victims Hope of South Carolina, a network that gives aid and comfort to victims of violent crime and their families. And on several occasions, Sheriff Metts asked Bob to accompany him when he had to notify the parents of murdered children.

IN APRIL 1987, THE SAME MONTH THAT THE HELMICK TRIAL CONCLUDED, THE BILLY Graham Crusade visited CCI. Dawn, a state celebrity because of her Miss South Carolina title, also appeared and spoke about the ordeal of Shari's abduction and murder. In addition to her many public performances and appearances, she began recording spiritual music, and on the third anniversary of Shari's death Dawn recorded a song she'd written, titled "Sisters."

On August 24, 1987, in a unanimous decision, the South

Carolina Supreme Court upheld Bell's convictions for kidnapping and murdering Shari Smith. Swerling's appeal had been
based mainly on what he considered Judge Smith's error in ruling Bell mentally competent to stand trial.

Another issue was whether the judge erred in allowing
Shari's family to testify about how her murder affected them.
There are a lot of people in the criminal justice world who don't
believe in victim impact statements because they can sway a
jury and therefore create an uneven playing field in sentencing,
even if two defendants are convicted of the same crime. From
my experience, I feel very strongly in the opposite direction.
Anytime an offender preys on a victim, he creates a "relationship" between the two of them; a relationship the victim does
not seek or want, but a relationship, nonetheless. Therefore, I
believe the aggrieved party has a definite stake in how that relationship is resolved. The judge is there to make sure the effect of the impact statement is not overweighted, but victims
should have rights in court just as defendants do.

With the loss on the state level, Swerling said he would now
go the federal appeals route. "We feel like there are some novel
issues involved here, and we'll keep trying," the defense attorney stated.

Then, in January 1988, the U.S. Supreme Court refused to
consider Bell's appeal, rejecting arguments that Bell's Sixth
Amendment rights were violated because he was denied a
"public trial" due to spectators not being allowed to enter or
leave the courtroom at certain times during the proceedings.

Another legal question that remained to be resolved was
whether Bell could be executed for the Smith murder before all
of his appeals were exhausted in the Helmick conviction. And

to show how convoluted the appeals process in a capital case can become, Swerling said he would bow out as Bell's attorney on further Smith case appeals because the next set of appeals for postconviction relief usually involve inadequate counsel at the trial.

"But I am still handling his appeal on the Helmick case," Swerling explained. "So, on one hand, I will be arguing his case in the South Carolina Supreme Court on the second conviction while, on the other hand, somebody else will be filing postconviction relief on the first conviction in which the effectiveness of my counsel will be questioned."

In April 1988, Tom Mims, the public defender for Edgefield, McCormick, and Saluda Counties, took over appeals in the Smith case.

The next month, Swerling argued before the South Carolina Supreme Court that the telephone call recordings should not have been admitted as evidence in the Helmick trial. He also argued against admission of the ropes and the collection of panties found in Bell's closet. Debra May's parents sat silently in the courtroom. As close as I could tell, Swerling and his co-counsel John Blume were claiming that the tapes were prejudicial because they called attention to the fact that Bell had already been tried and convicted in a previous and related murder. The logic was that Bell described to Dawn the manner in which Shari was killed, while there was no specific evidence to suggest how Debra May died. Therefore, admitting the tapes "allowed the jury to speculate what might have happened in the Helmick case, when there was no testimony about how she met her death."

Donnie Myers countered that prior court precedent allowed evidence from other cases if it showed "common scheme, plot or motive."

When you get to this point in the appeals process, unless you are claiming postconviction relief on the basis of "actual innocence," the arguments generally have more to do with legal procedure than with whether the defendant is guilty or not.

While all this was going on, from his prison cell, Larry Gene Bell joined the Broadacres Baptist Church in nearby Cayce. Some church members objected, but most felt it was a natural outgrowth of their ongoing prison ministry. Others felt it was a ploy by his attorneys to avoid execution. It is a fact that a lot of prisoners do find religion, or appear to, in prison, and since Bell had always claimed a special relationship with, and visions from, God, I was not surprised. He would be baptized at CCI.

In March 1989, Dawn married Will Jordan with her former roommate Julie as her matron of honor. At the ceremony, there was a special candle burning in Shari's memory. Among the cards she received was one from Larry Gene Bell on death row at CCI, congratulating her on her twenty-fifth birthday and marriage. She tried not to let it spoil the occasion for her. Together, Dawn and Will expanded what became Jordan Ministries, Inc., speaking and singing in churches and before civic groups with a message of faith and the ability to endure whatever life throws at us. Just as Dawn and Will were relocating to Fort Worth, Texas, for Will to work toward a master of divinity degree at Southwestern Baptist Theological Seminary, Dawn received a letter from Bell. It quoted Bible scripture about forgiveness and Dawn was affronted that he would dare to lecture her on the subject. But as she wrote in her book, she couldn't get the letter out of her mind and really had to confront herself about whether she had actually forgiven her sister's killer, and that even if she had, he had no way of knowing it.

She decided she had to write back to him, describing how God's grace had brought her through all the trials and "to this point in my life." She wrote that while she could never forget what he did to her family, she wanted him to know that she had forgiven him. She said she prayed for him and his family. "As I sat back and read over what I'd written," she related, "I felt as if a tremendous burden had lifted."

Near the end of February 1990, the South Carolina Supreme Court ruled on appeal that Bell had been properly convicted in the murder of Debra May Helmick, just as it had earlier upheld his conviction and death sentence for the murder of Shari Smith. In October, the U.S. Supreme Court let stand Bell's conviction in the Helmick case. So far, no court had found any reversible errors in any of his legal proceedings.

In June 1992, Charlotte police and the Cherokee County Sheriff's Office made plans to look near an abandoned well in the county. An informer told them that Bell had identified it to him as a place where he had dumped two bodies. One, they believed, could be that of Sandee Cornett; the other was unknown. The man said he had been hitchhiking as a fifteen-year-old with a companion along I-85 when Bell picked them up. Bell said he had seen two bodies stuffed down the well and had kept the secret for eight years, but that his conscience had finally gotten to him. The informant reported that when Bell showed them the location, he said, "If you don't do what I say, that's what will happen to you!"

Officials didn't know what they'd find, if anything, but the time frame matched up to when Cornett disappeared, and we knew that Bell enjoyed appealing to other people's emotions with his narratives of sex and violence.

Braving ticks, swarming bees, and heat, about twenty-five officers joined the search, trying to retrace what they thought was Bell's path through rural dirt roads and dense woods. They were guided by a helicopter that followed the hitchhiker's directions. Then, investigators employed a pump to remove twelve feet of water from what they believed to be the well the informant described, about four miles off I-85. Cornett's brother Larry accompanied the police as his parents waited at a nearby motel.

Police used a specialized camera to scan the well but came up with nothing. After two days, they called off the search. "We're pretty sure we've got the right area," Charlotte police sergeant Donna Job stated. "There's just so many wells." She said they would have to regroup, review their information, and see if it made sense to try again at other locations.

In April 1993, the U.S. Supreme Court once again refused to hear an appeal to Bell's sentence in the Smith case. By that time, Dawn and her husband, Will Jordan, were expecting their first child, a baby girl whom they had already decided to name Hannah Sharon.

The following October, a U.S. District Court judge denied another appeal in the Smith case.

But the story wasn't over yet.

CHAPTER 27

On April 4, 1995, which happened to be Dawn's birthday, Bob Smith suffered a heart attack while preparing dinner on the backyard grill. He had just returned from a business trip to Atlanta. Fortunately, he got to the hospital in time. His doctors attributed the attack to accumulated extreme stress.

On Friday, September 7, 1996, more than ten years after he was convicted of murdering Shari Smith, at the behest of Attorney General Charles "Charlie" Condon, the Supreme Court of South Carolina set the now forty-seven-year-old Bell's execution date for October 4. Noting that all of Bell's state and federal appeals had been denied, Condon commented, "The time is ripe to carry out the jury's judgment."

Bell's attorneys countered on September 10 with a request to the state circuit court for another mental competency hearing. Meanwhile, Bell had decided how he would die. Though Governor David Beasley had signed a bill in 1995 changing the state's method of execution from electrocution to lethal injection, those sentenced before that date could still opt for the previous method. Bell opted for the electric chair. I wondered whether, with his weird reasoning, it had anything to do with his pre-arrest profession as an electrician. He also seemed to liken the wooden-frame chair to the wood of Jesus's cross.

On Friday, September 27, after hearing from experts on both sides, Judge David Maring ruled that Bell was sane enough to meet the state's sanity test. Apparently agreeing with Myers, he stated that Bell "retains enough cognate thought to manipulate the system and get the results he wants."

Drilling down further, the judge said, "Although he is mentally ill, he still has the ability to manipulate and control his responses when he desires to do so. He can communicate much information to his attorneys."

FROM THE TIME HER DAUGHTER DIED, DEBRA HELMICK LOWE KEPT DEBRA MAY'S favorite doll, the mop-headed Scotty, in the bedroom of her Barnwell home. She was using her maiden name after divorcing Sherwood. So many times, I have seen the death of a child—particularly by violence—either draw a married couple closer together or tear them asunder. The Smiths were drawn together. The Helmicks weren't as fortunate.

Holding the doll, Debra told the *State* reporter John Allard, "It's a comfort to me. It's not like having her with me, but it's the next best thing. I still pray at night that she'll be taken care of." And on October 2, 1996, after the South Carolina Supreme Court refused to review a state judge's determination that Bell was mentally competent to be executed, Debra began to think that maybe the more than eleven-year ordeal was finally coming to an end. Meanwhile, Bell's attorneys were preparing another brief to present to the U.S. Court of Appeals for the Fourth Circuit and asking the U.S. Supreme Court to delay the execution, now scheduled for the early morning of Friday, October 4.

Debra said she planned to attend the execution, even though it was technically for the murder of Shari. "I just feel like I need to be there to satisfy myself. Every day, something goes on that makes me think of Debra." She acknowledged that she had forgiven Bell, though it was more nuanced than that. "I came to the realization I needed to forgive him to make myself right with God. But the execution won't stop me from wondering what Debra would be doing now."

Debra May's grandmother Ann Helmick said, "It won't be over for us until it's over for him. I feel like I will get a burden off me on Friday."

At this point, Larry Gene Bell had spent more time on death row than Debra May got to spend on earth.

Hilda Smith's brother Rick Cartrette planned to attend for the Smith family.

By this time, more of Bell's background had emerged, and little of it surprised me. In addition to his history of cruelty to small animals, as a teen and young adult he had sexually abused several female relatives, who were then pressured by the family not to report the assaults or press charges. One of those girls, now grown up, said he had fondled and stalked her from the ages of five to thirteen. At the latter age, she said he locked her in a bedroom and raped her.

"He always knew right from wrong," the *State*'s John Allard quoted her. "But he couldn't control his impulses. He got progressively worse and wouldn't get treatment. I wasn't surprised when I heard about his arrest for the murders. I knew he would eventually do something like that."

On Wednesday, October 2, 1996, the South Carolina Supreme Court refused to review Judge Maring's ruling that Bell was competent to be executed despite his mental illness. The U.S. Court of Appeals for the Fourth Circuit denied the defense team's last-minute appeals to stop or postpone the execution. Governor David Beasley did review the case and declined to grant clemency.

Investigators from Charlotte went down to Columbia, hoping to negotiate with Bell's attorneys for one final interview to see if they could get him to tell them anything about Sandee Cornett's disappearance, including if he actually knew where the body was; if he had any information about what happened to Denise Porch or Beth Marie Hagen; or if he could tell them anything about any other open cases.

Bell refused to speak with the Charlotte police detectives about Sandee Cornett or any of the cases. "I've talked to Sandee's family, and they are really crushed," Charlotte PD sergeant Rick Sanders said. "They know with his death dies the best chance of finding her so she can be buried."

Wearing a green jumpsuit, Larry Gene Bell went to the electric chair, which had originally been put into service in 1912, shortly after one A.M. on Friday, October 4, 1996. He seemed calm and resigned as he was strapped in and a three-part headpiece made up of a sponge, a metal ring, and a black leather outer layer was fitted onto his head to receive the electrical charge. A grounding wire was attached to a metal band around his right calf. He made no final statement and did not resist as the brown leather hood was placed over his head.

The protocol called for three anonymous executioners in a room with a one-way mirror onto the execution chamber to simultaneously press three red buttons on a small metal box. Only one of them would actually activate the electric chair, so each individual would never know who had effected the death.

Bell appeared to jerk as the 2,000-volt surge of electricity went through his body. His hands clenched and his back arched slightly. Then he went limp. He was declared dead at 1:12 A.M.

"He put us through days of hell," Sheriff Metts declared. "The Smith family forgives Bell. I can't."

EACH INDIVIDUAL WHO VIEWS THESE TRAGIC CASES CAN DECIDE FOR HIM- OR HER-self whether Larry Gene Bell was sufficiently mentally ill to avoid legal and moral responsibility for the kidnapping and murders of Shari Smith and Debra May Helmick. Since none of us can actually penetrate the mind of another person, there is no definitive way to be certain one way or another.

From my own perspective, I consider that he knew how long he could stay on the telephone before the calls could be traced and officers dispatched to each location, and he knew to wipe the phones clean of evidence. I consider that he thought to disguise his voice with an electronic device, before gaining confidence after eluding law enforcement. I consider that he planned the abductions and murders, waiting until he had a safe place to take his victims, and went to some lengths to conceal where he left the bodies until he knew decomposition would make evidence difficult to obtain. I consider how he thought ahead to change the license plates on the car he was driving to avoid detection. I consider how he repeatedly and cruelly manipulated the Smith family with the hope that Shari was still alive. I consider how anyone, no matter the extent of their mental or emotional abnormality, could possibly conceive that it is acceptable to kidnap, abuse, and murder two innocent girls, and I conclude that it is impossible. The offender did it because it fulfilled a need in him, even though he knew it was wrong and evil.

And I consider that no matter what hand life deals to each of us, we all have choices to make. Facing the horrible and premature end of her life, Shari Smith made her choice with almost unimaginable grace, dignity, and equanimity. I cannot even imagine what went through the mind of young Debra May Helmick, too young to understand what was happening to her beyond terror, fear, and pain. Throughout his far longer life, Larry Gene Bell made his own choices. They provide lessons for us all.

EPILOGUE

I n May 1997, while Bob was away on business in South Dakota, Hilda Smith developed a severe headache and nausea. Dawn insisted she get help and drove her to the emergency room at Lexington Medical Center. At the hospital, Hilda began to experience convulsions. It turned out she had suffered a brain aneurysm and would need surgery the next day. She was transferred by ambulance to Richland Memorial Hospital, accompanied by Dawn, who tracked down her father and told him to come right home. He drove through the night to Minneapolis and caught the first flight to Charlotte. By the time he arrived at the hospital, Hilda was already being prepared for surgery.

She spent eighteen days in the neurosurgical intensive care unit, coming close to death twice, and a total of forty-six days in the hospital. She and Bob, Dawn, and Robert all considered her recovery a miracle.

That same year, Will Jordan, by then an ordained pastor, walked away from his marriage with Dawn, saying he didn't love her anymore, leaving her with their two small children, ages one and four. He later remarried.

Debra Helmick Lowe married John Harmon Johnson on July 8, 1997.

On December 10, 1997, her daughter Rebecca, known as Becky, Debra May's younger sister, gave birth to a baby girl, whom she named Debra.

In 2003, Hilda Smith passed away after a two-year struggle with ovarian cancer.

In 2015, Sheriff James Metts was indicted for his role in a scheme to help illegal aliens held at the Lexington County Jail avoid federal detection. He agreed to plead guilty. At sixty-eight years of age, he had served as county sheriff since 1972, one of the longest public service tenures in state history, during which time he had taken the department from an ill-equipped and undertrained rural, twelve-deputy force into a modern, highly effective law enforcement agency with more than three hundred deputies. Despite over a hundred letters of support from the community and a request from both prosecution and defense attorneys that Metts not serve any prison time, Judge Terry L. Wooten of the U.S. District Court for the District of South Carolina sentenced him to one year and one day in prison and a $10,000 fine. Lewis McCarty took over as interim sheriff. Metts served ten months at the Butner Federal Prison Complex in North Carolina before early release in April 2016 for good behavior.

Lewis McCarty passed away in January 2018. He was seventy-six years old. He began his distinguished career in law enforcement as a patrolman in 1964, switching over to the Lexington County Sheriff's Department in 1972 and serving until his retirement in 1999.

The disappearances of Denise Newsome Porch in 1975, Beth Marie Hagen in 1980, and Sandee Elaine Cornett in 1984 remain unsolved.

ACKNOWLEDGMENTS

Once again, our admiration and heartfelt thanks go out to:

Our wonderful and discerning editor, Matt Harper, whose talent, insight and perspective guided us every step of the way; and the entire HarperCollins/William Morrow/Dey St. family, including Anna Montague, Andrea Molitor, Danielle Bartlett, Bianca Flores, Kell Wilson, and Beth Silfin.

Our amazing researcher and in-house Mindhunters editor Ann Hennigan, who has worked with us since the beginning and is an integral part of the team, one of the many reasons this book is dedicated to her.

Our ever supportive and resourceful agent, Frank Weimann, and his team at Folio Literary Management.

Mark's wife, Carolyn, our Mindhunters chief of staff and in-house counselor, among many other attributes.

Former special agent Ron Walker, John's partner on these cases, and all their colleagues at the FBI Academy.

Dawn Smith Jordan, and the entire Smith and Helmick families, for their courage, character, and cooperation.

Three books that proved to be invaluable resources and for which we are extremely grateful to their authors: Dawn's

Grace So Amazing (Crossways Books, Good News Publishers); her late mom Hilda Cartrette Smith's *The Rose of Shari* (America House Book Publishers); and Rita Y. Shuler's *Murder in the Midlands* (The History Press, Arcadia Publishing).

The journalists of the *Columbia Record*, the *State*, the Associated Press, and all of the newspapers that diligently covered what quickly became the largest manhunt and most newsworthy crime story in South Carolina history.

Maria Awes, Jen Blanck, and their team at Committee Films for their ongoing help, support, and encouragement.

And finally, the entire law enforcement and prosecution teams on the Smith and Helmick cases, especially James Metts, Donnie Myers, and the late Lewis McCarty and Leon Gasque. They and their colleagues dedicated their lives and careers to making their world a better and safer place.

ABOUT THE AUTHORS

JOHN DOUGLAS is a former FBI special agent, the bureau's criminal profiling pioneer, founding chief of the Investigative Support Unit at the FBI Academy in Quantico, Virginia, and one of the creators of the *Crime Classification Manual*. He has hunted some of the most notorious and sadistic criminals of our time, including the Trailside Killer in San Francisco, the Atlanta Child Murderer, the Tylenol Poisoning case perpetrator, the Unabomber, the man who hunted young women for sport in the woods of Alaska, and Seattle's Green River Killer, the case that nearly ended his own life. He holds a doctor of education degree, based on comparing methods of classifying violent crimes for law enforcement personnel. Today, he is a widely sought-after speaker and expert on criminal investigative analysis, having consulted on the JonBenet Ramsey murder, the civil case against O. J. Simpson, and the exoneration efforts for the West Memphis Three as well as Amanda Knox and Raffaele Sollecito. Douglas is the author, with Mark Olshaker, of seven previous books, including *Mindhunter*, the number one *New York Times* bestseller that is the basis for the hit Netflix series.

MARK OLSHAKER is a novelist, nonfiction author, and Emmy Award–winning filmmaker who has worked with John Douglas for many years, beginning with the PBS *Nova* Emmy-nominated documentary *Mind of a Serial Killer*. He has written and produced documentaries across a wide range of subjects, including for the Peabody Award–winning PBS series *Building Big* and *Avoiding Armageddon*. Olshaker is the author of highly praised suspense novels such as *Einstein's Brain*, *Unnatural Causes*, and *The Edge*. In another realm of life-threatening mysteries, he is coauthor with Dr. C. J. Peters of *Virus Hunter: Thirty Years of Battling Hot Viruses Around the World*, and with Dr. Michael Osterholm of *Deadliest Enemy: Our War Against Killer Germs*. His writing has appeared in the *New York Times*, the *Washington Post,* the *Wall Street Journal*, *USA Today*, the *St. Louis Post-Dispatch*, *Newsday*, *Time*, *Fortune*, and *Foreign Affairs*.

Both authors live with their wives in the Washington, D.C., area.